Current Debates in Comparative Politics

J. Tyler Dickovick

Washington and Lee University

Jonathan Eastwood

Washington and Lee University

New York   Oxford

OXFORD UNIVERSITY PRESS

Oxford University Press is a department of the University of Oxford. It furthers the University's objective of excellence in research, scholarship, and education by publishing worldwide.

Oxford   New York
Auckland   Cape Town   Dar es Salaam   Hong Kong   Karachi
Kuala Lumpur   Madrid   Melbourne   Mexico City   Nairobi
New Delhi   Shanghai   Taipei   Toronto

With offices in
Argentina   Austria   Brazil   Chile   Czech Republic   France   Greece
Guatemala   Hungary   Italy   Japan   Poland   Portugal   Singapore
South Korea   Switzerland   Thailand   Turkey   Ukraine   Vietnam

For titles covered by Section 112 of the US Higher Education Opportunity Act, please visit www.oup.com/us/he for the latest information about pricing and alternate formats.

Published in the United States of America by
Oxford University Press
198 Madison Avenue, New York, NY 10016
http://www.oup.com

Library of Congress Cataloging-in-Publication Data
Dickovick, James Tyler, 1973-
    Current debates in comparative politics / J. Tyler Dickovick, Washington and Lee University, Jonathan Eastwood, Washington and Lee University.
       pages cm
    Includes bibliographical references and index.
    ISBN 978-0-19-934135-1 (alk. paper)
    1. Comparative government. I. Eastwood, Jonathan. II. Title.
    JF51.D54 2015
    320.3--dc23
                                                    2013046991

Printing number: 9 8 7 6 5 4 3 2 1

Printed in the United States of America
on acid-free paper

Brief Contents

Contents

Preface

This reader is for use in undergraduate courses in comparative politics. It is based on the premise that engaging with contemporary world affairs is a good strategy for beginning to learn the discipline. The book is designed in parallel with our textbook, *Comparative Politics: Integrating Theories, Methods, and Cases*, and can be fruitfully read alongside that work. However, the current volume can also be read as a stand-alone text.

Comparative politics is not just a subfield of political science but an analytical technique and a method for solving problems. The core of this method is the attempt to ask and answer "why questions" through making systematic comparisons. The purpose is to make arguments about cause and effect and to back these arguments with empirical evidence. As such, it should be useful to you whether you go on to become a professional political scientist or (more likely) choose some other career.

Just the same, political scientists use the method to understand the contemporary political world, and we want you to see how interesting, important, and, yes, fun this can be. Political scientists try to figure out the answers to questions like why some states are "strong" (e.g., the France, Japan, or Chile) relative to others that are "weak" or "failed" (e.g., Somalia, Chad). We try to determine why some regimes are highly democratic (e.g., the Scandinavian countries) and others are highly authoritarian (e.g., North Korea). We want to know why some countries have achieved high levels of economic development (e.g., Germany, Singapore) whereas others remain very poor (e.g., Bangladesh, Bolivia, Democratic Republic of the Congo). We hope to figure out why events like terrorist attacks, democratic revolutions, and coups d'état take place as well as what influences processes like the expansion of women's political representation, institutional reforms like decentralization, and the creation and elimination of welfare state institutions.

Most political scientists are doubly motivated to try to answer questions like these. First of all, we are curious about them. If you think about such questions, we think you will discover that you are curious about them as well, especially when you think about how they relate to current events. Why do some revolutions succeed while others fail? This matters for understanding the Arab Spring of 2011. Why does democratization happen in "waves"? This mattered for understanding changes in Eastern Europe in 1989, Africa in the early 1990s, and maybe even whether it will happen in China in the future. What causes differences in levels of public corruption? This matters greatly to people living in India and Nigeria—among other countries—today. At the same time, most political scientists care about these questions because we want to produce *useful knowledge*. That is, our hope is that if we can answer some of these questions, policy makers will be able to use the answers to govern more effectively for the greater good. For example, if we can learn that designing electoral institutions in certain ways will make for greater citizen representation, constitutional reformers might use this information to design their institutions optimally. If we know that certain factors increase the likelihood of intergroup conflict and genocide, leaders and citizens can work to reduce or eliminate them.

Much of the debate about these matters among political scientists and other academics takes place in scholarly journals such as *World Politics* or the *American Political Science Review*. Many of the articles appearing in those journals are highly technical, often relying on mathematically sophisticated formal models and systematically collected empirical data. This work is important, and if you want to go on and become a political scientist, you are going to want to learn how to read, analyze, and even produce such works (don't be discouraged—it's not as hard as it sounds!).

Happily for introductory students, though, many of the same theories and arguments are considered in more "popular" (yet still sophisticated) sources like *Foreign Affairs*, *The Economist*, and *The New York Times*, among other places. This volume brings together readings of this latter sort. The goal in selecting these readings is to allow you to focus on the questions posed and the answers given as prominent scholars, journalists, and public figures think about issues in comparative politics. We also hope this approach allows you to think about the policy implications of different analyses in political science. We also encourage you to keep an open mind to multiple sides of current debates and not simply to try to confirm the beliefs you had prior to reading the book.

The book follows the organizational structure of *Comparative Politics: Integrating Theories, Methods, and Cases*, dividing readings into fifteen sections. A brief editorial essay precedes each section: it aims to draw your attention to the key themes raised in that section. The first two sections deal with theoretical and methodological issues and the remaining thirteen sections deal with "substantive" issues in comparative political science: the modern state; economic development; democracy; authoritarianism; constitutions and constitutional design; legislatures; executives; interest groups and parties; revolutions and other forms of contention; national identity; race, gender and ethnicity; religion and ideology; and the relationship between domestic and international issues in global politics.

Taken together, we hope this set of readings will help you become ready, willing, able, and eager to make your own contributions to current debates in comparative politics.

Acknowledgments

The authors would like to thank many people who assisted in the development of this book. We wish first to thank the reviewers who gave constructive commentary and feedback that helped improve the book considerably. They are: Cheryl L. Brown, University of North Carolina at Charlotte; Matthew Fails, Oakland University; Therese M. Hammond, Penn State Lehigh Valley; Pawel Lutomski, University of San Francisco and Stanford University; Satoshi Machida, University of Nebraska at Kearney; Susan Matarese, University of Louisville; Anthony M. Messina, Trinity College, Hartford, CT; Diane L. Parness, Sonoma State University; Dagmar Radin, Mississippi State University; Adriana Seagle, Virginia Tech; Heidi Swarts, Rutgers University-Newark; Ronald W. Vardy, University of Houston.

At Washington & Lee University, we would like to thank many people who have supported this work: June Aprille, Bob Strong, Daniel Wubah, Larry Peppers, Hank Dobin, Suzanne Keen, Mark Rush, Lucas Morel, David Novack, and Krzysztof Jasiewicz. We would like to acknowledge the summer Lenfest Grant program for support of this work. We also want to thank two former Washington and Lee students—Ali Greenberg and Natasha Lerner—who helped us prepare the selections and offered their informed perspective on the readings chosen.

We also owe gratitude to our families for their patience and support during work on these materials. We are especially thankful to our spouses, María Emilia Nava and Alessandra Del Conte Dickovick, as well as our children: Gabriela Eastwood, Carolina Dickovick, Gabriela Dickovick, Samuel Eastwood, and Alexander Eastwood. We also wish to thank our parents and extended families, of course.

Last but not least, we would like to thank two people at Oxford University Press for their contributions and efforts. Jennifer Carpenter had the original idea for creating the book, encouraged us to pursue it, and shepherded the project through its early stages. As the manuscript was being prepared, Maegan Sherlock then put remarkable effort into ensuring that the book came to fruition. We are thankful to both of them.

Critical Thinking and the Comparative Approach

This first section is designed to get you thinking about the context in which we do comparative politics and how it relates to your life as a student and as a citizen. Comparative politics is a method used in the social sciences, which are part of the broader set of fields known as the "liberal arts." As you pursue your education, you are hopefully thinking about your future and trying to acquire useful skills and knowledge. We think comparative politics can help! Hopefully, though, you are also trying to get a good education, part of which involves developing your sense of your own beliefs, values, commitments, and goals. There will be plenty of time over the course of this book to read and think about the various topics and themes of comparative politics: we think you will be well served by first reflecting a bit about why you are taking this course and reading this book and what you can take away from the experience.

In this section we have three readings that directly and indirectly address these issues. The first, by the *Atlantic* correspondent Lane Wallace, argues that polarization, conflict, and other ills might be reduced if we become better "critical thinkers." Liberal arts education should help us not just to deconstruct arguments but also to see the world as "gray" and complex and to recognize our own views as themselves subject to potential critique. Wallace notes some research suggesting that not everyone who goes to college (or teaches at one!) has fully mastered this difficult set of skills. Do you agree, though, that subjecting our own perspectives to critical scrutiny ought to be one of our chief aims in a course like this one?

The remaining two selections address comparative politics more specifically and why it matters, especially by considering how it relates to the actual practice of politics and the efforts to use knowledge to solve problems. Most people who do comparative politics are both intrinsically interested in the questions they ask and also want to solve them for practical reasons: to make our lives and the lives of others better in some way.

The first of these two selections is a column by the journalist and author David Brooks, "The Underlying Tragedy." This piece reminds us of the human costs inflicted in recent years by the combination of economic underdevelopment and natural disasters in Haiti. We include it for three reasons. First, Brooks is asking "our kind" of question: a "why" question about a topic in comparative politics. Unlike the sorts of questions often asked in the humanities and related fields, Brooks's question is one that, in principle, we could answer on the basis of empirical evidence. Second, Brooks uses a simple illustration of the comparative method to address his "why question." Notice how he compares and contrasts Haiti with other countries nearby, pointing to both similarities and differences and attempting to examine the logical implications of each. Third, he offers a (debatable) pessimistic perspective on the record of that research, drawing several lessons that you can evaluate and discuss with your fellow students. Do Brooks's four conclusions make sense to you? How does he argue for them, and what sort of evidence does he present?

The second of these selections is a lecture delivered by Fernando Henrique Cardoso, the former president of Brazil, who also happens to be a social scientist. This lecture, given in honor of another great scholar of comparative politics—one whose name will surface again later in this book—reflects on a number of important themes. First, note that it picks up on questions raised by Brooks about the relationship between culture and economic performance, drawing on Lipset's work to cast some doubt on the claim that religious and cultural values make the most difference (these questions will be addressed in more detail in Section 4 of this book). Cardoso hints that factors like when a country industrializes and how land and other resources are distributed there also matter. He also follows Lipset in suggesting that societies with different cultures might "modernize" economically in different but overlapping ways. Perhaps equally important, Cardoso raises the question of the relationship between social scientific knowledge and political leadership. How does Cardoso feel that the rise of social science has changed the nature and requirements of political leadership? What does he tell us about the relationship between knowledge and ethics in politics?

After thinking about this, we encourage you to think a bit about your own views about why doing research on these subjects might be important. Why are you taking this class and reading this book? We encourage you to "be intentional" about it. Don't just go through the motions and follow instructions—think about what you are doing and why. What do you hope to accomplish by learning about comparative politics?

The Importance of Critical Thinking

LANE WALLACE

In a column that came out yesterday in the *New York Times*, Nicholas Kristof explored some of the emotional "hot buttons" that separate the thinking of "liberals" and "conservatives." (The column was a follow-up to an earlier column he wrote about how people tend to use the internet to seek news and information that reinforces already-held positions.) Part of the reason the two groups have difficulty engaging in meaningful discussion, Kristof said, was that the two camps don't just think differently. They *feel* differently. They react strongly, and in different ways, to different scenarios and cues.

No big news flash there. What any of us hold as core values . . . emotional or otherwise . . . informs our worldview, and influences how we interpret information or events.

More interesting to me was Kristof's take on a solution to the impasse. "How do we discipline our brains to be more open-minded, more honest, more empirical?" Kristof asked. How, indeed?

A prerequisite for any progress, he acknowledged, is an admission that the "other" side of an argument has at least some legitimate concerns. But Kristof also quoted University of Virginia psychology professor Jonathan Haidt, who said that "our minds were not designed by evolution to discover the truth; they were designed to play social games." Therefore, according to Haidt, "the best way to open the mind is through the heart." Kristof expanded on this to suggest finding moderates on the "other" side and eating meals with them to build emotional bonds that allow a differing point of view to make it through to the other side.

I'm not sure I agree with Haidt about our minds being designed solely (if, in fact, he meant that) for social games. Our ability to reason is as legendary as our ability to manipulate. By the same token, the number of people who like me very much but won't for two seconds entertain a discussion point that challenges a position they hold is legion. Which means . . . what?

Well, for one thing, it means that I'm not sure lunches or emotional bonds alone . . . while certainly helpful additions to the equation . . . are enough to tip the balance, or create suddenly-improved communication between opposing camps.

In my experience, there are two factors that seem to make the biggest difference as to whether or not two people can have a meaningful and productive discussion from different points of view (assuming both are fairly self-assured and reasonable beings):

1. The first factor is whether the people involved see the world in black-and-white terms, or in more complex shades of gray. For those who see the world in absolute terms of black and white (on the left or the right), the only choice of movement is all the way to the other side. Which is an awfully long distance to move an opinion. People who are more inclined to see the world in nuanced shades of gray, on the other hand, can consider a slightly different shade without feeling their basic values threatened. The options for movement, and therefore their potential willingness to consider another perspective, are far greater.

2. The second factor is how skilled, practiced, and comfortable both participants are in the art of critical thinking. The website criticalthinking.org offers more definitions of what critical thinking consists of than anyone probably needs. But at its most exemplary, the site says, critical thinking is based on "clarity, accuracy, precision, consistency, relevance, sound evidence, good reasons, depth, breadth, and fairness." Critical thinkers "avoid thinking simplistically about complicated issues and strive to appropriately consider the rights and needs of relevant others." And "they realize that no matter how skilled they are as thinkers . . . they will at times fall prey to mistakes in reasoning, human irrationality, prejudices, biases, distortions, uncritically accepted social rules and taboos, self-interest, and vested interest."

Which is to say, people skilled in the art of critical thinking make a practice of questioning everything. Even their own opinions. They don't necessarily sit in the middle ground of any debate, but they understand the potential fallibility of sources, and acknowledge the legitimate existence of other points of view . . . subject to examination, along with their own. Meaningful exploration and discussion of issues, therefore, becomes possible. Even productive.

In theory, this is the strength and purpose of a liberal arts education (one intended to provide general knowledge and foster intellectual capabilities and reasoned, rational thought). And to the degree that this teaching happens, I think it *is* a strong and important argument for a liberal arts education.

But here's the bad news. How many of us actually put our "gut" opinions or the information that comes at us daily through the rigorous filters of a critical thinker? I don't have the answer to that, but the results of a 1995 study done by the Center for Critical Thinking aren't encouraging. In a study of 140 professors at 66 public and private universities in California, the researchers found that while an overwhelming majority (89%) claimed that critical thinking was a primary objective of their instruction, only a small percentage (19%) could give a clear explanation of what critical thinking

was. And from the respondents' answers, the researchers concluded that only 9% were teaching with a view toward critical thinking on a typical day in class. And that's professors tasked with *teaching* the subject. How must the rest of us fare?

Granted, that's only one study. And clearly, there's a lot more to the subject than one column or post can cover. Like so many issues in the world, it's complex. But developing the ability to step back a step and question where opinions come from; objectively consider and dissect an argument for its strengths and flaws, look at what the source of any information is and through what biases, values, assumptions, or lenses we or others are filtering that information, consider what other information might exist to counter or support any given "fact" . . . and, yes, consider that we, too, might have to adjust our views or thinking in the end . . . is central to upgrading both the level and of productivity of discourse in this country.

Critical thinking acumen doesn't get mentioned as often as the other skills we test for or examine in education debates. But it's essential if we want to "discipline our brains to be more open-minded, more honest, more empirical." And it's every bit as important as math, science, reading or writing in terms of being an informed, discerning citizen in an increasingly complex world.

The Underlying Tragedy

DAVID BROOKS

On Oct. 17, 1989, a major earthquake with a magnitude of 7.0 struck the Bay Area in Northern California. Sixty-three people were killed. This week, a major earthquake, also measuring a magnitude of 7.0, struck near Port-au-Prince, Haiti. The Red Cross estimates that between 45,000 and 50,000 people have died.

This is not a natural disaster story. This is a poverty story. It's a story about poorly constructed buildings, bad infrastructure and terrible public services. On Thursday, President Obama told the people of Haiti: "You will not be forsaken; you will not be forgotten." If he is going to remain faithful to that vow then he is going to have to use this tragedy as an occasion to rethink our approach to global poverty. He's going to have to acknowledge a few difficult truths.

The first of those truths is that we don't know how to use aid to reduce poverty. Over the past few decades, the world has spent trillions of dollars to generate growth in the developing world. The countries that have not received much aid, like China, have seen tremendous growth and tremendous poverty reductions. The countries that have received aid, like Haiti, have not.

In the recent anthology "What Works in Development?," a group of economists try to sort out what we've learned. The picture is grim. There are no policy levers that consistently correlate to increased growth. There is nearly zero correlation between how a developing economy does one decade and how it does the next. There is no consistently proven way to reduce corruption. Even improving governing institutions doesn't seem to produce the expected results.

The chastened tone of these essays is captured by the economist Abhijit Banerjee: "It is not clear to us that the best way to get growth is to do growth policy of any form. Perhaps making growth happen is ultimately beyond our control."

The second hard truth is that micro-aid is vital but insufficient. Given the failures of macrodevelopment, aid organizations often focus on microprojects. More than 10,000 organizations perform missions of this sort in Haiti. By some estimates, Haiti has more nongovernmental organizations per capita than any other place on earth. They are doing the Lord's work, especially these days, but even a blizzard of these efforts does not seem to add up to comprehensive change.

Third, it is time to put the thorny issue of culture at the center of efforts to tackle global poverty. Why is Haiti so poor? Well, it has a history of oppression, slavery and colonialism. But so does Barbados, and Barbados is doing pretty well. Haiti has endured ruthless dictators, corruption and foreign invasions. But so has the Dominican Republic, and the D.R. is in much better shape. Haiti and the Dominican Republic share the same island and the same basic environment, yet the border between the two societies offers one of the starkest contrasts on earth—with trees and progress on one side, and deforestation and poverty and early death on the other.

As Lawrence E. Harrison explained in his book "The Central Liberal Truth," Haiti, like most of the world's poorest nations, suffers from a complex web of progress-resistant cultural influences. There is the influence of the voodoo religion, which spreads the message that life is capricious and planning futile. There are high levels of social mistrust. Responsibility is often not internalized. Child-rearing practices often involve neglect in the early years and harsh retribution when kids hit 9 or 10.

We're all supposed to politely respect each other's cultures. But some cultures are more progress-resistant than others, and a horrible tragedy was just exacerbated by one of them.

Fourth, it's time to promote locally led paternalism. In this country, we first tried to tackle poverty by throwing money at it, just as we did abroad. Then we tried microcommunity efforts, just as we did abroad. But the programs that really work involve intrusive paternalism.

These programs, like the Harlem Children's Zone and the No Excuses schools, are led by people who figure they don't understand all the factors that have contributed to poverty, but they don't care. They are going to replace parts of the local culture with a highly demanding, highly intensive culture of achievement—involving everything from new child-rearing practices to stricter schools to better job performance.

It's time to take that approach abroad, too. It's time to find self-confident local leaders who will create No Excuses countercultures in places like Haiti, surrounding people—maybe just in a neighborhood or a school—with middle-class assumptions, an achievement ethos and tough, measurable demands.

The late political scientist Samuel P. Huntington used to acknowledge that cultural change is hard, but cultures do change after major traumas. This earthquake is certainly a trauma. The only question is whether the outside world continues with the same old, same old.

Scholarship and Statesmanship

FERNANDO HENRIQUE CARDOSO

Adapted from the first annual Seymour Martin Lipset Lecture on Democracy in the World, delivered by Fernando Henrique Cardoso on 6 December 2004.

I first came to know Professor Seymour Martin Lipset in the mid-1960s, when I contributed a chapter to a book that he and the Paraguayan sociologist Aldo Solari were preparing on the topic of elites in Latin America.[1] I was by then a full-time researcher at the University of São Paulo, where I was studying the roles and ideologies of industrial elites in Brazil (as well as Argentina, Chile, and Mexico).

As this was the subject on which I had just written an academic thesis, it was very rewarding for me to be engaged in the broader debate that Professor Lipset was leading on the ethical or "values" orientation of Latin American elites. His views could not have been more straightforward. Building on concepts developed by Talcott Parsons, Lipset argued that economic factors alone could not fully explain the relative backwardness of Latin America. Attention would have to be paid as well to the attachment of local elites to values that inhibited the systematic accumulation of capital.

Latin Americans, it was often said, were anything but enthusiastic supporters of the principles of achievement, universalism, and egalitarianism. These were the basic principles that Talcott Parsons had stressed in some of his very important contributions to sociological theory. They were, moreover, principles from which Latin America had always seemed a little distant, which explains why the prospect of cultural change in the region was of such interest. The most obvious route to change lay through improving and diversifying the content of the educational system, or through transforming the social structure in order to marginalize traditional powerholders, addicted as they were to ascription, particularism, and elitism—the opposites of the Parsonian principles.

Despite the influential idea, most famously associated with Max Weber, that the rise of Protestantism (or more specifically Calvinism) was crucial to the rise of systematic capital accumulation in certain European societies, Lipset held that inculcating a Protestant ethic in Latin Americans would be unnecessary. He pointed to nineteenth-century Meiji Japan as a case where a shift from tradition to modernity had occurred within the context of a single, continuous cultural environment, and he felt that the same sort of process could unfold in Latin America. The Japanese had become efficient and competitive in a modern economic sense without having to abandon the samurai ethic of militancy.

In short, Lipset argued that achievement-oriented values could prosper in Latin America without having to displace basic cultural and religious tenets. This was very important at the time, because it suggested that modernization did not have to mean the complete abandonment of one cultural pattern and the complete embrace of another and radically different one, but instead could proceed in a more measured fashion, producing a blend of tradition and modernity that would lay a sounder foundation for the pursuit of freedom and prosperity across the whole region.

In the essay which I wrote for that 1967 book, I tried to stress that the theories coined to explain the historical evolution of elites in older industrialized countries were insufficient to account for the formation and ideology of industrial communities in "peripheral" countries outside the already-developed world. Favorable conditions for development in Latin America would not be secured simply by updating the thinking of entrepreneurs through the assimilation of values friendlier to the spirit of capitalism. If we were to grasp the situation and prospects of local industrial elites, I was convinced that it would be essential to consider the specific structural and historical patterns that entrepreneurial activity had taken in the region. At least a couple of variables that had been absent in the industrialization of developed countries would need to be taken into account, all of which limited the chances that entrepreneurs could act as "demiurgic" forces for change.

First, basic conditions of production and marketing, including technology and trading methods, were "givens" already laid down by developed economies. Also relevant was the influence of other groups, such as labor unions, that applied pressure on or by means of the state in order to restrict industry's freedom of action. Finally, the expansion of markets and the crafting of industrial-development policies were not priorities for those in power. Governments were more likely to focus instead on ending domination by large landowners and securing international rules to advance the industrialization process. Such circumstances made it difficult if not impossible for Latin American industrialists to play a role comparable in dynamism to the roles that North American or European industrialists had played in developing capitalism in their own regions. The prevailing values in the industrial community were certainly evolving away from the mindset of the traditional patron and toward that of the modern professional entrepreneur, but this was occurring in rather irregular and contradictory ways, precisely because of the practical factors and constraints that I have just mentioned. Modern and traditional mentalities existed side-by-side—sometimes in a sort of functional relationship, as if they were somehow meant to reinforce one another.

This is not the occasion to evaluate in detail whether the views that Professor Lipset and I held in the mid-1960s still hold any hermeneutical value. The point is that at the time, our respective approaches to the subject were very similar. Lipset had already gained considerable experience studying Canada, and was always comparing Canada to the United States. He also had enormous experience in analyzing Europe, and he was *starting* to understand Latin America, producing in the process his fresh and remarkable view that industrial modernity and key parts of Latin America's traditional cultural heritage could combine in new ways.

It goes without saying that entrepreneurial practices and values in Latin America have changed dramatically over the decades since Professor Lipset and I worked together on that book. The reasons for the changes are many, and include the new wave of globalization that has swept the world in recent years. The revolution in information technology and the internationalization of production processes have helped to bring about an extraordinary convergence of methods and perceptions among business communities everywhere. Despite the continued relevance of national and regional characteristics, business circles today are definitely sharing a common code of procedures and concepts, much to the benefit of general levels of productivity. Latin America is no exception to that trend.

Of course, the region is not a homogeneous whole. Indicators vary from one country to another, being more positive in nations that can count upon a significant scientific and technological base. Brazil fares well in this regard, as shown, for instance, by the number of doctorates earned in the country every year, a figure that totals around six thousand. This is basically the same number that Italy or Canada produces. Most of these new doctorates, moreover, come in areas that are directly relevant to economic development. One such area is that of the agricultural sciences. The country's most important research center in this field—the Brazilian Enterprise on Agricultural Research—has more than a thousand people with doctorates on its payroll. Brazilian agribusiness, not surprisingly, breaks productivity records year after year, with the country ranking first or second among commodity producers in many areas (soy, coffee, sugar, maize, and meat, among others).

Knowledge and Values

Whether or not the scenario that Professor Lipset and I sketched in the 1960s is outdated, I am certain that the subject area on which we chose to focus continues to be as important as ever. Studies of ethical and values orientations remain highly relevant not only to the study of economic processes, but also—and perhaps even more importantly—to the study of political agency. Governments no longer seem to derive their legitimacy from upholding the "right" cause or "fighting the good fight," but from doing a good job of delivering what their constituents want and expect. Today's motto is not "what to do," but "how to do it" in the most efficient and cost-effective manner possible. Yet this in no way implies that values or ethical considerations do not matter to public agency. Politics has not been and cannot be reduced to a technical matter of optimizing defined interests. Values continue to be of the utmost importance to politics, but they come to bear in a different way. Political agents are now supposed to engage in deliberative exercises with a multitude of actors in order to define the common good. The general will, rather than being a predetermined variable, as Rousseau and his followers would have it, is now seen as the outcome of extensive and open-ended deliberation. This is why it is so important that the "modern prince" should have a republican turn of mind and a clear view of the ultimate values that political decisions should promote. Otherwise, the prince risks being held hostage by corporatist interests. As never before, virtue is expected to prevail over vice in the conduct of public affairs—in the eyes of diverse peoples all over the world, corruption is becoming less and less tolerable, and good governance more and more a *sine qua non* of national life lived to the full.

Here again, the prince is supposed to be not only morally but also technically more enlightened today than in the past. The work of fitting many conflicting demands into policies that serve the common interest can succeed only if the necessary expertise to evaluate and fine-tune the various inputs is available. To be meaningful, republicanism must also be effectual. There is no cultivating public virtues in the abstract. They presuppose technical competence as applied to actual cases. The good news is that the same trends that hem in the modern prince also open up new areas of initiative and action. Suffice it to mention the extraordinary resources that the new wave of technology has put at the disposal of the public power to better meet social demands. As far as public policies are concerned, the Internet not only serves the demand side by conveying requests, but also assists the supply side, helping governments to deliver everything from distance learning to mail. E-government has brought the state as a provider of public goods closer to the citizenry at large, enhancing social control of public policies and thereby boosting transparency and democratic accountability.

Here again, people in virtually every quarter expect the upshot to be a more selective and cost-effective use of public funds. It is as if all roads lead to Rome. From whatever perspective we take on the conditions that currently govern political life—the number and variety of social demands, the deliberative nature of decision making, or the impact of new technologies on society and the state—we find ourselves concluding that public agency fares better with rather than without technical knowledge. What balance, then, should be struck between values and facts for a ruler to be successful? I need not stress that there seems to be no clear and definite answer. But allow me to venture some additional remarks.

The first is that the relationship between ethics and objective knowledge is not static. It changes over time for obvious reasons. Knowledge in the social sciences is anything but time-proof. What appears to be the state of the art today might not look that way tomorrow as new data and assumptions filter into the picture. Let us recall, for example, how views of the market and its effects upon the social fabric have shifted over the last several centuries. Montesquieu spoke of *le doux commerce* ("gentle commerce"). The luminaries of the Scottish Enlightenment followed him in thinking of trade as a way to civilize people, for regular commercial exchange presupposes habits of conversation, negotiation, and compromise. So, for the leading thinkers of the Enlightenment, commerce comes to light as a powerful tool for building a better world characterized by more peace, prosperity, and civilized refinement. Markets, if allowed to operate free of undue political or other constraints, should help to temper passions and constrain the arbitrary use of authority.

As the eighteenth century gave way to the nineteenth and the human and social costs of the Industrial Revolution became more evident, however, a change in mentality began to take place. The market then came to be portrayed as a locus of violence and oppression. The emergence of imperialism made things worse, as not only individuals but entire nations could be said to be under the severe yoke of capital. The state was then praised as the necessary countervailing force to market excesses. The welfare state follows from this critique, resting on the premise that there should be a safety net in place to catch those whose socioeconomic fall is unchecked by the market's invisible hand. The financial collapse of state-run welfare systems in the 1980s, however, led to the rediscovery of the market's virtues. The World Bank and the International Monetary Fund took the lead in spreading the so-called Washington Consensus, which steered numerous developing countries toward smaller, less ambitious states and freer markets. Thus the cycle has gone through a full turn, from the original idea that commerce and markets would make a better world, through the idea of the market as a problem and the state as the solution for improving the human condition, and now again back to praise of the market as a crucial force countervailing the state and its tendency toward arbitrariness. There is nothing wrong with this shift of perceptions. Changing realities require a constant updating of theories and concepts, if these are to bear any hermeneutical or practical value. What would be wrong would be to ignore this lesson and to approach contingent notions as truths for all time. Ideas are to be understood in light of the circumstances that they are meant to explain and address. Only then can we intelligently put ideas to work for our chosen causes.

Suppose, for example, that one settles on a social-democratic program as the best option for one's country? Would it be sufficient to assemble, based on theory and the experiences of other nations, a set of rules establishing an appropriate balance between the market and the state? Or should other variables that are specific to local circumstances—national history, particular distributions of power, and social expectations—also figure in the account? How far ought one to go in sacrificing universal principles to national particularities, and vice-versa? Is it unnecessary to be concerned with local specificities, provided that public deliberations are broad and open enough to encompass views from all across society and the nation? For those who hold the latter view, the outcome of a truly representative deliberative process will inevitably bear the national imprint. An appropriate method, in other words, will produce an appropriate result.

Statesmanship and Political Judgment

Yet it goes without saying that even a truly representative process is insufficient to ensure that the expectations of the majority will be met. For a leader to safeguard national interests and achieve national goals, there is an additional requirement. Updated knowledge, republican values, and a good deliberative process, important though they are, may not be enough to produce a successful statesman. The missing quality is what Isaiah Berlin identified as the capacity for good "political judgment." This entails not only the discernment to avoid the opposite risks of impractical idealism and uninspiring realism, but also the practical wisdom to grasp the character of a particular situation or moment in history and to seize the opportunities or confront the challenges that it presents. It is the capacity to reach into the chaotic flow of experience and sift out what matters, to see what fits with what, what springs from what, and what leads to what. It is a sense for what is qualitative rather than quantitative, a proven capacity for synthesis rather than analysis. Berlin goes so far as to equate that gift with the talent displayed by great novelists such as Proust or Tolstoy, who convey a sense of direct acquaintance with the texture of life.

Those who lack this gift, no matter how clever, learned, imaginative, and noble they may be, lack the sense of what will make a difference in history and what will not. One may add that while political judgment always matters, it matters even more so at times of transition. It is true that in democracies, all moments are in some way transitional, for democracies are constantly reinventing themselves. Yet no moment is perhaps so critical as that of democratic consolidation, when progressive trends struggle daily with regressive ones, and the outcome is by no means certain. A true statesman will know how to foster the former and inhibit the latter, or at least how to put any such backwardness as cannot be uprooted at the service of progress, for the benefit of institution-building. For it is only institutions, and not individuals, that can reliably sustain democracy over the long haul.

Perhaps the best use that statesmen can make of political acumen in such moments is precisely that of making their nations less reliant on themselves and more dependent on institutions. How George Washington did this for the sake of the young United States of America is the great theme of Lipset's 1998 *Journal of Democracy* essay on the first U.S. president as a democratic founder.[2]

These are the thoughts that I wanted to share with you today as a tribute to Seymour Martin Lipset, a great patriot, scholar, and friend of democracy who has never been moved solely by what Weber called the "ethics of conviction." Ever mindful of the "ethics of responsibility," Lipset has never let the political implications of his work escape from his sight.

To paraphrase Ludwig Wittgenstein, let me say that Seymour Martin Lipset's words have also been deeds, and they have benefited such important causes as democracy in Latin America and peace in the Middle East. Lipset has always been alive to history and to the ethical dimension of human life, and on top of that, always concerned with some sense of the qualitative, of how to judge, and to judge well. I felt that quoting Isaiah Berlin in this context was fitting because Berlin and Lipset are such kindred spirits. Lipset understands, as Berlin understood, that even if you intend to bring together the scientist's passionate concern for understanding with the citizen's passionate concern for social affairs and political life, you also need to have a sense that does not necessarily come from formal knowledge, but flows instead from another kind of sprit—a quality of mind, but also of heart. In order to honor Seymour Martin Lipset, I would like to recall this very simple idea. The worldwide honor and recognition that he now enjoys are his just deserts. We are all in his debt.

NOTES

1. Seymour Martin Lipset and Aldo Solari, eds., *Elites in Latin America* (New York: Oxford University Press, 1967).

2. Seymour Martin Lipset, "George Washington and the Founding of Democracy," *Journal of Democracy* 9 (October 1998): 24–38.

DISCUSSION QUESTIONS

1) Based on what you have read in this section, what would you say is the difference between "critical thinking" and "being critical"? Does critical thinking necessarily involve negative evaluation? Does it necessarily involve value judgments? Why or why not?

2) David Brooks begins his short essay with the discussion of a humanitarian disaster and this leads him to make a series of claims about social science (including comparative politics). He seems to be implying that there is a relationship between the moral seriousness of the problems in Haiti and other parts of the developing world and a responsibility of scholars to do good science. How do these things (moral seriousness and scholarly responsibility) relate? How important do you think ethical goals should be to comparative political analysis?

3) What does former Brazilian president Fernando Henrique Cardoso add to the discussion of the relationship between "knowledge" and "values"? As both a prominent global politician and a well-known social scientist, how does *he* see the proper relationship between articulating and pursuing values and carrying out comparative political analysis? Do you agree? What can politicians learn from social scientists? Is there anything important to major decisions that social science *cannot* teach them?

Theories, Hypotheses, and Evidence

In this section we look at the formulation and application of *theories*. Theories are general strategies of explanation in science. They consist of accounts of why things happen as they do, and they typically aim to be applicable in many places and for many time periods. Theories generally become prominent when they are supported by at least some accumulated evidence and have been tested over time. Examining theories often involves testing specific hypotheses about cases. Hypotheses can be potential answers about why certain events happened at certain places and certain times; in comparative politics, we develop hypotheses to test possible answers about why something happened or tends to happen, using empirical evidence about one or more specific case studies. Thus, generally speaking, we might say that theories are tentative answers to "big" why questions, and hypotheses are tentative answers to "little" why questions.

The section begins with a short piece from the satirical online periodical *The Onion* called "I'm Very Interested in Hearing Some Half-Baked Theories." We include this piece because we think it is kind of funny (we hope you agree) but also because it indirectly highlights key features of good scientific theories by describing their *opposite*. The fictitious author and self-described "ill-informed pseudo-intellectual with a particular interest in the unverifiable" asks us to accept untestable and outlandish claims and to then jump to the conclusion that they are correct without attempting to test them against empirical evidence.

This sort of reminder of what scientific theory is *not* would be unnecessary if thinking scientifically were easy, but it is hard. In reality, we have all kinds of "biases" and make use of mental shortcuts that influence our thinking. A different kind of authority, Comedy Central's Stephen Colbert, has pointed to something similar in his notion of "truthiness," basically the idea that media can create the sensation that something is true. The second short reading in this section describes research carried out by Australian scholars that seems to show that Colbert is right about this. Just attaching a photograph to a claim about a person being alive or dead had an effect on people's assessment of whether the claim was probably true!

As citizens, this suggests, we need to be really careful, critical consumers of truth claims. And as scientists (including social scientists!) we need to be careful about how we formulate and present our results, so that we aim at conveying truth and not just truthiness. The third short excerpt in this section, by Notre Dame philosopher Gary Gutting, reflects on these issues, noting inadequacies in much media coverage of scientific studies and clearing up a couple of common misconceptions about science. We encourage you to be especially attentive to his argument about the nature of science: "it's not that it's infallible but that it's self-correcting." Here Gutting succinctly paraphrases Karl Popper's "critical rationalist" approach to science, which is widely adopted by scholars in comparative politics. We can never prove our theories right. Rather, we try to prove them wrong. It may seem surprising or counterintuitive that we try to see where we are wrong. But this is most often how science advances. The theories that we have trouble proving wrong over the course of time have a greater probability of being true. Very strong theories, like the theory of evolution, are those that have survived huge numbers of attempts at refutation: about these we can have great confidence. Also think about Gutting's claims about how hard it might be to establish law like-generalizations in the social sciences and the implications of this for the application of social-scientific knowledge to policy.

I'm Very Interested in Hearing Some Half-Baked Theories

ROBERTA FOIT

As an ill-informed pseudo-intellectual with a particular interest in the unverifiable, I'm always on the lookout for some partially thought out misinformation. So, if you have an uninformed solution to a dilemma that doesn't actually exist, don't bother double-checking your information. I'm all ears.

However, I must warn you: If you want to convince me of anything, you better be prepared to back up your claims with rumor, circumstantial evidence, or hard-to-make-out photographic proof. I may also need friend-of-a-friend corroboration or several signed testimonials all written in the same unmistakably spidery handwriting. I'm a quasi-critical-thinker. Things have to add up more or less in my head before I let myself be taken in by some baloney story.

Take Atlantis, for example. When I first heard about this lost civilization, I was suspicious to say the least. But then someone made a good point: Prove that it didn't exist. I was hard-pressed to find a comeback to that.

But if Atlantis really did exist, then where did it go? It couldn't have just disappeared without an unreasonable explanation. I was about to give up on the whole matter when suddenly it hit me: It probably washed away, and it's too deep underwater for scientists to find it. All it takes is a little supposition mixed with critical theorizing and you can easily stumble on a tenuous half-truth that really makes you think.

Over time, I've also learned that slapdash research is key before jumping to any conclusion. While I've always postulated the existence of gnomes, it wasn't until I researched the topic on AskJeeves.com that I realized it's a well-documented medical condition.

As important as research is, it's all about common sense in the end. If you can't cool your apartment by leaving the refrigerator open, how's it keeping all that produce fresh? Think about it. If you can't really read the world's great works of literature in only five minutes using a system peddled on TV, how do you explain that gentleman on the infomercial who aces those tests? Would extraterrestrials travel millions of light years just to abduct a non-trustworthy human for their series of intrusive tests? Yes.

[…]

Now, if you have a half-baked theory that you'd like to disclose, please be so kind as to skirt around the issue. I'll only listen to your elaborate webs of presumption and hearsay if you promise to veer unexpectedly and pointlessly off course at every opportunity. Prose density is part of what makes a half-baked theory fascinating.

Only last week, my friend Janet gave me a book that teaches how, through a diet of salmon and romaine lettuce, you can shave 20 years off your appearance. However, before we got to the hardcore salmon-and-lettuce, face-lifting theory, I was taken through a series of anecdotes, solicited testimonials, and long-winded circular logic proving the author's qualifications by citing the medical establishment's fear of his simple brilliance. It was an eye-opener.

I encourage people endowed with a gift for half-baked theories to inform as many unsuspecting strangers as possible. That's how I'm most interested in being exposed to shaky new ideas. At the bus station, on the street corners, wherever strikes your fancy.

[…]

Only then will we continue to safeguard the free exchange of erroneous fallacy so vital to maintaining a freethinking, uneducated society. Thank you.

Stephen Colbert's "Truthiness" Theory Holds True

PHOEBE HO

U.S. news satirist Stephen Colbert's "truthiness" theory might have some truth in it after all, according to a study conducted by researchers from Canada and New Zealand.

The word was used by Colbert to describe a gut feeling that often trumps facts, or "subjective feelings of truth".

A recent study, called 'Non-probative photographs (or Words) inflate truthiness,' conducted by five scientists from the Victoria University of Wellington, B.C's Kwantlen Polytechnic University and University of Victoria, is giving Colbert's theory some scientific credit.

Researchers found that people were more likely to believe a claim when they're shown a photograph through a series of experiments.

In one experiment, subjects were asked to respond with a "true" or "false" to the claim "this famous person is alive".

"We use names of fairly obscure celebrities, they're names most people are vaguely familiar with" said University of Victoria's Steve Lindsay, one of the study's researchers.

The result was that students were most likely to answer "true" when they were shown a photo of the celebrity.

But Lindsay said the result of that experiment wasn't too surprising, since the photo could suggest that the celebrity was in fact alive. What did surprise him were the results they got when they asked a different group to respond "true" or "false" to the claim "this famous person is dead".

"People were more likely to say yes, that the person is dead if the name is accompanied with the photo," said Lindsay. "What that suggested was that it's not an aliveness bias, it's a "truthiness" bias. Whatever the claim is, people are more likely to believe it's true if a photo is present than if it isn't."

According to Lindsay, when people were given names of celebrities they didn't know much about, they tend to try and generate images or evidence that's consistent with whatever the hypothesis is.

"Our default while making these judgments tend to be to generate evidence that's consistent with the hypothesis, and if we can generate a lot of evidence, then we think, 'oh it must be true,'" he said.

What Do Scientific Studies Show?

GARY GUTTING

As any regular reader of news will know, popular media report "scientific results" nearly every day. They come delivered in news reports and opinion pieces, and are often used to make a variety of points concerning important matters like health, parenting, education, even spirituality and self-knowledge. How seriously should we take them?

The key feature of empirical testing is not that it's infallible but that it's self-correcting.

For example, since at least 2004, we have been reading about studies showing that "vitamin D may prevent arthritis." A 2010 Johns Hopkins Health Alert announced, "During the past decade, there's been an explosion of research suggesting that vitamin D plays a significant role in joint health and that low levels may be a risk factor for rheumatologic conditions such as rheumatoid arthritis and osteoarthritis." However, in February 2013, a more rigorous study called the previous studies into serious question. Similarly, despite many studies suggesting that taking niacin to increase "good cholesterol" would decrease heart attacks, a more rigorous study showed the niacin to have no effect.

Such reports have led many readers to question the reliability of science. And given the way the news is often reported, they seem to have a point. What use are scientific results if they are so frequently reversed? But the problem is typically not with the science but with the reporting.

In both the above examples, earlier studies had shown a *correlation* but not a *causal connection*. They had not shown that, for example, taking vitamin D was the *only relevant difference* between those whose pain decreased and those whose pain did not decrease. Perhaps, for example, those taking vitamin D also exercised more, and this was the cause of the pain decrease. Typically, the best way to establish a cause rather than a correlation is to perform a randomized controlled experiment (R.C.T.), where we know that only one possibly relevant factor distinguishes the two groups. In both the vitamin D and the niacin cases, there was an R.C.T. that showed that the earlier results had been merely correlations.

R.C.T.s are often very difficult to set up properly and can take many years to carry out. As a result, most research we read about involves just correlational studies. John Ioannidis, in a series of highly regarded analyses, has shown that, in published medical research, 80 percent of non-randomized studies (by far the most common) are later found to be wrong. Even 25 percent of randomized studies and 15 percent of large randomized studies—the best of the best—turn out to be inadequate. (For details, see Ioannidis's seminal paper, "Why Most Published Research Findings Are False," and David H. Freedman's Atlantic article on Ioannidis's work.)

Why, then, do scientists even bother with correlational studies, most of which they know will turn out to be wrong? One reason is that such studies are excellent starting points for deciding which

hypotheses to evaluate with the more rigorous R.C.T.s. (Correlational studies are also important in a number of other ways.) Contrary to what many non-scientists seem to believe, the key feature of empirical testing is not that it's infallible but that it's self-correcting. As the physicist John Wheeler said, "Our whole problem is to make mistakes as fast possible." Indeed, Karl Popper built an illuminating philosophy of science on the idea that science progresses precisely by trying as hard as it can to falsify its hypotheses.

The trouble with much science reporting is that it does not do enough to ensure that the public can tell just how significant a scientific result is. The better reports will implicitly hedge results that are merely correlational, saying, for example, that vitamin D "may" decrease arthritis pain or that niacin "can" prevent heart attacks. But they seldom explain how preliminary and unreliable most correlational studies are. They don't explain the specific limited role such studies usually play in the overall scientific process.

There's another crucial limitation that science reporting—especially in psychology and the social sciences—often ignores. Even when we have R.C.T.s that decisively establish a scientific law, it doesn't follow that we can appeal to this result to guide practical decisions. As Nancy Cartwright, a prominent philosopher of science, has recently emphasized, the very best randomized controlled test in itself establishes only that a cause has a certain effect in a particular kind of situation. For example, a feather and a lead ball dropped from the same height will reach the ground at the same time—but only if there is no air resistance. Typically, scientific laws allow us to predict a specific behavior only under certain conditions. If those conditions don't hold, the law doesn't tell us what will happen.

In dealing with the natural world, we are often in a position to establish conditions that are sufficiently close to those that make a law relevant. In the human (and, especially the social) world the high degree of complexity and interconnectedness makes this extremely hard to do. A method of teaching fifth-grade math that has been rigorously shown to be highly effective for the students and teachers in one school district may well not work for the students and teachers in another. As Cartwright puts it, all a randomized controlled test tells us is that "this works here." It is another—and often very difficult—matter to conclude that "this will work there."

It follows then that even when we have reliable results from "pure science," we need engineers who can tell us whether and how these results apply to the situations we are dealing with. For the natural sciences (physics, chemistry, biology) we have well-established methods of engineering. But the engineering equivalent for the human world is, with few exceptions, still a long way off. Reporting of "breakthroughs" in the human sciences needs to make clear the gap between science and application.

Media tend to present almost any scientific result they report as valuable for guiding our lives, with the entire series of reports accumulating a vast body of practical knowledge. In fact, most scientific results are of no immediate practical value; they merely move us one small step closer to a final result that may be truly useful. Too many news reports present experimental results as providing good advice on which we can reliably act. In most cases those results would be better viewed as mistakes pointing to a next step that will be a bit less mistaken.

Science reporting would be much improved if we had a labeling system that made clear a given study's place in the scientific process. Is it *merely a preliminary result* (a small-scale heuristic study meant to suggest a hypothesis that will itself require many stages of further testing before we have a reliable conclusion)? Is it a *larger-scale observational study* (showing a correlation but by no means establishing a causal connection)? Is it a *large-sample randomized controlled test* (establishing a causal connection, given specific conditions)? Or, finally, is it a *well-established scientific law that we know how to apply in a wide range of conditions*?

Of course, the above categories are just an outsider's rough suggestions. The various scientific disciplines (through their governing organizations) should set professional labeling standards for material discussed in popular media. Some such system is essential because many if not most people who read popular reports of scientific work are looking for results on which they can rely in making practical decisions about personal life, work or public policy.

Unfortunately, such results are far less common than the many highly fallible preliminary studies that contribute to the complex process leading to reliable results. Media reports saying "studies show . . ." are most often giving us highly tentative results—indeed, results that are likely to be false. They need to be labeled as such.

DISCUSSION QUESTIONS

1) The reading from *The Onion*, ostensibly by Rebecca Foit, is a kind of absurdist argument in support of the position opposite to the one it seems to express. Articulate that position: What are the qualities of *good* theories and of good efforts to test them?

2) Stephen Colbert has given us the concept of "truthiness," which refers to a situation in which something *seems* likely to be true or as if it were true. One of the readings in this section points to scientific research showing that Colbert is on to something. The perception that something is true is not just a function of its likely truth-value but of heuristics like "if the statement is accompanied with a picture, it seems true." What are the implications of our tendency to fall victim to "truthiness" for comparative political science? How might we avoid mistaking "truthiness" for truth?

3) According to Gary Gutting, what are some of the limitations of correlational analysis? What are they nonetheless good for?

4) Discuss the implications of Gary Gutting's argument about the nature of science for comparative politics specifically.

The Modern State

One of the most important subjects in comparative politics is the state. Think about all of the things a state does: the provision of defense, internal policing, economic regulation and management, and, in most contemporary cases, the provision of a variety of "welfare services" (this is by no means an exhaustive list!).

Given the centrality of the state in contemporary politics, there are many questions that social scientists ask about it. One fundamental question is why the state emerged and became the dominant way of organizing politics across the globe. Here, though, we include readings that focus on two other questions that are likely of greater interest to students of *contemporary* politics: (a) the determinants of a state's strength, weakness, or "failure"; and (b) the development and fate of the "welfare state," which attempts to provide a basic safety net and services for citizens. We have two readings on each of these themes.

Discussion of the first theme begins with an article from *The Economist*, which discusses the concept and realities of so-called "failed states." Political scientists often speak of strong states as those with a high "capacity" to accomplish their objectives. Thus a strong state has not only an effective army for external defense but functional internal policing and judicial bureaucracies (with relatively low corruption), an effective system of taxation, and an electoral/political system that is stable and open for citizen participation. Weak states have difficulty meeting these thresholds, and "failed states" are incapable of meeting many or most of them. As you read this piece, think about what sorts of factors might predict state strength or weakness. Think also about whether "state failure" is a useful concept or whether the concept's utility is limited.

This is followed by a somewhat longer piece by Shannon O'Neill on what she takes to be the relative success of state strengthening and social and economic development in recent years in Mexico, a country where state weakness has often been a source of concern especially due to the rise of criminality. How does she document and measure success? More important, what is her explanation of increasing Mexican state capacity and economic performance? As you read this, think back to Gutting's argument about science in the last section: Could these processes be reproduced in other countries that face different issues and have different cultures? Why or why not?

We begin this section's second theme with a piece written in *The Economist* on the welfare state model of the Nordic countries. For many years, Scandinavian welfare states were held up by champions of activist states as ideals and criticized by libertarians as wasteful and excessive. According to this piece, however, they have changed, and in many ways this change splits the difference between these perspectives. Scandinavian welfare states remain robust but now spend considerably less as a percentage of GDP than they once did, and they have been fiscally sound, perhaps even conservative. This discussion is important beyond just a consideration of these particular cases, among other reasons because it may tell us something about the welfare state's future.

The final piece is another entry from *The Economist*, this one focusing on the ongoing spread of welfare state institutions in the developing world, specifically in parts of Asia. This is of contemporary interest because Asia is a world region where the development of the welfare state has lagged behind Europe. What do you think are the implications of the fact that new welfare states are still being created? What does the article suggest about lessons that their architects might learn from the European experience?

Where Life Is Cheap and Talk Is Loose

Modish Jargon or A Useful Category? The Term "Failed State" Conceals Many Tangles

THE ECONOMIST

© The Economist Newspaper Limited, London (March 7, 2011).

The annals of diplomacy recorded something startling in February. Saying, in effect, that it was in danger of collapse, the West African state of Guinea voluntarily turned to a United Nations agency that deals with failed or failing states. Like most of its neighbours Guinea has a history of violence, weak governance, poverty and destructive competition for natural resources. Its new government sought help from the UN Peacebuilding Commission, an unwieldy body that duly set up a task force known as a "country-specific configuration" to bolster the government in Conakry. It is already involved in shoring up half a dozen other countries, all African, at the behest of the Security Council; but this was the first time a country owned up to being at risk.

Such honesty is rare, but states that cannot control their territories, protect their citizens, enter or execute agreements with outsiders, or administer justice are a common and worsening phenomenon. Robert Gates, America's defence secretary, says "fractured or failing states" are "the main security challenge of our time." The term now extends beyond the poor world: American officials have applied it to the Italian region of Calabria.

The problem has attracted lots of wonkish experts, who have offered their expertise to the American government. As a scholar, Susan Rice used to berate the Bush administration for calling broken states a deadly threat but failing to fix them. Now she is her country's envoy to the UN. As a Princeton professor, Anne-Marie Slaughter was a leading academic authority on benighted places; till last month, she was a policy planner at the State Department.

This brainpower has yet to turn the tide of anarchy. In places where the state is chronically weak, it is not improving much. The spectre of state failure is haunting hitherto calm locations too. An annual ranking published by the Fund for Peace, a

think-tank in Washington DC, always features the usual black spots: Somalia, Congo, Afghanistan, Haiti. Applying a fairly strict standard, it finds that most countries in the global South face some threat to their proper functioning.

Politics can complicate diagnosis and prescription. In a topical bit of scaremongering a Texas-based think-tank, Stratfor, has voiced fears that the drug-related mayhem engulfing parts of Mexico could end in state collapse. But the State Department would never bring that language to a delicate relationship. In some contexts, the use or non-use of words is a political choice. Last year, when Russia's President Dmitry Medvedev suggested that Kyrgyzstan was at risk of failing, he wasn't engaging in political analysis but hinting that Moscow's fatherly hand might again be needed to keep order.

Some semantic history may help. "Failed state" entered the political lexicon with the (ill-fated) American-led venture in Somalia in 1992. With cold-war patrons gone, so the theory went, many poor states were at risk of collapsing into Hobbesian anarchy, with dire results for their own inhabitants and neighbouring lands. Robert Kaplan, an American writer, captured and somewhat exaggerated an important truth by describing the chaos engulfing Liberia and Sierra Leone and warning of the "coming anarchy" in other parts of the world.

When Words Become Deeds

No sooner was the term "state failure" born than political scientists began picking it apart. "Failure" may misleadingly imply that a government is trying to function but not managing. In fact, dysfunctional statehood may suit the powerful. As Ken Menkhaus of Davidson College in North Carolina has written*, the last thing a kleptocrat needs is

*Ending Wars, Consolidating Peace: Economic Perspectives, ed Berdal and Wennmann, IISS.

good judges, or robust ministries that could be power bases for rival robber barons. "Where governments have become deeply complicit in criminal activities ... perpetuation of state failure is essential for the criminal enterprise to operate."

Yet even fairly bad rulers, say African or Afghan warlords or corrupt provincial governors in Russia, may feel the need to provide certain public goods, if only to further their own interests. Such public services might range from half-decent roads to the suppression (or perhaps limitation through taxing) of petty crime. What those rulers will not do, though, is create an arena in which other economic or political players can emerge. Is that a success or a failure, then?

The English word "fail" can imply a status: a binary category into which you (or your exam paper) either fall or don't fall. Or it can be a process of indefinite duration. The second sense is more useful when discussing the welfare of states, where no bright line separates success and failure. Nor is there a continuum stretching from dismal failure to blessed success. The conditions are mixed in a variety of ways.

In the case of Mexico, it is hard to deny that governance is failing at some levels: some municipal police and councils, and authorities in certain states, have been infiltrated by the narco-mafia, becoming useless or worse in any fight against the drug trade. But the government can still marshal a formidable array of forces against the traffickers; that is quite a different situation from the anomie of Congo or Somalia.

Calling Afghanistan a failed state seems less controversial, but in a land where central power has always been weak, what does success mean? The American-led coalition's goals include the defeat of the Taliban, the interdiction of the opium business and the bolstering and cleaning up of the government in Kabul. But such aims may be hard to

Country (Population, m)	Failed states index, score*	Life expectancy, years	Symptoms
Somalia (9.4)	114.3	51.5	Anarchy, civil war, piracy
Chad (11.5)	113.3	50.0	Desertification, destitution, meddling neighbours
Sudan (43.2)	111.8	59.8	Ethnic, religious strife, illiteracy, tyranny
Zimbabwe (12.6)	110.2	50.4	Economic collapse, kleptocracy, oppression
Congo (67.8)	109.9	48.8	Civil war, massacres, mass rape, looting
Afghanistan (29.1)	109.3	45.5	Civil war, drugs, no infrastructure, terrorism
Iraq (31.5)	107.3	70.2	Ruined infrastructure, sectarian strife, terrorism
Central African Republic (4.5)	106.4	48.6	Desertification, destitution, disease, terrorism
Guinea (10.3)	105.0	60.1	Destitution, drugs, kleptocracy
Pakistan (184.8)	102.5	68.0	Coups, drugs, illiteracy, terrorism
Haiti (10.2)	101.6	62.1	Deforestation, destitution, crime
Côte d'Ivoire (21.6)	101.2	59.6	Incipient civil war, post-election deadlock

Sources: The Fund for Peace, *Foreign Policy*; UN; *The Economist*

Figure 3.1   Anarchy's Anatomy
Failed States, 2010
Sources: The Fund for Peace; Foreign Policy; *UN; The Economist*

reconcile, argues Jonathan Goodhand of London's School of Oriental and African Studies. The drug economy may have had a stabilising effect on some parts of Afghanistan, he has written; the only plausible hope of a functioning state may rest on a compromise among regional barons whose power rests on narcotics.

If this is even half-right, then success is hard to imagine, let alone achieve. And many an outsider has grown cynical about the prospects of even partial success in establishing a clean government in Kabul. Local support for clean governance is too weak; many hidden channels link the state, the drug lords and even the Taliban.

Another category of states, hard to place on any spectrum of success or failure, could be described as "brittle" dictatorships, like the communist regime that once ruled Albania or the one that still holds sway in North Korea. Such regimes are successful in the sense that they manage, as long as they last, to make people do what they are told; but once they fall, such polities can shatter into a thousand pieces.

Beyond Good and Evil

Nor is there anything simple or Manichean about the standoff between the state on the one hand and its would-be wreckers on the other. States that are fighting either terrorist or criminal groups often respond by sponsoring their own terrorist or criminal protégés. At that point it can be hard to make any moral distinction between pro- and anti-state forces.

Moreover, anti-state forces (such as the Tamil Tigers, the IRA in Northern Ireland, or the Kosovo Liberation Army) often function rather like states in the territory they control, operating welfare services and primitive justice systems, while at the same time engaging in crime, from organ-snatching to bank heists, to keep their coffers full. Such organisations may "go straight" when they gain a degree of formal political power. Or they may not.

Given the messy intractability of state failure, who or what has a chance of solving it? Coaxing states in the direction of success, so that relatively clean institutions drive out the dirtiest ones, may

be the most realistic goal. But if dozens of the world's states are in some sense failed, and may well have a stake in covering up the failure of others, then help offered by yet more governments, or inter-governmental agencies, is unlikely to be a panacea.

To see the difficulties of what pundits call a "state-centric approach", consider the history of the UN Peacebuilding Commission. It was one of the big ideas to emerge from a reflection on the UN's future by the global great and good in 2005. As first conceived, it would have had enforcement powers and tried to pre-empt state failure, not just cure it. But many governments, jealously guarding the cloak of statehood, lobbied to keep the commission weak.

To have any hope of success, state-mending efforts must tackle benighted places as they really are, says James Cockayne, who co-directs a New York think-tank called the Centre on Global Counterterrorism Co-operation. They must cope with local power-brokers with no particular link to state capitals; and also with anti-state forces with global connections that could never be trumped by a single national government, even a clean one.

The clearest cases of such transnational statespoilers concern the drug trade. As long as Latin American narco-lords find it easy to sell cocaine and buy guns in the United States, no government to the south can eliminate them. Whether in Latin America, in Afghanistan or in the emerging narcostates of West Africa, purely national attempts to deal with drugs can be counter-productive; they just drive up prices or create new networks.

In many other cases the wreckers are too effectively globalised for any one state to take them on, adds Mr Cockayne. Examples include Somali warlords with deep ties to the diaspora and Western passports; Congolese militia leaders who market the produce of tin and coltan mines to end-users in China and Malaysia; Tamil rebels who used émigré links to practise credit-card fraud in Britain; or Hezbollah's cigarette smuggling in the United States.

No worthy effort to train civil servants in just one capital will be of much use in neutralising these global networks. Last November the UN Security Council took a step towards recognising this. It passed a resolution telling buyers of tin not to source their raw material from mines controlled by Congolese militia leaders.

It was highly unusual for the council to issue an order to anybody except governments. Global Witness, an anti-corruption outfit, has reported that the resolution has been badly enforced, with only half-hearted efforts at self-policing by the tin industry. But at least the UN may be edging away from the fiction that governments, and people under their orders, are the only factors that determine the fate of nations.

Mexico Makes It
A Transformed Society, Economy, and Government

SHANNON K. O'NEILL

Reprinted by permission of FOREIGN AFFAIRS, Volume 92, Number 2, March/April 2013. Copyright © 2013 by the Council on Foreign Relations, Inc. www.ForeignAffairs.com.

Four tons of cocaine confiscated by U.S. authorities off the California coast; 35 bodies dumped by the side of a busy Veracruz highway in broad daylight; an attack by gunmen on a birthday party in Ciudad Juárez killing 14, many of them teenagers: tragedies like these, all of which occurred over the past two years and were extensively covered by the media, are common in Mexico today. Prominent Mexican news organizations and analysts have estimated that during the six-year term of Mexico's last president, Felipe Calderón, over 60,000 people were killed in drug-related violence, and some researchers have put the number at tens of thousands more. Mexico's crime rates are some of the worst in the Western Hemisphere. According to Latinobarómetro, an annual regionwide public opinion poll, over 40 percent of Mexicans say that they or a family member has been the victim of a crime at some point in the last year.

Hidden behind the troubling headlines, however, is another, more hopeful Mexico—one undergoing rapid and widespread social, political, and economic transformation. Yes, Mexico continues to struggle with grave security threats, but it is also fostering a globally competitive marketplace, a growing middle class, and an increasingly influential pro-democracy voter base. In addition, Mexico's ties with the United States are changing. Common interests in energy, manufacturing, and security, as well as an overlapping community formed by millions of binational families, have made Mexico's path forward increasingly important to its northern neighbor.

For most of the past century, U.S.-Mexican relations were conducted at arm's length. That began to change, however, in the 1980s and, even more, after the 1994 North American Free Trade Agreement (NAFTA) spurred greater bilateral economic engagement and cooperation. Mexico's democratic transition has further eased the wariness of some skeptics in Washington. Still, the U.S.-Mexican relationship is far from perfect. New bilateral policies are required, especially to facilitate the movement of people and goods across the U.S.-Mexican border. More important, the United States needs to start seeing Mexico as a partner instead of a problem.

Economic Revolution

Three decades ago, Mexico had an inward-looking, oil-dominated economy. The Institutional Revolutionary Party (PRI), which ruled the country for 71 years, maintained a stranglehold on the economy and the country as a whole. PRI presidents championed domestic industries with high tariffs, generous domestic subsidies, and export and production quotas. These policies limited trade, with primarily machinery, chemicals, and metals coming in, and oil, which accounted for three out of every four dollars of Mexico's exports, going out. State-owned enterprises controlled economic sectors as diverse as telecommunications, sugar, airlines, hotels, steel, and textiles. These state-sponsored monopolies provided employment for almost one million Mexicans, as well as patronage to party officials and union leaders. But they also weighed down the economy with overpriced goods, inefficient policies, and corruption, triggering repeated booms and busts.

Today, Mexico has shaken off this volatile past to become one of the most open and globalized economies in the world. It maintains free-trade agreements with over 40 countries. The country's trade as a percentage of GDP—a useful measure of economic openness—is 65 percent, compared with 59 percent in China, 32 percent in the United States, and 25 percent in Brazil. No longer addicted to oil, Mexico's export economy is now driven by manufacturing, especially of cars, computers, and appliances. The shift from commodities and agriculture to services and manufacturing has catapulted the country forward, and Mexico is outpacing many other emerging-market countries, including China, India, and Russia, in making this economic transition.

These fundamental changes began in 1982, at the onset of the Latin American debt crisis. Hit by rising interest rates and declining oil prices, the Mexican government stopped payment on some $80 billion in foreign obligations, mostly to U.S. commercial banks. The ensuing financial crisis further crippled the economy and cost millions their livelihoods, but it also forced the government to consider drastic economic reforms. President Miguel de la Madrid led the charge after 1982, cutting public spending, reducing subsidies, and signing the General Agreement on Tariffs and Trade (the predecessor of the World Trade Organization), which committed Mexico to lowering tariffs and trade barriers. His successor, Carlos Salinas, was even more aggressive. He eradicated the traditional *ejido* (communal landholding) system, privatized

hundreds of public companies, and negotiated NAFTA with the United States and Canada, a treaty that was, at the time, the most comprehensive and ambitious free-trade agreement in the world.

These policies helped, but in 1994, Mexico stumbled again. An overvalued peso, a weak banking sector, dwindling foreign reserves, and the PRI's elevated preelection spending led to yet another financial mess. The peso lost half its value in just weeks, GDP fell by seven percent, inflation soared to triple digits, and over one million Mexicans lost their jobs. Fortunately, due to the trade security provided by NAFTA and earlier reforms that had opened the economy, the recession was relatively short, with recovery beginning in 1996. Even better, Mexico emerged with a strong fiscal management system, including an independent central bank dedicated to curbing inflation and a finance ministry committed to balancing the federal budget.

The combination of permanent access to the world's largest consumer market, through NAFTA, and currency devaluation made Mexican businesses more globally competitive and led to a manufacturing boom and a fourfold surge in exports between 1990 and 2000. Industries producing goods such as auto parts, electronics, and apparel added some 800,000 jobs, pushing the total number of factory workers to well over one million. Foreign direct investment poured in, averaging $11 billion a year in the late 1990s.

Other economic transformations also accelerated during this time. Over two million farmers were put out of work as small-scale agriculture became unprofitable in the face of subsidized U.S. agribusiness. This reflects the harsh implications of NAFTA, but it is also a trend that is common to many industrializing economies, in which manufacturing and services replace agriculture as the drivers of economic growth and employment. In addition, oil became much less important to the economy. To be sure, it still funds over a third of the federal budget, but as a share of GDP, it fell from a peak of nearly 20 percent in 1981 to around six percent today.

Mexico's Middle

Along with these economic reforms came significant social changes, especially the rise of Mexico's middle class. By the early 1980s, the country's middle class had grown to about a third of the population, thanks to the PRI's commitment to accessible education and the expansion of public-sector employment. But the 1982 financial crisis and the subsequent reforms of the late 1980s and early 1990s hurt the government-nurtured middle class by trimming public-sector jobs and government subsidies and largess.

At the same time, these reforms opened up the space for a more diverse, less PRI-dependent middle class to grow. The past 15 years of economic stability have bettered the lives of many Mexicans, whose savings and investments are no longer repeatedly wiped out by financial crises. NAFTA has both increased investment in the economy and lowered costs for average Mexicans. A study by Tufts University's Global Development and Environment Institute shows that the agreement has lowered the price of basic goods in Mexico by some 50 percent, making salaries go much further than in the past. In addition, growing access to credit has enabled millions of Mexicans to buy their own homes and start or expand businesses.

As a result, modern Mexico is a middle-class country. The World Bank estimates that some 95 percent of Mexico's population is in the middle or the upper class. The Organization for Economic Cooperation and Development (OECD) also puts most of Mexico's population on the upper rungs, estimating that 50 percent of Mexicans are middle class and another 35 percent are upper class. Even the most stringent measurement, comparing incomes alongside access to health care, education, social security, housing, and food, finds that just over 45 percent of Mexicans are considered poor— meaning that almost 55 percent are not.

According to the World Bank, more than three-quarters of Mexicans are city dwellers, and the growing middle class is a decidedly urban phenomenon. Today's middle-class Mexicans are also much less dependent on the government than their parents were, as most work in the private sector. These professionals frequently fill jobs as accountants, lawyers, engineers, entrepreneurs, specialized factory workers, taxi drivers, or midlevel managers in Mexico's growing service and manufacturing sectors.

In addition, Mexico's workforce includes more women than ever before. Forty-five percent of Mexican women now work outside their homes— more than double the rate of 30 years ago. Although there are fewer dual-income households in Mexico than in many other developing countries, they are increasingly common. This trend is tied to a change in average family size, which has allowed women to pursue their own careers. In the 1970s, the typical Mexican family included seven children. Today, most women have only two children, which is the average in the United States. And Mexican children now spend much more time in school than they did in the past. In 1990, most children made it through only the primary grades. Today, the majority remain through high school.

As the number of Mexicans with greater earnings has increased, so, too, has consumption. With middle-class annual individual incomes estimated at somewhere between $7,000 and $85,000, households now earn enough to buy modern appliances, such as refrigerators, televisions, and washing machines. Approximately 80 percent of all Mexicans own a cell phone, half own a car, and nearly a third own a computer. The media might depict Mexico as a crime-ridden battlefield, but the country boasts a middle-income, emerging-market economy.

Not Your Parents' PRI

As Mexico's economy and society have changed, so has its politics. For decades, the PRI maintained political control through what the Peruvian writer Mario Vargas Llosa dubbed "the perfect dictatorship": buying votes, co-opting the opposition, and cracking down on dissidents. The seeds of democracy were planted in the 1980s, when voters, frustrated with the status quo, started supporting opposition candidates in regional elections. Political change gained momentum after the 1994 economic crisis, when dissatisfaction with the regime escalated. The PRI's control suffered a further blow from a 1996 electoral reform that made voter fraud harder to commit. In the late 1990s, the growing middle class abandoned the PRI altogether, first in the 1997 congressional elections and then in the 2000 presidential contest, in which it helped elect Vicente Fox of the National Action Party.

In 2012, voters, concerned about waning economic growth and unrelenting drug violence, ushered the PRI back into the executive branch. Some worry that the party's return has sounded the death knell for Mexico's democracy. Sure enough, President Enrique Peña Nieto's administration includes some old-guard politicos not known for championing democratic ideals. But Mexico's political system has changed since the PRI last held high office. Both the legislative and the judicial branches of government now provide checks and balances against presidential power. Congress was once filled with a permanent majority of PRI delegates who rarely questioned the edicts of their president. Today, the PRI holds a plurality, not a majority, in both houses, which means the party will have to negotiate with the opposition to pass legislation.

The Supreme Court provides another check on executive power. In the old days, the justices blessed whatever legislation came their way. But thanks to President Ernesto Zedillo's overhaul of the justice system in the mid-1990s, the court has become an independent and final arbiter on many contentious issues. The court has passed judgment on topics as diverse as the constitutionality of new legislation, the rules governing elections, and the jurisdiction of civilian courts over the military. It even overturned the controversial "Televisa law," passed by Congress in 2006, which assured the continued duopoly of the two dominant television networks.

Since 2000, power has also become increasingly decentralized and regionalized. At one time, a president could dismiss half of Mexico's sitting governors without a hint of blowback, as Salinas did during his 1988–94 term. Today, states and their elected leaders are more independent, both politically and, increasingly, economically. Some worry that decentralization might bolster local authoritarianism, but in reality, it will prevent the return of the old political model; because regional executives are more autonomous now, they can stand up to federal politicians.

Other developments, especially the expansion of an independent press, have further enriched Mexico's democracy. A few decades ago, if PRI leaders were displeased with news coverage, they could literally stop the presses, because the party held a monopoly on newsprint. Subsequent economic crises, however, and declining political power lessened the PRI's control of the media. Today, Mexico has a vibrant and fiercely independent press, led by publications such as *El Universal*, *Reforma*, and *La Jornada*. With the proliferation of social media and with information now publicly available through Mexico's freedom of information law, passed in 2002, Mexican civil-society organizations and individual voters can criticize and shame corrupt bureaucrats and politicians. Bulwarked by such fundamentals—checks and balances, an independent press, and a growing civil society—Mexican democracy seems here to stay.

Roadblocks

Still, many problems hold Mexico back. In recent decades, Mexico City has done little to bust the monopolies and oligopolies that hobble the country's growth, and in some cases, it has strengthened them. In addition to the state's control of energy, one or just a few companies still dominate the production of goods such as cement, glass, soft drinks, flour, sugar, and bread. The OECD estimates that these monopolies increase basic costs for Mexican families by some 40 percent. The Peña Nieto administration has promised to open up the energy sector, and some initial steps have been taken by regulators and the Supreme Court to break up these concentrations of economic power. Much more needs to happen, however, to level the economic playing field.

Shoddy infrastructure further limits Mexico's progress. Just over a third of its roads are paved, and its railways, ports, and airports fall short of filling the country's growing needs. There is little hope that this will improve anytime soon. Despite the promises of successive governments and leaders, from the PRI and the opposition alike, the World Bank estimates that public spending in Mexico is only half of what is needed for basic transportation maintenance, never mind necessary additions.

Plans for aggressive spending have failed in the past—first because of a lack of technically savvy bureaucrats able to take charge and push the projects through and later because of the global economic crisis. As a result, even though Mexico has advanced in the World Economic Forum's annual *Global Competitiveness Report* on measures such as access to financing and technology, it has stagnated in its infrastructure ranking.

Mexico's educational system is also subpar. Children now stay in school longer, but they do not seem to be getting much for their time. On tests by the Program for International Student Assessment, which compare academic performance, Mexico's students score lower than students from all the other OECD countries in reading, math, and science. Employers and graduates complain about the mismatch between training and opportunities: too many political science majors, for example, and not enough engineers. According to a study by Mexico's National Association of Universities and Higher Education Institutions, 40 percent of Mexican university graduates over the last ten years are now unemployed or working in a different field from the one they studied. Mexico needs to develop a properly trained work force if it is to ensure future prosperity.

Even more pressing, Mexico must deal with its crime problem. Extortion, kidnapping, and theft, not to mention rampant assault and murder, stunt economic growth—particularly that of small and medium-sized enterprises (the job creators in most economies), which cannot afford private security. Violence discourages domestic and foreign investment, preventing the construction of new factories that would provide jobs and boost local economies. Estimates by the Mexican government, as well as by private-sector investors, such as J.P. Morgan, suggest that insecurity shaves more than one percent off Mexico's GDP annually.

Crippled by corruption and impunity, the state fails to provide basic safety for many of its citizens. Several parts of the country lack effective police forces and sound court systems. New tools, such as the freedom of information act and enhanced press coverage, have helped expose wrongdoing, but such liberties are often fitfully employed, especially at the state and local level, where politicians and vested interests push back. So far, only a few heavy hitters have been successfully prosecuted for their misdeeds. Mexico's ban on the reelection of any official, from the local mayor to the president, makes politicians more concerned with pleasing party leaders (who can nominate them for their next position) than with serving their constituents. Civil-society leaders have called for a reform of this part of the constitution, but so far their efforts have failed.

Mexico City has taken some corrective steps in recent years, and levels of violence are declining in hotspots such as Ciudad Juárez and seem to have plateaued nationally. But the process of fundamentally transforming Mexico's law enforcement and justice systems is still ongoing. Mexico needs to expand its police training and reforms beyond the national level to reach state- and local-level forces and to finish revamping its justice system, creating courts that can punish the guilty and free the innocent. Although the new government has promised both, it remains to be seen if Peña Nieto will do what is necessary, throwing the full force of his administration behind these efforts.

If Mexico addresses these challenges, it will emerge as a powerful player on the international stage. A democratic and safe Mexico would attract billions of dollars in foreign investment and propel the country into the world's top economic ranks. Robust growth would both reduce northbound emigration and increase southbound trade, benefiting U.S. employers and employees alike. Already influential in the G-20 and other multilateral organizations, Mexico could become even more of a power broker in global institutions and help construct new international financial, trade, and climate-change accords.

After three transformative decades, Mexico is still forging its geopolitical, economic, and social identity. It can continue down the path toward becoming a top-ten world economy, a strong democracy with a middle-class society, and a confident global player. Or it can be consumed by its challenges—violence, crime, crumbling infrastructure, a weak educational system, economic roadblocks, and persistent corruption. Either way, Mexico's future will affect the United States.

Border Buddies

Since NAFTA was passed, U.S.-Mexican trade has more than tripled. Well over $1 billion worth of goods crosses the U.S.-Mexican border every day, as do 3,000 people, 12,000 trucks, and 1,200 railcars. Mexico is second only to Canada as a destination for U.S. goods, and sales to Mexico support an estimated six million American jobs, according to a report published by the Woodrow Wilson International Center's Mexico Institute. The composition of that bilateral trade has also changed in recent decades. Approximately 40 percent of the products made in Mexico today have parts that come from the United States. Many consumer goods, including cars, televisions, and computers, cross the border more than once during their production.

Admittedly, this process has sent some U.S. jobs south, but overall, cross-border production is good for U.S. employment. There is evidence that U.S. companies with overseas operations are more likely to create domestic jobs than those based solely in the United States. Using data collected confidentially from thousands of large U.S. manufacturing firms, the scholars Mihir Desai, C. Fritz Foley, and James Hines upended the conventional wisdom in a 2008 study, which found that when companies ramp up their investment and employment internationally, they invest more and hire more people at home, too. Overseas operations make companies more productive and competitive, and with improved products, lower prices, and higher sales, they are able to create new jobs everywhere. Washington should welcome the expansion of U.S. companies in Mexico because increasing cross-border production and trade between the two countries would boost U.S. employment and growth. Mexico is a ready, willing, and able economic partner, with which the United States has closer ties than it does with any other emerging-market country.

Familial and communal ties also unite the United States and Mexico. The number of Mexican immigrants in the United States doubled in the 1980s and then doubled again in the 1990s. Fleeing poor economic and employment conditions in Mexico and attracted by labor demand and family and community members already in the United States, an estimated ten million Mexicans have come north over the past three decades. This flow has recently slowed, thanks to changing demographics and economic improvements in Mexico and a weakening U.S. economy. Still, some 12 million Mexicans and over 30 million Mexican Americans call the United States home.

For all these reasons, the United States should strengthen its relationship with its neighbor, starting with immigration laws that support the binational individuals and communities that already exist in the United States and encourage the legal immigration of Mexican workers and their families. U.S. President Barack Obama has promised to send such legislation to Congress, but a strong anti-immigrant wing within the Republican Party and the slow U.S. economic recovery pose significant barriers to a comprehensive and far-reaching deal.

Nevertheless, the United States and Mexico urgently need to invest in border infrastructure, standardize their customs forms, and work to better facilitate legal trade between them. Furthermore, getting Americans to recognize the benefits of cross-border production will be an uphill battle, but it is one worth fighting in order to boost the United States' exports, jobs, and overall economic growth.

On the security front, U.S. efforts must move beyond cracking down on drug trafficking to helping Mexico combat crime more generally. Security links have expanded since 2007, when Washington and Mexico City began taking on drug traffickers together. Today, Obama should support Peña Nieto's strategy of cracking down on violence rather than try to eliminate the drug trade. Washington should also expand its law enforcement training programs, currently conducted primarily at the federal level, to Mexico's state and local police forces and justice systems. Washington and Mexico City should also invest together in border community projects and programs that support social and economic development in often neglected and crime-ridden areas.

New administrations are beginning their terms in both countries. In Mexico, Peña Nieto has six years to overcome his country's remaining economic, social, and political barriers. Obama has the opportunity to strengthen U.S. manufacturing, production, and security by working with the United States' increasingly prosperous neighbor. It is in the interests of both countries to form a lasting partnership now.

Rethinking the Welfare State: Asia's Next Revolution

Countries across the Continent Are Building Welfare States—with a Chance to Learn from the West's Mistakes

THE ECONOMIST

© The Economist Newspaper Limited, London (September 8, 2012).

Asia's economies have long wowed the world with their dynamism. Thanks to years of spectacular growth, more people have been pulled from abject poverty in modern Asia than at any other time in history. But as they become more affluent, the region's citizens want more from their governments. Across the continent pressure is growing for public pensions, national health insurance, unemployment benefits and other hallmarks of social protection. As a result, the world's most vibrant economies are shifting gear, away from simply building wealth towards building a welfare state.

The speed and scale of this shift are mind-boggling. Last October Indonesia's government promised to provide all its citizens with health insurance by 2014. It is building the biggest "single-payer" national health scheme—where one government outfit collects the contributions and foots the bills—in the world. In just two years China has extended pension coverage to an additional 240m rural folk, far more than the total number of people covered by Social Security, America's public-pension system. A few years ago about 80% of people in rural China had no health insurance. Now virtually everyone does. In India some 40m households benefit from a government scheme to provide up to 100 days' work a year at the minimum wage, and the state has extended health insurance to some 110m poor people, more than double the number of uninsured in America.

If you take Germany's introduction of pensions in the 1880s as the beginning and Britain's launch of its National Health Service in 1948 as the apogee, the creation of Europe's welfare states took more than half a century. Some Asian countries will build theirs in a decade. If they get things wrong, especially through unaffordable promises, they could wreck the world's most dynamic economies. But if they create affordable safety nets, they will not just improve life for their own citizens but also become role models themselves. At a time when governments in the rich world are failing to re-design states to cope with ageing populations and gaping budget deficits, this could be another area where Asia leapfrogs the West.

Beyond Bismarck and Beveridge

History offers many lessons for the Asians on what to avoid. Europe's welfare states began as basic safety nets. But over time they turned into cushions. That was partly because, after wars and the Depression, European societies made redistribution their priority, but also because the recipients of welfare spending became powerful interest groups. The eventual result, all too often, was economic sclerosis with an ever-bigger state. America has kept its safety net less generous, but has made mistakes in creating its entitlements system—including making unaffordable pension and health-care promises, and tying people's health insurance to their employment.

The record in other parts of the emerging world, especially Latin America, is even worse. Governments have tended to collect insufficient tax revenue to cover their spending promises. Social protection often aggravated inequalities, because pensions and health care flowed to affluent urban workers but not the really poor. Brazil famously has a first-world rate of government spending but third-world public services.

Asia's governments are acutely conscious of all this. They have little desire to replace traditions of hard work and thrift with a flabby welfare dependency. The region's giants can seek inspiration not from Greece but from tiny Singapore, where government spending is only a fifth of GDP but schools and hospitals are among the best in the world. So far, the safety nets in big Asian countries have generally been minimalist: basic health insurance and pensions which replace a small fraction of workers' former income. Even now, the region's social spending relative to the size of its economies is only about 30% of the rich-country average and lower than any part of the emerging world except sub-Saharan Africa.

That leaves a fair amount of room for expansion. But Asia also faces a number of peculiarly tricky problems. One is demography. Although a few countries, notably India, are relatively youthful, the region includes some of the world's most rapidly ageing populations. Today China has five workers for every old person. By 2035 the ratio will have fallen to two. In America, by contrast, the baby-boom generation meant that the Social Security system had five contributors per beneficiary in 1960, a quarter of a century after its introduction. It still has three workers for every retired person.

Another problem is size, which makes welfare especially hard. The three giants—China, India and Indonesia—are vast places with huge regional income disparities within their borders. Building a welfare state in any one of them is a bit like creating a single welfare state across the European Union. Lastly, many Asian workers (in India it is about 90%) are in the "informal" economy, making it harder to verify their incomes or reach them with transfers.

Cuddly Tigers, Not Flabby Cats

How should these challenges be overcome? There is no single solution that applies from India to South Korea. Different countries will, and should, experiment with different welfare models. But there are three broad principles that all Asian governments could usefully keep in mind.

The first is to pay even more attention to the affordability over time of any promises. The size of most Asian pensions may be modest, but people collect them at an early age. In China, for example, women retire at 55; in Thailand many employees are obliged to stop work at 60 and can withdraw their pension funds at 55. That is patently unsustainable. Across Asia, retirement ages need to rise, and should be indexed to life expectancy.

Second, Asian governments need to target their social spending more carefully. Crudely put, social provision should be about protecting the poor more than subsidising the rich. In fast-ageing societies, especially, handouts to the old must not squeeze out investment in the young. Too many Asian governments still waste oodles of public money on regressive universal subsidies. Indonesia, for instance, last year spent nine times as much on fuel subsidies as it did on health care, and the lion's share of those subsidies flows to the country's most affluent. As they promise a broader welfare state, Asia's politicians have the political opportunity, and the economic responsibility, to get rid of this kind of wasteful spending.

Third, Asia's reformers should concentrate on being both flexible and innovative. Don't stifle labour markets with rigid severance rules or over-generous minimum wages. Make sure pensions are portable, between jobs and regions. Don't equate a publicly funded safety net with government provision of services (a single public payer may be the cheapest way to provide basic health care, but that does not have to mean every nurse needs to be a government employee). And use technology to avoid the inefficiencies that hobble the rich world's public sector. From making electronic health records ubiquitous to organising transfer payments through mobile phones, Asian countries can create new and efficient delivery systems with modern technology.

In the end, the success of Asia's great leap towards welfare provision will be determined by politics as much as economics. The continent's citizens will have to show a willingness to plan ahead, work longer and eschew handouts based on piling up debt for future generations: virtues that have so far eluded their rich-world counterparts. Achieving that political maturity will require the biggest leap of all.

Northern Lights

The Nordic Countries Are Reinventing Their Model of Capitalism

THE ECONOMIST

Thirty years ago Margaret Thatcher turned Britain into the world's leading centre of "thinking the unthinkable." Today that distinction has passed to Sweden. The streets of Stockholm are awash with the blood of sacred cows. The think-tanks are brimful of new ideas. The erstwhile champion of the "third way" is now pursuing a far more interesting brand of politics.

Sweden has reduced public spending as a proportion of GDP from 67% in 1993 to 49% today. It could soon have a smaller state than Britain. It has also cut the top marginal tax rate by 27 percentage points since 1983, to 57%, and scrapped a mare's nest of taxes on property, gifts, wealth and inheritance. This year it is cutting the corporate-tax rate from 26.3% to 22%.

Sweden has also donned the golden straitjacket of fiscal orthodoxy with its pledge to produce a fiscal surplus over the economic cycle. Its public debt fell from 70% of GDP in 1993 to 37% in 2010, and its budget moved from an 11% deficit to a surplus of 0.3% over the same period. This allowed a country with a small, open economy to recover quickly from the financial storm of 2007–08. Sweden has also put its pension system on a sound foundation, replacing a defined-benefit system with a defined-contribution one and making automatic adjustments for longer life expectancy.

Most daringly, it has introduced a universal system of school vouchers and invited private schools to compete with public ones. Private companies also vie with each other to provide state-funded health services and care for the elderly. Anders Aslund, a Swedish economist who lives in America, hopes that Sweden is pioneering "a new conservative model"; Brian Palmer, an American anthropologist who lives in Sweden, worries that it is turning into "the United States of Swedeamerica."

There can be no doubt that Sweden's quiet revolution has brought about a dramatic change in its economic performance. The two decades from 1970 were a period of decline: the country was demoted from being the world's fourth-richest in 1970 to 14th-richest in 1993, when the average Swede was poorer than the average Briton or Italian. The two decades from 1990 were a period of recovery: GDP growth between 1993 and 2010 averaged 2.7% a year and productivity 2.1% a year, compared with 1.9% and 1% respectively for the main 15 EU countries.

For most of the 20th century Sweden prided itself on offering what Marquis Childs called, in his 1936 book of that title, a "Middle Way" between capitalism and socialism. Global companies such as Volvo and Ericsson generated wealth while enlightened bureaucrats built the *Folkhemmet* or "People's Home." As the decades rolled by, the middle way veered left. The government kept growing: public spending as a share of GDP nearly doubled from 1960 to 1980 and peaked at 67% in 1993. Taxes kept rising. The Social Democrats (who ruled Sweden for 44 uninterrupted years from 1932 to 1976 and for 21 out of the 24 years from 1982 to 2006) kept squeezing business. "The era of neo-capitalism is drawing to an end," said Olof Palme, the party's leader, in 1974. "It is some kind of socialism that is the key to the future."

The other Nordic countries have been moving in the same direction, if more slowly. Denmark has one of the most liberal labour markets in Europe. It also allows parents to send children to private schools at public expense and make up the difference in cost with their own money. Finland is harnessing the skills of venture capitalists and angel investors to promote innovation and entrepreneurship. Oil-rich Norway is a partial exception to this pattern, but even there the government is preparing for its post-oil future.

This is not to say that the Nordics are shredding their old model. They continue to pride themselves on the generosity of their welfare states. About 30% of their labour force works in the public sector, twice the average in the Organisation for Economic Development and Co-operation, a rich-country think-tank. They continue to believe in combining open economies with public investment in human capital. But the new Nordic model begins with the

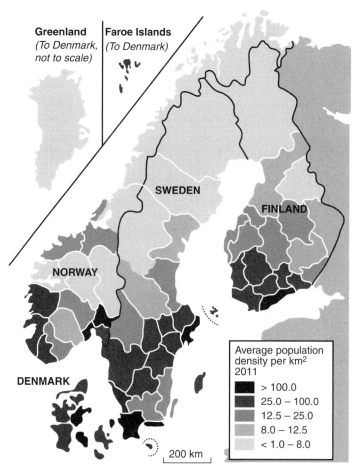

Figure 3.2 Map of Greenland, Faroe Islands, Denmark, Norway, Sweden, and Finland
Sources: Nordregio & NLS Finland

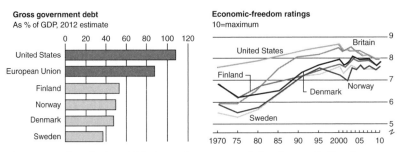

	Population 2012, m	GDP per person 2012, $'000	GDP, average annual growth rate 2002-12, %
Denmark	5.6	55.4	0.6
Finland	5.4	45.5	1.6
Norway	5.0	99.3	1.6
Sweden	9.5	54.9	2.2

All figures are estimates

Gross government debt
As % of GDP, 2012 estimate

Economic-freedom ratings
10=maximum

Figure 3.3   Population, GDP, Gross Government Debt, Economic Freedom Ratings
Sources: IMF; national sources; Fraser Institute; OECD

individual rather than the state. It begins with fiscal responsibility rather than pump-priming: all four Nordic countries have AAA ratings and debt loads significantly below the euro-zone average. It begins with choice and competition rather than paternalism and planning. The economic-freedom index of the Fraser Institute, a Canadian think-tank, shows Sweden and Finland catching up with the United States (see chart). The leftward lurch has been reversed: rather than extending the state into the market, the Nordics are extending the market into the state.

Why are the Nordic countries doing this? The obvious answer is that they have reached the limits of big government. "The welfare state we have is excellent in most ways," says Gunnar Viby Mogensen, a Danish historian. "We only have this little problem. We can't afford it." The economic storms that shook all the Nordic countries in the early 1990s provided a foretaste of what would happen if they failed to get their affairs in order.

There are two less obvious reasons. The old Nordic model depended on the ability of a cadre of big companies to generate enough money to support the state, but these companies are being slimmed by global competition. The old model also depended on people's willingness to accept direction from above, but Nordic populations are becoming more demanding.

Small Is Powerful

The Nordic countries have a collective population of only 26m. Finland is the only one of them that is a member of both the European Union and the euro area. Sweden is in the EU but outside the euro and has a freely floating currency. Denmark, too, is in the EU and outside the euro area but pegs its currency to the euro. Norway has remained outside the EU.

But there are compelling reasons for paying attention to these small countries on the edge of Europe. The first is that they have reached the future first. They are grappling with problems that other countries too will have to deal with in due course, such as what to do when you reach the limits of big government and how to organise society when almost all women work. And the Nordics are coming up with highly innovative solutions that reject the tired orthodoxies of left and right.

The second reason to pay attention is that the new Nordic model is proving strikingly successful. The

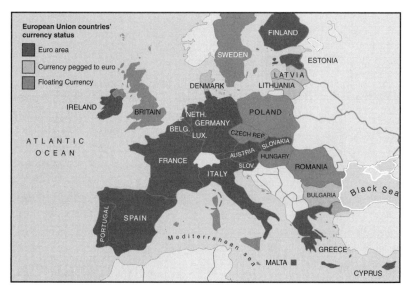

Figure 3.4   Europe's Economies
Source: The Economist

Nordics dominate indices of competitiveness as well as of well-being. Their high scores in both types of league table mark a big change since the 1980s when welfare took precedence over competitiveness.

The Nordics do particularly well in two areas where competitiveness and welfare can reinforce each other most powerfully: innovation and social inclusion. BCG, as the Boston Consulting Group calls itself, gives all of them high scores on its e-intensity index, which measures the internet's impact on business and society. Booz & Company, another consultancy, points out that big companies often test-market new products on Nordic consumers because of their willingness to try new things. The Nordic countries led the world in introducing the mobile network in the 1980s and the GSM standard in the 1990s. Today they are ahead in the transition to both e-government and the cashless economy. Locals boast that they pay their taxes by SMS. This correspondent gave up changing sterling into local currencies because everything from taxi rides to cups of coffee can be paid for by card.

The Nordics also have a strong record of drawing on the talents of their entire populations, with the possible exception of their immigrants. They have the world's highest rates of social mobility: in a comparison of social mobility in eight advanced countries by Jo Blanden, Paul Gregg and Stephen Machin, of the London School of Economics, they occupied the first four places. America and Britain came last. The Nordics also have exceptionally high rates of female labour-force participation: in Denmark not far off as many women go out to work (72%) as men (79%).

Flies in the Ointment

This special report will examine the way the Nordic governments are updating their version of capitalism to deal with a more difficult world. It will note that in doing so they have unleashed a huge amount of creativity and become world leaders in reform. Nordic entrepreneurs are feeling their oats in a way not seen since the early 20th century. Nordic writers and artists—and indeed Nordic chefs and game designers—are enjoying a creative renaissance.

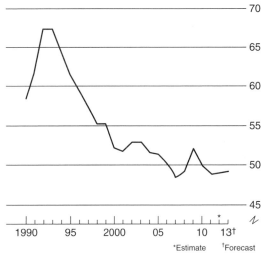

                        *Estimate   †Forecast

Figure 3.5   It Can Be Done
Sweden's Government Spending as % of GDP
Source: IMF

attack in 2011, but also on a more mundane level every day. Sweden is finding it particularly hard to integrate its large population of refugees.

The Nordic model is still a work in progress. The three forces that have obliged the Nordic countries to revamp it—limited resources, rampant globalisation and growing diversity—are gathering momentum. The Nordics will have to continue to upgrade their model, but they will also have to fight to retain what makes it distinctive. Lant Pritchett and Michael Woolcock, of the World Bank, have coined the term "getting to Denmark" to describe successful modernisation. This report will suggest that the trick is not just to get to Denmark; it is to stay there.

The final caveat is about learning from the Nordic example, which other countries are rightly trying to do. Britain, for example, is introducing Swedish-style "free schools." But transferring such lessons is fraught with problems. The Nordics' success depends on their long tradition of good government, which emphasises not only honesty and transparency but also consensus and compromise. Learning from Denmark may be as difficult as staying there.

The report will also add caveats. The growing diversity of Nordic societies is generating social tensions, most horrifically in Norway, where Anders Breivik killed 77 people in a racially motivated

DISCUSSION QUESTIONS

1) The first reading in this section discussed the concept of "failed states." It questions the utility of this idea. How can we tell if a social scientific concept like "failed states" is good or useful?

2) This section's second reading deals with the case of Mexico, a state that has both faced serious security problems and made major social and economic advances in recent years. What does the reading's author, Shannon O'Neill, think best accounts for these developments?

3) One of the major questions of contemporary global politics concerns the fate of the welfare state. On the one hand, there is a debate about what is happening or should happen to the established welfare states in the advanced industrial and postindustrial world. Some have argued that they will need to be scaled back, and others that they can and should be maintained. At the same time, a number of developing countries are still working to construct welfare states. Put these two processes together and assess their combined implications for the likely future of the welfare state.

Development

This section focuses on explanations of development. As with the subjects of other units in this book, there are many questions we could ask here. Traditionally, though, the core question of development studies asks why some countries are wealthier than others.

This section examines this question by looking at an example of theoretical debate from the public forum. In July 2012, presidential candidate Mitt Romney, during a trip to Israel, made a statement about the role "culture" plays in the disparity in development and standards of living between Israelis and Palestinians. After some outcry, Romney wrote a follow-up article in which he asked a question that has long been debated in the study of development: "But what exactly accounts for prosperity if not culture?" Essentially, Romney argued that wealth and poverty are, at least in part, products of cultural differences. This was controversial because the word "culture" is used in many different ways, and some thought (inaccurately, we think) that Romney was impugning ways of life and beliefs of entire peoples. What Romney was really asserting is that certain values are good for development and that others increase the likelihood of poverty and economic stagnation. This places Romney's ideas in a tradition of thought that goes back to Max Weber's famous argument about capitalism and the "Protestant ethic."

We find scholars' responses to Romney's comments compelling because they show a major comparative politics debate coming out of the ivory tower and into the public forum. We include three selections that illustrate different perspectives on the causes of variations in development. As you read each one, don't just focus on their critique of the cultural values argument. Rather, look at what the authors say about their own theories. First, Daron Acemoglu and James Robinson offer a critical account that emphasizes that *institutions* matter more than values. Then, Jared Diamond offers a critique emphasizing the importance of *geography*. Finally, the journalist Charles Kenny draws on the research of several scholars to circle back to "culture." He tries to provide different, and more limited, arguments about the possible role of norms and values in producing economic growth and suggests that such factors matter less and less as time goes on, in part, perhaps, because of global cultural convergence on key matters. As you read these short pieces, try to think like a scientist—keep an open mind. Knowing which of these theories works best will require some empirical analysis. Rather than trying to decide who you agree with, try to figure out how we could determine, on the basis of evidence which of the development theories mentioned here are best.

We do not want you to draw the conclusion that all of development studies in comparative politics focus on the debate about "culture," "institutions," and geography. The section concludes with one final reading, which looks more concretely at development trends in sub-Saharan Africa, and argues for ten major claims about the region. Many of these suggest that Africa—which has long been the world's least developed continent by most measures—is moving toward a more dynamic phase of development in the future. If so, this could dramatically change common perceptions about the continent.

Uncultured: Mitt Romney Doesn't Know Much about Economic History

DARON ACEMOGLU AND JAMES A. ROBINSON

"Culture makes all the difference," Mitt Romney told an intimate gathering of Israeli businessmen at Jerusalem's posh King David Hotel. "And as I come here and I look out over this city and consider the accomplishments of the people of this nation, I recognize the power of at least culture and a few other things."

The U.S. Republican presidential hopeful, whose own net worth is estimated at roughly $250 million, went on to compare Israelis' economically comfortable existence with the more straitened circumstances in Palestinian areas. The comment predictably drew the ire of Palestinian leaders, with one senior official deriding it as "racist."

Despite the controversy, Romney then doubled down on his argument in a short op-ed for the *National Review*, asking, "But what exactly accounts for prosperity if not culture?" Unfortunately for Romney, the answer is: quite a lot. True, his cultural explanation for why Israel is richer than Palestine has sparked an important debate that rarely occurs in the parochial, U.S.-centric world of American presidential elections. And given the important role the United States plays in global affairs, a presidential candidate's views about why the United States is more economically successful than most parts of the world are an important indicator of how he would approach the job.

Unfortunately, Romney's views are seriously out of sync with those of the great mass of social scientists. For one, as his more extended argument in the *National Review* illustrates, he confuses "culture" with institutions. By culture, social scientists mean people's values and beliefs. Romney refers to Americans' "work ethic," which is cultural, but he also claims that political and economic freedoms are the real keys to economic success. But political and economic freedom are not guaranteed by (or even related to) culture but by institutions, such as the U.S.

Constitution or its system of property rights. Romney did cite Harvard University historian David Landes, who did indeed argue that values and beliefs are crucial for economic development, as providing the intellectual origins of his views—but his focus on institutions is much more in line with our book *Why Nations Fail* than with Landes. Indeed, the facts on the ground in the Middle East illustrate the power not of culture, but of institutions.

It is true, of course, that living standards are much higher in Israel than in Gaza or the West Bank—the gap is even wider, in fact, than Romney claimed. Israelis have much higher levels of educational attainment and better technology, and they benefit from much better provision of public services—for example, roads, health care, and water—than their Palestinian neighbors. There is also no denying that there are important cultural differences between Palestinians and Israelis: For instance, the former are primarily Muslims, while the latter are primarily Jewish.

But is there any cause-and-effect relationship between these cultural realities and differences in prosperity? The evidence suggests not. In fact, as economists Maristella Botticini and Zvi Eckstein point out in their recent book, *The Chosen Few: How Education Shaped Jewish History*, the origins of the high human-capital levels of Jews are in the historical adoption of educational institutions in Jewish society that induced people to become highly educated. This decision then led Jews to have a comparative advantage in trade and commerce—specializations that have served them well in the modern world. This is where the roots of Israel's current prosperity lie, because these highly educated people migrated there, bringing their institutions with them. There was no cultural proclivity that led Jews to introduce or sustain these rules forcing Jews to educate their children. Rather, they emerged out of a political struggle between the Pharisees and the Sadducees to control Jewish society.

These new Israelis migrated to a place that had suffered a long history of colonial exploitation under the Ottomans and the British, who created extractive political and economic institutions—in other words, political institutions that concentrated power narrowly and economic institutions designed to redistribute income and power to themselves at the expense of society. The Israelis replaced these with mostly inclusive institutions that encouraged technological progress and economic growth and created the Middle East's first democracy, but did not spread it to the Palestinians.

This happened for several reasons, none of them cultural. Let's start with the long history of Arab-Israeli enmity: The existence of the state of Israel was contested by the surrounding Arab states, leading to a long series of conflicts and Israel's capture of the West Bank and Gaza in 1967. It is hardly surprising that the Palestinian territories—under occupation and geographically separated from each other—were unable to develop inclusive political and economic institutions under such circumstances. The effects of the conflict haven't just been limited to the Palestinians: Several authoritarian Arab governments have used it to divert the attention of their citizens and consolidate their corrupt grip on power.

The Middle East conflict extracts political and economic costs on the Palestinians to this day. Israel continues to expropriate large tracts of land in the West Bank for settlements, and of course such insecure property rights have been disastrous for investment and prosperity on the Palestinian side. Both territories have also had serious economic restrictions imposed on them by the Israeli government, not to mention the destruction of infrastructure and buildings.

All this may be justified as necessary to maintain the security of the Israeli state, but it has obvious consequences for Palestinian prosperity. In addition, the Palestinians have not done well at creating the type of inclusive political institutions that are critical for generating economic development. This is mostly because the conflict and struggle for statehood damages accountability and creates serious political polarization, not due to any innate cultural differences.

Leaving aside the case of Israel and Palestine, we show in *Why Nations Fail* that Romney's ideas about "freedom" are much closer to the right way to think about relative prosperity than his ones about "culture." Rich countries are those that have created inclusive political and economic institutions. These spread political power broadly in society and make it accountable; they create an economy that can harness the talents, skills, and creativities of the vast mass of their citizens. We also show that cultural differences simply cannot account for the differences in economic prosperity we see today. They are either irrelevant, as in the case of the Israelis and the Palestinians, or they are themselves the product of institutional differences.

The most dramatic example of this is the divide between North and South Korea—a previously cohesive cultural entity driven apart by war and radically different institutions. Since their split six decades ago, the South has prospered under its inclusive system, while the North—with its extractive institutions based on central planning and continuous repression—has been driven to the brink of famine. Bizarrely, Romney cites the case of the Koreas to support his culturalist argument. But the divergence of these two countries obviously cannot be blamed on deeply rooted cultural factors—the only explanation is institutional differences and geopolitical realities. If Romney truly wants to understand the irrelevance of cultural factors to countries' success or failure, it's not Jerusalem he should've visited—it's the Demilitarized Zone.

Romney Hasn't Done His Homework

JARED DIAMOND

Mitt Romney's latest controversial remark, about the role of culture in explaining why some countries are rich and powerful while others are poor and weak, has attracted much comment. I was especially interested in his remark because he misrepresented my views and, in contrasting them with another scholar's arguments, oversimplified the issue.

It is not true that my book "Guns, Germs and Steel," as Mr. Romney described it in a speech in Jerusalem, "basically says the physical characteristics of the land account for the differences in the success of the people that live there. There is iron ore on the land and so forth."

That is so different from what my book actually says that I have to doubt whether Mr. Romney read it. My focus was mostly on biological features, like plant and animal species, and among physical characteristics, the ones I mentioned were continents' sizes and shapes and relative isolation. I said nothing about iron ore, which is so widespread that its distribution has had little effect on the different successes of different peoples. (As I learned this week, Mr. Romney also mischaracterized my book in his memoir, "No Apology: Believe in America.")

That's not the worst part. Even scholars who emphasize social rather than geographic explanations—like the Harvard economist David S. Landes, whose book "The Wealth and Poverty of Nations" was mentioned favorably by Mr. Romney—would find Mr. Romney's statement that "culture makes all the difference" dangerously out of date. In fact, Mr. Landes analyzed multiple factors (including climate) in explaining why the industrial revolution first occurred in Europe and not elsewhere.

Just as a happy marriage depends on many different factors, so do national wealth and power. That is not to deny culture's significance. Some countries have political institutions and cultural practices—honest government, rule of law, opportunities to accumulate money—that reward hard work. Others don't. Familiar examples are the contrasts between neighboring countries sharing similar environments but with very different institutions. (Think of South Korea versus North Korea, or Haiti versus the Dominican Republic.) Rich, powerful countries tend to have good institutions that reward hard work. But institutions and culture aren't the whole answer, because some countries notorious for bad institutions (like Italy and Argentina) are rich, while some virtuous countries (like Tanzania and Bhutan) are poor.

A different set of factors involves geography, which embraces many more aspects than the physical characteristics Mr. Romney dismissed. One such geographic factor is latitude, which has big effects on wealth and power today: tropical countries tend to be poorer than temperate-zone countries. Reasons include the debilitating effects of tropical diseases on life span and work, and the average lower productivity of agriculture and soils in the tropics than in the temperate zones.

A second factor is access to the sea. Countries without a seacoast or big navigable rivers tend to be poor, because transport costs over land or by air are much higher than transport costs by sea.

A third geographic factor is the history of agriculture. If an extraterrestrial had toured earth in the year 2000 B.C., the visitor would have noticed that centralized government, writing and metal tools were already widespread in Eurasia but hadn't yet appeared in the New World, sub-Saharan Africa or Australia. That long head start would have let the visitor predict correctly that today, most of the world's richest and most powerful countries would be Eurasian countries (and their overseas settlements in North America, Australia and New Zealand).

The reason is the historical effect of geography: 13,000 years ago, all peoples everywhere were hunter-gatherers living in sparse populations without centralized government, armies, writing or metal tools. These four roots of power arose as consequences of the development of agriculture, which generated human population explosions and accumulations of food surpluses capable of feeding full-time leaders, soldiers, scribes and inventors. But agriculture could originate only in those few regions endowed with many wild plant and animal species suitable for domestication, like wild wheat, rice, pigs and cattle.

In short, geographic explanations and cultural-institutional explanations aren't independent of each other. Of course, not all agricultural regions developed honest centralized government, but no nonagricultural region ever developed any centralized government, whether honest or dishonest. That's why institutions promoting wealth today arose first in Eurasia, the area with the oldest and most productive agriculture.

What does this mean for Americans? Can we assume that the United States, blessed with temperate location and seacoasts and navigable rivers, will remain rich forever, while tropical or landlocked countries are doomed to eternal poverty?

Of course not. Some tropical and subtropical countries have become richer despite geographic limitations. They've invested in public health to overcome their disease burdens (Botswana and the Philippines). They've invested in crops adapted to the tropics (Brazil and Malaysia). They've focused their economies on sectors other than agriculture (Singapore and Taiwan).

Conversely, geographic advantages don't guarantee permanent success, as the growing difficulties in Europe and America show. We Americans fail to provide superior education and economic incentives to much of our population. India, China and other countries that have not been world leaders are investing heavily in education, technology and infrastructure. They're offering economic opportunities to more and more of their citizens. That's part of the reason jobs are moving overseas. Our geography won't keep us rich and powerful if we can't get a good education, can't afford health care and can't count on our hard work's being rewarded by good jobs and rising incomes.

Mitt Romney may become our next president. Will he continue to espouse one-factor explanations for multicausal problems, and fail to understand history and the modern world? If so, he will preside over a declining nation squandering its advantages of location and history.

Culture Matters—Just Not as Much as Romney Thinks

CHARLES KENNY

Mitt Romney created a stir this week when he pointed to the immense difference in wealth between Israel and the Palestinian territories and explained it with his interpretation of Harvard economic historian David Landes's work that "culture makes all the difference."

By now there is wide agreement that Romney used a pretty terrible example to illustrate Landes's point. And yet the proposition that "culture" is a factor in long-term economic performance is increasingly accepted among development economists.

What Romney seems to have missed is that culture is a declining barrier to development worldwide.

After his remarks in Jerusalem set off a media firestorm, candidate Romney attempted to clarify them in interviews and a blog post in the *National Review*. When he talked about culture, what he meant was liberty: Pointing to the U.S., Romney suggested that "Free people and their free enterprises are what drive our economic vitality" and that these were features Israel shares. With regard to Israel and the Palestinians, his clarifications did not help bolster the case, not least because the freedom of people and enterprise in the West Bank has been considerably constrained by Israel itself. The World Bank's latest report on Palestine suggests that sustainable economic growth "necessitates a lifting of Israeli restrictions on access to land, water, a range of raw materials, and export markets."

As for the broader argument that norms and inherited behavior matter to long-run economic performance, Romney's comments weren't entirely off-base. In a recent paper, Enrico Spolaore and Romain Wacziarg of the National Bureau of Economic Research review evidence of the "deep roots" of development. They note the considerable number of studies pointing to the importance of ethnic and linguistic factors on economic outcomes within and between countries—not least analysis by economists Stelios Michalopoulos and Elias Papaioannou suggesting that levels of regional economic development in Africa today are determined more by which ethnic group lived in the region before colonization than by which country currently controls the land.

Spolaore and Wacziarg also note that countries that are rich today are usually full of people descended from places where states were centralized; agriculture developed early; and such technologies as the wheel and the compass spread 1,000-plus years ago. Norms and values transmitted across generations may help account for that finding. Their research suggests that "genetic distance"—a measure of when two present-day populations shared common ancestors—helps to predict the difference in economic outcomes among countries. The smaller the genetic distance between two populations, the more similar their modern condition incomes.

The researchers suggest that this may be because genetically closer populations share similar cultural values, and that means technologies will spread between them more easily. An example: In the Eurovision Song Contest—a cross between *American Idol* and the Olympics for Europop stars—viewers in Cyprus give 7.4 points more to Greek singers than the average viewer, and Greek viewers award Cypriot singers 6.3 additional points. Such cultural affinity translates into more trade than would be predicted by standard economic models and doubtless, easier technology transfer as well.

At the same time, Spolaore and Wacziarg note that culture is less a barrier to development than it used to be. They suggest that genetic proximity has around one-half the influence on income differences today as it did in 1870. They also accept that deep historical factors such as embedded culture account for only a proportion—probably the minority—of modern variation in income across countries. One reason for this declining influence is that a range of different populations has overcome the barrier of cross-cultural technology diffusion, lowering in turn the barriers for those that follow. (Think Japan, followed by much of South Asia and East Asia.) This alone, they argue, should mean that genetic distance should eventually have no effect on income differences as more and more societies reach the global technological frontier.

A further factor behind the declining impact of culture on levels of development may be that global cultural change is itself increasingly rapid—and converging. Think about attitudes toward gay people, for example: Across the globe, discriminatory opinions have been declining as they have in the U.S. The proportion of Indians saying homosexuality is "never justifiable" has dropped from 89 percent in 1990 to 48 percent in 2008. Worldwide attitudes on issues from the importance of girls' education to voting have dramatically changed over the last 50 years as well. As a result, most countries see gender parity in education as a worthwhile goal, and democracy has never been as widespread. Both developments may have helped level disparities between rich and poor nations.

Perhaps the most unfortunate aspect of Romney's comments on "culture" and development was his failure to recognize how much potential exists for development in the Palestinian territories—if Israel and the Palestinians can ever forge a durable peace. In today's world, "culture" is a less-important factor than ever before, which means change can be incredibly rapid when circumstances allow. That's reason for hope, even in the seeming morass of the Middle East.

Lions on the Move: 10 Things You Don't Know about Africa's Booming Economy

SUSAN LUND AND AREND VAN WAMELEN

Republished with permission of *Foreign Policy*, from "Lions on the Move," Susan Lund and Arend van Wamelen, © 2012; permission conveyed through Copyright Clearance Center, Inc.

Africa is no longer the "lost continent" of popular imagination. The region has been growing rapidly for over a decade, the private sector is expanding, and a new class of consumers is wielding considerable spending power. And because of its young and growing population, the sky is the limit for future growth: Between 2010 and 2020, the continent is set to add 122 million people to its labor force. An expansion of this magnitude should set the stage for dynamic growth, but capturing this potential will require a change in economic development strategy. At its current pace, Africa is not generating wage-paying jobs rapidly enough to absorb its massive labor force, which will be the largest in the world by 2035.

Across Africa's diverse mosaic of countries, the challenge is the same: to create the kind of jobs that will ensure continued prosperity and stability for its citizens and enable Africa to become a major player in the world economy. If current trends continue, it will take the continent half a century to reach the same share of its labor force in stable, paying jobs as we see in East Asia today. Africa's most developed economies have a better record in producing wage-based employment, but shortfalls persist even in countries like South Africa, Egypt, and Morocco. Without wage-paying jobs, millions will be forced to turn to subsistence activities to survive, squandering vast potential.

To change this picture, Africa's leaders must move to accelerate job creation in order to entrench economic growth and continue to expand Africa's emerging consuming class. But it won't be easy. To illuminate the opportunities and challenges ahead, here are 10 things you might not know about Africa's economic landscape:

1. Africa is booming.

Africa has been the second-fastest-growing region in the world over the past 10 years. It has posted average annual GDP growth of 5.1 percent over the past decade, driven by greater political stability and economic reforms that have unleashed the private sector in many of the continent's varied mosaic of economies.

Poverty is also on the retreat. A new consuming class has taken its place: Since 2000, 31 million African households have joined the world's consuming class. At this point, when their household incomes exceed $5,000, measured at purchasing power parity, consumers begin to direct more than half their income to things other than food and shelter. The continent now has around 90 million people who fit this definition. That figure is projected to reach 128 million by 2020.

Africa now has considerable discretionary spending power. Indeed, contrary to conventional wisdom, the majority of Africa's growth has come from domestic spending and non-commodity sectors, rather than the resources boom.

2. Africa is poised to have the largest labor force in the world.

By 2035, Africa's labor force will be bigger than that of any individual country in the world—even bigger than economic behemoths like India and China. That offers the continent a chance to reap a demographic dividend, using its young and growing workers to boost economic growth.

The story varies from country to country. Nigeria and Ethiopia, Africa's most populous countries, will together add 30 million workers—an increase in their workforces of about 35 percent by 2020—while South Africa is expected to add 2 million workers, growth of only 13 percent.

As Africa's workforce grows, the number of children and retired people that each worker supports will fall from the highest level in the world today to a level on a par with the United States and Europe in 2035—the other part of the demographic dividend.

With fewer mouths to feed and fewer dependents to support, African households will begin to enjoy even greater discretionary spending power, furthering driving economic growth.

3. African workers are better educated than ever before.

Today 40 percent of Africans have some secondary or tertiary education—and that share is rising fast. By 2020, the share of workers with some secondary or tertiary education will rise to nearly half.

While education rates are higher than many outside observers might assume, this is still an area where African countries need to make further progress to remain economically competitive. While 33 percent of Africans in the labor force receive some secondary education, 39 percent of Indian workers receive education at this level. In China, the share is an impressive 66 percent.

Today, educational attainment and skills are not perceived as a major obstacle for employers, as a new McKinsey survey of more than 1,300 African employers reveals. However, this is likely to be an increasingly important factor as the continent's economies develop—employers in the survey from South Africa, for example, did cite difficulty in finding workers with the specific skills needed as a barrier to business. Across the continent, the right kind of education and practical training programs can give the next generation of workers the soft skills needed to do any kind of job—not just basic literacy and numeracy, but also punctuality, communication, and dependability.

4. Steady work is still hard to come by in Africa.

But here's the bad news: Only 28 percent of Africans currently have stable, wage-paying jobs. To reap the benefits of its positive demographics and advancements in education, Africa needs to quickly create more jobs. Although Africa has created 37 million "stable" wage-paying jobs over the past decade, 91 million people have been added to its labor force.

As a result, 9 percent of the workforce is officially unemployed, and nearly two-thirds of African workers sustain tvhemselves through subsistence activities and low-wage self-employment—so-called "vulnerable" jobs. Poverty may be decreasing, but it remains stubbornly high.

Youth unemployment is also a major challenge. In Egypt, one of the flash points of the Arab Spring, the adult unemployment rate is moderate—but youth unemployment is sharply higher at 25 percent. For the sake of social and political stability, Africa needs to accelerate its creation of stable jobs that are the route to lasting prosperity and an expanding consuming class.

5. With a few reforms, massive job growth is within Africa's reach.

The experience of other emerging economies shows that Africa could accelerate its creation of stable jobs dramatically. When they were at a similar stage of development as Africa today, Thailand, South Korea, and Brazil generated jobs at double or triple the rate as Africa. If current trends and policies continue, Africa looks set to create around 54 million more stable jobs by 2020, boosting the share of Africans with stable employment to 32 percent of the labor force. But if Africa were to match the efforts of Thailand, South Korea, and Brazil, it could create 72 million new stable jobs—raising the portion of Africans with stable employment to 36 percent.

This would lift millions more Africans out of poverty and vault millions of others into the consuming class. It would also cut the time needed to reach East Asia's percentage of stable employment by more than half—from over 50 years to just 20 years. Africa's most developed economies—such as South Africa, Morocco, and Egypt—are on track to create more wage-paying jobs than new entrants to the workforce, thereby reducing the ranks of the unemployed and vulnerable employed. Three sectors in particular already have a proven capacity to create jobs in Africa and can do so in the future: agriculture, manufacturing, and retail and hospitality.

6. Africa can become the world's breadbasket.

Africa has about 60 percent of the world's unused cropland, providing it with a golden opportunity to simultaneously develop its agricultural sector and reduce unemployment. On current trends,

African agriculture is on course to create 8 million wage-paying jobs between now and 2020.

With two important reforms, however, Africa could add 6 million more jobs. First, policymakers could encourage expansion of large-scale commercial farming onto uncultivated land. African countries need to reform land rights and water management, build up their infrastructure, and improve access to inputs such as seeds, finance, and insurance in order to give a boost to agriculture. Such steps have allowed Mali, which built integrated road, rail, and sea links to transport refrigerated goods, to increase its mango exports to the European Union sixfold in just five years.

Second, African economies can move from producing low-value grain to higher-value crops such as horticultural crops and biofuels. This will not only boost GDP, but provide much-needed jobs: Staples such as grains employ up to 50 people per 1,000 hectares while horticultural products need up to 800.

7. It's often cheaper for Africans to buy goods made in China than those made at home.

African manufacturing is declining as a share in most economies, and that needs to stop. Africa is on course to generate 8 million new manufacturing jobs by 2020 but could nearly double that tally if it can reverse this trend.

Rising labor costs and exchange rates across Asia give African economies an ideal opportunity to expand their manufacturing industries. There is already anecdotal evidence that Asian businesses are setting up factories in some African countries to regain their competitive advantage.

High transportation and input costs, duties, and bureaucracy are some of the obstacles that have hindered African manufacturing in the past. The continent needs to open itself up to foreign investment too. Lesotho, a country of just 2 million people, has 100 times South Africa's exports of apparel to the United States on a per capita basis because it made investment attractive to foreign players and put the necessary rail and distribution infrastructure in place. Apparel manufacturing is Lesotho's largest employer, providing 40,000 workers with stable jobs.

Prospects for manufacturing vary according to the country. Large, diversified economies like South Africa have relatively high labor costs, more skilled workers, and developed infrastructure, and need to move into higher-value-added production. Morocco has done this in auto parts and assembly. But less-developed African countries still have competitive wages and productivity and could develop as low-cost manufacturing hubs.

8. Nigeria's four largest cities still have only six shopping malls.

Africa's rising number of consumers is already driving growth in retailing, but the sector could grow much faster. The potential of retail still goes largely unrealized: In Ethiopia, Egypt, Ghana, and Nigeria, nearly three-quarters of groceries are bought in tiny informal outlets. If barriers to foreign players were removed and action was taken to boost the share of modern retail outlets, this industry could finally hit its stride.

Hospitality and tourism is another major potential growth area. Africa's advanced economies now receive around 70 percent of international visitors, but less developed countries can quickly improve their appeal to tourists. Take the case of Cape Verde, which offered investors a tax holiday, exemption from import duties, and free expatriation to foreign investors, laying the groundwork for its currently booming tourism industry. Today, tourism employs one in five people in the island nation. Retail and hospitality together could add up to 14 million jobs throughout Africa by 2020 if the necessary reforms were undertaken.

9. Africa needs more than petrodollars.

Mining, oil, and gas contribute significantly to Africa's GDP, but these sectors employ less than 1 percent of the workforce.

Africa needs a job strategy, not just a growth strategy. Countries in this region need explicit programs to create jobs, targeted at labor-intensive sectors that enjoy comparative advantage. Governments, working with private companies, need to improve access to finance in those sectors, build the necessary infrastructure, cut unnecessary regulation and bureaucracy and create a more business-friendly environment, and develop the skills needed to support the industries of the future.

Morocco's auto-parts industry is an example of success. Realizing the country's unique advantage of proximity to the large market of high-income earners in Europe, the Moroccan government set a goal for the country to become the industrial automotive supplier for Europe. Morocco analyzed its comparative advantage for more than 600 automotive parts and eventually chose around 100 parts on which to focus. It then created two free trade zones dedicated to the automotive industry. Today, the sector employs more than 60,000 people, and this year saw the opening of a 1 billion euro assembly plant by Renault.

10. The future for Africa looks bright—but there's still a lot of work to be done.

More than 300 million Africans will remain in vulnerable jobs in 2020. And even if African governments are successful at promoting job creation, the number of Africans in vulnerable employment will keep on rising for at least another 20 years because the labor force is expanding so quickly.

Africans in vulnerable jobs—and those with no jobs at all—will need government support. African governments can use their newfound resources to mitigate some of the pain of this process: They should invest in programs that help organize subsistence employment more effectively, as well as invest in health and education for the vulnerable.

Africa's employment challenge is daunting, but it is not unique. Many other emerging markets have transformed their employment landscapes and made sweeping gains in economic growth, and with the right policies in place, Africa has the right ingredients to produce similar success. Businesses and investors are beginning to take note of the continent's potential—not only its wealth of natural resources but its vast human capital. Africa may, in fact, prove to be one of the next great global stories.

DISCUSSION QUESTIONS

1) Three selections here (those by Acemoglu and Robinson, Diamond, and Kenny) offer three different perspectives on whether development is shaped mainly by culture, by institutions, or by geography and other conditions that cannot be altered. Which of these perspectives is most intuitively appealing to you? Now assume that a classmate finds another perspective more appealing. What are the challenges that would arise if you try to "prove" to her or him your preferred theory is the most effective? Do these challenges imply that debates of this kind cannot be resolved?

2) How could one use comparison to test which theories are the most effective at explaining the causes of development? In considering this, focus in particular on two or more countries that have different levels of development. How would a brief comparison help you to set up a research design to explore this question in greater depth?

3) Consider the article on Africa by Lund and van Wamelen. Do you believe the positive trends mentioned here are sustainable? Why or why not? Can you link these claims about contemporary Africa to major theories or explanations of why development happens?

Democracy and Democratization

One of the topics of greatest interest in comparative politics is democracy and democratization. Indeed, it seems likely that many political scientists enter the field because they value democracy highly and wish to see it succeed and grow.

Scholars debate what democracy is and how we should measure it. Some are proponents of minimal or "procedural definitions," which stipulate that a country is democratic if certain procedures are followed (elections that are regular and fair, with multiple parties allowed to compete, and so forth). Others favor "substantive definitions," which judge a country to be democratic not just to the extent that certain rules are followed but which, rather, stress the importance of certain outcomes like citizen equality, high levels of participation, and so forth. These differences mean that reasonable people can disagree about just how democratic certain countries are, and we can debate whether borderline cases are democracies at all. But almost every political scientist would agree that certain countries are clearly authoritarian: think of North Korea, Cuba, or Syria under Bashar al-Assad. By the same token, some countries are clearly democratic: think of Canada, France, or Chile after the transition from the Pinochet regime in the late 1980s.

Much of the world today is democratic, but there are still plenty of authoritarian regimes, and even hybrid or, to use Steven Levitsky and Lucan Way's phrase, "competitive authoritarian" cases that blend democratic and authoritarian features. Comparative politics scholars are interested in trying to understand why the world has become more democratic, in part so they can make predictions about whether and when those remaining authoritarian regimes are likely to undergo democratization. Indeed, some hope that comparative politics can uncover lessons that will help democratizers and their supporters strategize about how best to accomplish this.

There are many patterns of democratic transition. In this section we include readings that will allow you to focus on two types by examining current processes. The wave of contention known as the Arab Spring is an example of a revolutionary transition, one that may or may not lead to successful consolidation of democracies in several predominantly Arab countries. Our selection on this subject, by Fouad Ajami, recounts the basic story of the Arab Spring and sets it against its region-wide historical background. Be attentive to Ajami's views of both why the revolts took place and where they are likely to lead.

Often, though, democratic transitions take place not through revolution but through a process of negotiation and exchange between elements of the authoritarian regime and those pressing for democratic institutions. We include a reading on recent events in Myanmar, which *may* exemplify this pattern (again, as with the Arab Spring, because these events are still playing out there is no way to know for sure if we are witnessing a successful or failed case of democratization). The piece by Aung Zaw gives a brief overview of the situation in Burma (also called Myanmar) and asks whether what we are witnessing is a democratic transition. As you read this piece, be attentive to the explicit and implicit theoretical claims about *why* these events are happening.

Scholars in comparative politics seek to explain how democratization has taken place when and where it does. One of the most established theories is modernization theory, which says that economic development is a major cause of democracy. In our final reading in this section, Daron Acemoglu asks whether economic development alone is sufficient to promote democracy, focusing on the case of Turkey.

Looking at this set of readings, notice that even where these scholars take factors like economic development and history very seriously, there seems to be a way in which each focuses on the decisions of individual politicians or key groups. In other words, these authors seem to argue in different ways that the specific politics of certain moments matter most in determining outcomes, often emphasizing decisions made by key leaders and groups.

The Arab Spring at One: A Year of Living Dangerously

FOUAD AJAMI

Reprinted by permission of FOREIGN AFFAIRS, Volume 91, Number 2, March/April 2012. Copyright © 2012 by the Council on Foreign Relations, Inc. www.ForeignAffairs.com.

Throughout 2011, a rhythmic chant echoed across the Arab lands: "The people want to topple the regime." It skipped borders with ease, carried in newspapers and magazines, on Twitter and Facebook, on the airwaves of al Jazeera and al Arabiya. Arab nationalism had been written off, but here, in full bloom, was what certainly looked like a pan-Arab awakening. Young people in search of political freedom and economic opportunity, weary of waking up to the same tedium day after day, rose up against their sclerotic masters.

It came as a surprise. For almost two generations, waves of democracy had swept over other regions, from southern and eastern Europe to Latin America, from East Asia to Africa. But not the Middle East. There, tyrants had closed up the political world, become owners of their countries in all but name. It was a bleak landscape: terrible rulers, sullen populations, a terrorist fringe that hurled itself in frustration at an order bereft of any legitimacy. Arabs had started to feel they were cursed, doomed to despotism. The region's exceptionalism was becoming not just a human disaster but a moral embarrassment.

Outside powers had winked at this reality, silently thinking this was the best the Arabs could do. In a sudden burst of Wilsonianism in Iraq and after, the United States had put its power behind liberty. Saddam Hussein was flushed out of a spider hole, the Syrian brigades of terror and extortion were pushed out of Lebanon, and the despotism of Hosni Mubarak, long a pillar of Pax Americana, seemed to lose some of its mastery. But post-Saddam Iraq held out mixed messages: there was democracy, but also blood in the streets and sectarianism. The autocracies hunkered down and did their best to thwart the new Iraqi project. Iraq was set ablaze, and the Arab autocrats could point to it as a cautionary tale of the folly of unseating even the worst of despots. Moreover, Iraq carried a double burden of humiliation for Sunni Arabs: the bearer of liberty there was the United States, and the war had empowered the Shiite stepchildren of the Arab world. The result was a standoff: the Arabs could not snuff out or ignore the flicker of freedom, but nor did the Iraqi example prove the subversive beacon of hope its proponents had expected.

It was said by Arabs themselves that George W. Bush had unleashed a tsunami on the region. True, but the Arabs were good at waiting out storms, and before long, the Americans themselves lost heart and abandoned the quest. An election in 2006 in the Palestinian territories went the way of Hamas, and a new disillusionment with democracy's verdict overtook the Bush administration. The "surge" in Iraq rescued the American war there just in time, but the more ambitious vision of reforming the Arab world was given up. The autocracies had survived the brief moment of American assertiveness. And soon, a new standard-bearer of American power, Barack Obama, came with a reassuring message: the United States was done with change; it would make its peace with the status quo, renewing its partnership with friendly autocrats even as it engaged the hostile regimes in Damascus and Tehran. The United States was to remain on the Kabul hook for a while longer, but the greater Middle East would be left to its Furies.

When a revolt erupted in Iran against the theocrats in the first summer of his presidency, Obama was caught flatfooted by the turmoil. Determined to conciliate the rulers, he could not find the language to speak to the rebels. Meanwhile, the Syrian regime, which had given up its dominion in Lebanon under duress, was now keen to retrieve it. A stealth campaign of terror and assassinations, the power of Hezbollah on the ground, and the subsidies of Iran all but snuffed out the "Cedar Revolution" that had been the pride of Bush's diplomacy.

Observers looking at the balance of forces in the region in late 2010 would have been smart to bet on a perpetuation of autocracy. Beholding Bashar al-Assad in Damascus, they would have been forgiven the conclusion that a similar fate awaited Libya, Tunisia, Yemen, and the large Egyptian state that had been the trendsetter in Arab political and cultural life. Yet beneath the surface stability, there was political misery and sterility. Arabs did not need a "human development report" to tell them of their desolation. Consent had drained out of public life; the only glue between ruler and ruled was suspicion and fear. There was no public project to bequeath to a generation coming into its own—and this the largest and youngest population yet.

And then it happened. In December, a despairing Tunisian fruit vendor named Mohamed Bouazizi took one way out, setting himself on fire to protest the injustices of the status quo. Soon, millions of his unnamed fellows took another, pouring into the streets. Suddenly, the despots, seemingly secure in their dominion, deities in all but name, were on the run. For its part, the United States scurried to catch up with the upheaval. "In too many places, in too many ways, the region's foundations are sinking into the sand," U.S. Secretary of State Hillary Clinton proclaimed in Qatar in mid-January 2011, as the storm was breaking out. The Arab landscape lent her remarks ample confirmation; what she omitted was that generations of American diplomacy would be buried, too.

The Fire This Time

The revolt was a settlement of accounts between the powers that be and populations determined to be done with despots. It erupted in a small country on the margins of the Arab political experience, more educated and prosperous and linked to Europe than the norm. As the rebellion made its way eastward, it skipped Libya and arrived in Cairo, "the mother of the world." There, it found a stage worthy of its ambitions.

Often written off as the quintessential land of political submission, Egypt has actually known ferocious rebellions. It had been Mubarak's good fortune that the land tolerated him for three decades. The designated successor to Anwar al-Sadat, Mubarak had been a cautious man, but his reign had

sprouted dynastic ambitions. For 18 magical days in January and February, Egyptians of all walks of life came together in Tahrir Square demanding to be rid of him. The senior commanders of the armed forces cast him aside, and he joined his fellow despot, Tunisia's Zine el-Abidine Ben Ali, who had fallen a month earlier.

From Cairo, the awakening became a pan-Arab affair, catching fire in Yemen and Bahrain. As a monarchy, the latter was a rare exception, since in this season it was chiefly the republics of strongmen that were seized with unrest. But where most monarchies had a fit between ruler and ruled, Bahrain was riven by a fault line between its Sunni rulers and its Shiite majority. So it was vulnerable, and it was in the nature of things that an eruption there would turn into a sectarian feud. Yemen, meanwhile, was the poorest of the Arab states, with secessionist movements raging in its north and south and a polarizing leader, Ali Abdullah Saleh, who had no skills save the art of political survival. The feuds of Yemen were obscure, the quarrels of tribes and warlords. The wider Arab tumult gave Yemenis eager to be rid of their ruler the heart to challenge him.

Then, the revolt doubled back to Libya. This was the kingdom of silence, the realm of the deranged, self-proclaimed "dean of Arab rulers," Muammar al-Qaddafi. For four tormenting decades, Libyans had been at the mercy of this prison warden, part tyrant, part buffoon. Qaddafi had eviscerated his country, the richest in Africa yet with an abysmally impoverished population. In the interwar years, Libya had known savage colonial rule under the Italians. It gained a brief respite under an ascetic ruler, King Idris, but in the late 1960s was gripped by a revolutionary fever. *Iblis wa la Idris*, went the maxim of the time, "Better the devil than Idris." And the country got what it wanted. Oil sustained the madness; European leaders and American intellectuals alike came courting. Now, in 2011, Benghazi, at some remove from the capital, rose up, and history gave the Libyans a chance.

The Egyptian rulers had said that their country was not Tunisia. Qaddafi said that his republic was not Tunisia or Egypt. Eventually, Assad was saying that Syria was not Tunisia, Egypt, or Libya. Assad was young, not old; his regime had more legitimacy because it had confronted Israel rather than collaborated with it. He spoke too soon: in mid-March, it was Syria's turn.

Syria was where Islam had made its home after it outgrew the Arabian Peninsula and before it slipped out of the hands of the Arabs into those of the Persians and the Turks. Yet decades earlier, Bashar al-Assad's father, Hafez—a man of supreme cunning and political skill—had ridden the military and the Baath Party to absolute power, creating a regime in which power rested with the country's Alawite minority. The marriage of despotism and sectarianism begat the most fearsome state in the Arab east.

When the rebellion broke out there in 2011, it had a distinct geography, as the French political scientist Fabrice Balanche has shown, based in the territories and urban quarters of the country's Sunni Arabs. It erupted in Dara'a, a remote provincial town in the south, then spread to Hamah, Homs, Jisr al-Shughour, Rastan, Idlib, and Dayr az Zawr—skipping over Kurdish and Druze areas and the mountain villages and coastal towns that make up the Alawite strongholds. The violence in the Syrian uprising has been most pronounced in Homs, the country's third-largest city, because of its explosive demographics—two-thirds Sunni, one-quarter Alawite, one-tenth Christian.

Sectarianism was not all, of course. Syria has had one of the highest birthrates in the region, with its population having almost quadrupled since Hafez seized power in 1970. The arteries of the regime had hardened, with a military-merchant complex dominating political and economic life. There was not much patronage left for the state to dispose of, since under the banner of privatization in recent years, the state had pulled off a disappearing act. The revolt fused a sense of economic disinheritance and the wrath of a Sunni majority determined to rid itself of the rule of a godless lot.

Where Things Stand

There has, of course, been no uniform script for the Arab regimes in play. Tunisia, an old state with a defined national identity, settled its affairs with relative ease. It elected a constituent assembly in which al Nahda, an Islamist party, secured a plurality. Al Nahda's leader, Rachid al-Ghannouchi, was a shrewd man; years in exile had taught him caution, and his party formed a coalition government with two secular partners.

In Libya, foreign intervention helped the rebels topple the regime. Qaddafi was pulled out of a drainage pipe and beaten and murdered, and so was one of his sons. These were the hatreds and the wrath that the ruler himself had planted; he reaped what he had sown. But wealth, a sparse population, and foreign attention should see Libya through. No history in the making there could be as deadly to Libyans, and others, as the Qaddafi years.

The shadows of Iran and Saudi Arabia hover over Bahrain. There is no mass terror, but the political order is not pretty. There is sectarian discrimination and the oddness of a ruling dynasty, the House of Khalifa, that conquered the area in the late years of the eighteenth century but has still not made peace with the population. Outsiders man the security forces, and true stability seems a long way off.

As for Yemen, it is the quintessential failed state. The footprint of the government is light, the rulers offer no redemption, but there is no draconian terror. The country is running out of water; jihadists on the run from the Hindu Kush have found a home: it is Afghanistan with a coastline. The men and women who went out into the streets of Sanaa in 2011 sought the rehabilitation of their country, a more dignified politics than they have been getting from the cynical acrobat at the helm for more than three decades. Whether they will get it is unclear.

Syria remains in chaos. Hamas left Damascus in December because it feared being left on the wrong side of the mounting Arab consensus against the Syrian regime. "No Iran, no Hezbollah; we want rulers who fear Allah," has been one of the more meaningful chants of the protesters. Alawite rule has been an anomaly, and the regime, through its brutal response to the uprising, with security forces desecrating mosques, firing at worshipers, and ordering hapless captives to proclaim, "There is no God but Bashar," has written its own regional banishment. Hafez committed cruelties of his own, but he always managed to remain within the Arab fold.

Bashar is different—reckless—and has prompted even the Arab League, which has a history of overlooking the follies of its members, to suspend Damascus' membership.

The fight still rages, Aleppo and Damascus have not risen, and the embattled ruler appears convinced that he can resist the laws of gravity. Unlike in Libya, no foreign rescue mission is on the horizon. But with all the uncertainties, this much can be said: the fearsome security state that Hafez, the Baath Party, and the Alawite soldiers and intelligence barons built is gone for good. When consent and popular enthusiasm fell away, the state rested on fear, and fear was defeated. In Syria, the bonds between the holders of power and the population have been irreparably broken.

What Follows Pharaoh

Egypt, meanwhile, may have lost the luster of old, but this Arab time shall be judged by what eventually happens there. In the scenarios of catastrophe, the revolution will spawn an Islamic republic: the Copts will flee, tourism revenues be lost for good, and Egyptians will yearn for the iron grip of a pharaoh. The strong performance of the Muslim Brotherhood and of an even more extremist Salafi party in recent parliamentary elections, together with the splintering of the secular, liberal vote, appears to justify concern about the country's direction. But Egyptians have proud memories of liberal periods in their history. Six decades of military rule robbed them of the experience of open politics, and they are unlikely to give it up now without a struggle.

The elections were transparent and clarifying. Liberal and secular forces were not ready for the contest, whereas the Brotherhood had been waiting for such a historic moment for decades and seized its opportunity. No sooner had the Salafists come out of the catacombs than they began to unnerve the population, and so they pulled back somewhat from their extreme positions. The events in Tahrir Square transfixed the world, but as the young Egyptian intellectual Samuel Tadros has put it, "Egypt is not Cairo and Cairo is not Tahrir Square." When the dust settles, three forces will contest Egypt's future—the army, the Brotherhood, and a broad liberal and secular coalition of those who want a civil polity, the

separation of religion and politics, and the saving graces of a normal political life.

The Brotherhood brings to the struggle its time-honored mix of political cunning and an essential commitment to imposing a political order shaped by Islam. Its founder, Hasan al-Banna, was struck down by an assassin in 1949 but still stalks the politics of the Muslim world. A ceaseless plotter, he talked of God's rule, but in the shadows, he struck deals with the palace against the dominant political party of his day, the Wafd. He played the political game as he put together a formidable paramilitary force, seeking to penetrate the officer corps—something his inheritors have pined for ever since. He would doubtless look with admiration on the tactical skills of his successors as they maneuver between the liberals and the Supreme Council of the Armed Forces, partaking of the tumult of Tahrir Square but stepping back from the exuberance to underline their commitment to sobriety and public order.

The plain truth of it is that Egypt lacks the economic wherewithal to build a successful modern Islamic order, whatever that might mean. The Islamic Republic of Iran rests on oil, and even the moderate ascendancy of the Justice and Development Party, or AKP, in Turkey is secured by prosperity stemming from the "devout bourgeoisie" in the Anatolian hill towns. Egypt lies at the crossroads of the world, living off tourism, the Suez Canal, infusions of foreign aid, and remittances from Egyptians abroad. Virtue must bow to necessity: in the last year, the country's foreign reserves dwindled from $36 billion to $20 billion. Inflation hammers at the door, the price of imported wheat is high, and the bills have to be paid. Four finance ministers have come and gone since Mubarak's fall. A desire for stability now balances the heady satisfaction that a despot was brought down.

There are monumental problems staring Egypt's leaders in the face, and the reluctance of both the Brotherhood and the armed forces to assume power is telling. Good sense and pragmatism might yet prevail. A plausible division of spoils and responsibility might give the Brotherhood the domains of governance dearest to it—education, social welfare, and the judiciary—with the military getting defense, intelligence, the peace with Israel, the military ties to the United States, and a retention of the officer corps' economic prerogatives. Liberal secularists would have large numbers, a say in the rhythm of daily life in a country so hard to regiment and organize, and the chance to field a compelling potential leader in a future presidential election.

For two centuries now, Egypt has been engaged in a Sisyphean struggle for modernity and a place among the nations worthy of its ambitions. It has not fared well, yet it continues to try. Last August, a scene played out that could give Egyptians a measure of solace. The country's last pharaoh—may it be so—came to court on a gurney. "Sir, I am present," the former ruler said to the presiding judge. Mubarak was not pulled out of a drainage pipe and slaughtered, as was Qaddafi, nor did he hunker down with his family and murder his own people at will, as has Assad. The Egyptians have always had, in E. M. Forster's words, the ability to harmonize contending assertions, and they may do so once again.

The Third Great Awakening

This tumult, this awakening, is the third of its kind in modern Arab history. The first, a political-cultural renaissance born of a desire to join the modern world, came in the late 1800s. Led by scribes and lawyers, would-be parliamentarians and Christian intellectuals, it sought to reform political life, separate religion from politics, emancipate women, and move past the debris of the Ottoman Empire. Fittingly enough, that great movement, with Beirut and Cairo at the head of the pack, found its chronicler in George Antonius, a Christian writer of Lebanese birth, Alexandrian youth, a Cambridge education, and service in the British administration in Palestine. His 1938 book, *The Arab Awakening*, remains the principal manifesto of Arab nationalism.

The second awakening came in the 1950s and gathered force in the decade following. This was the era of Gamal Abdel Nasser in Egypt, Habib Bourguiba in Tunisia, and the early leaders of the Baath Party in Iraq and Syria. No democrats, the leaders of that time were intensely political men engaged in the great issues of the day. They came from the middle class or even lower and had dreams of power, of industrialization, of ridding their people of the sense of inferiority instilled by Ottoman and then colonial rule. No simple audit can do these men justice: they had monumental accomplishments, but then, explosive demographics and their own authoritarian proclivities and shortcomings undid most of their work. When they faltered, police states and political Islam filled the void.

This third awakening came in the nick of time. The Arab world had grown morose and menacing. Its populations loathed their rulers and those leaders' foreign patrons. Bands of jihadists, forged in the cruel prisons of dreadful regimes, were scattered about everywhere looking to kill and be killed. Mohamed Bouazizi summoned his fellows to a new history, and across the region, millions have heeded his call. Last June, the Algerian author Boualem Sansal wrote Bouazizi an open letter. "Dear Brother," it said,

> I write these few lines to let you know we're doing well, on the whole, though it varies from day to day: sometimes the wind changes, it rains lead, life bleeds from every pore. . . .

But let's take the long view for a moment. Can he who does not know where to go find the way? Is driving the dictator out the end? From where you are, Mohamed, next to God, you can tell that not all roads lead to Rome; ousting a tyrant doesn't lead to freedom. Prisoners like trading one prison for another, for a change of scenery and the chance to gain a little something along the way.

"The best day after a bad emperor is the first," the Roman historian Tacitus once memorably observed. This third Arab awakening is in the scales of history. It has in it both peril and promise, the possibility of prison but also the possibility of freedom.

Burma's Tightrope

Burma's Mysterious President Insists That He Wants Democracy. But Can He Deliver?

AUNG ZAW

One sweltering day in August of last year, Burmese opposition leader and Nobel Peace Prize laureate Aung San Suu Kyi arrived for the first time in the capital of her country. The city of Naypyidaw, inaugurated six years ago by Burma's mercurial military rulers, is a supremely artificial creation, a place of vacant boulevards and echoing plazas built in the foothills some 200 miles away from the old capital of Rangoon. Rangoon is the city that Aung San Suu Kyi calls home, and it is there that she had spent 15 of the past 22 years under house arrest.

She had come to Naypyidaw to meet the man who had orchestrated her release from detention 10 months earlier. Burmese President Thein Sein, like most of the men who have ruled the country since World War II, spent almost his entire adult life as an army officer. Then, in 2010, he took off his uniform, assumed the leadership of the ruling political party, and led it to victory in an election denounced by most international observers as a sham. He then took office as the head of the first ostensibly civilian government in Burma (also known as Myanmar) in 49 years and announced that he was preparing to lead the country toward democracy.

Aung San Suu Kyi was understandably cautious as she went into her meeting with the president. She and her fellow activists have watched Burma's leaders break promises for decades. Was this one really any different?

To her surprise, the president welcomed her warmly, lavishing praise upon her father Aung San, a hero of Burma's anti-colonial struggle in the 1940s. Two decades ago, wary of the late Aung San's continuing star power (and that of his daughter, who entered politics after the 1988 uprising), the military junta had erased his image from the national currency. Now, in demonstrative contrast, the president insisted that he and Aung San Suu Kyi pose for an official photo beneath a portrait of her father. Later that evening Thein Sein's wife welcomed Aung San

Suu Kyi to a "family dinner" in the presidential palace. She greeted Burma's leading dissident with a warm embrace.

In the weeks that followed, the opposition leader told her colleagues that it was time to take the president's promises of reform for real. She moved to obtain official registration for her political party, the National League for Democracy (NLD), and stated that she wanted to see it participate in parliamentary by-elections to be held on April 1 of this year. Even if the NLD wins every seat at stake, it would still fall short of anything like a legislative majority. Victory, though, could ensure an important opposition voice in the hitherto docile body. On Jan. 10, after weeks of uncertainty, she finally announced that she will run for a seat in the parliament.

Allowing the NLD to participate is merely the latest in a series of dramatic moves made by the president. Since Thein Sein took power in March 2010, he has freed hundreds of political prisoners, initiated discussions about legalizing trade unions, and loosened censorship. Over the past year the new Burmese government has taken more steps toward political reform than the previous military regime took in over two decades.

Yet none of this can disguise the fact that Burma is still a country under authoritarian rule, and that means its further progress depends to a critical extent on the motives and capabilities of the man who holds its highest office. Many observers wonder whether Thein Sein is committed to meaningful progress or is simply serving as the public face of the old junta in its quest to retain power under a quasi-civilian government. Once a pillar of the old regime, he was one of its highest-ranking generals when in 2007 he assumed the office of prime minister, a post that he retained throughout the government's crackdown on pro-democracy protests that year.

There are also questions about the extent to which Thein Sein is truly in control. Several leaders of the military regime still hold positions in his government. (In a recent interview with the Associated Press, Aung San Suu Kyi cautioned that the generals still wield enormous power despite the veneer of democracy provided by the elections. "I am concerned about how much support there is in the military for changes," she said. "In the end that's the most important factor, how far the military are prepared to cooperate with reform principles.") Although the government denies it, former junta chief Senior Gen. Than Shwe, a master political chess player, continues to exercise considerable influence behind the scenes, say some experts.

The culture of secrecy surrounding Burma's military rulers makes it especially difficult to gauge just how far they will allow the current opening to go. But Thein Sein's biography provides some intriguing clues. The son of peasants from the Irrawaddy Delta, he graduated from the country's elite military academy in 1968. As a young officer in the 1970s, he was sent to the front lines of the Burmese military campaign against the Chinese-backed communist insurgency. Retired Lt. Gen. Chit Swe, under whom Thein Sein served in the 1980s, describes the president as someone who rarely shows his emotions, is notably devoid of arrogance, and is usually willing to listen to differing opinions.

Development Won't Ensure Democracy in Turkey

DARON ACEMOGLU

For the past few years, there has been a general optimism about Turkish democracy in Western capitals, especially in Washington, thanks to the economic strides made by Prime Minister Recep Tayyip Erdogan's Justice and Development Party, known as the A.K.P.

These optimists, and even those who admit that Turkish democracy has its shortcomings, tend to subscribe to the political scientist Seymour Martin Lipset's famous modernization theory—the idea that greater democratization follows automatically as a country becomes more prosperous. Turkey has been growing rapidly and steadily over the last 11 years, the theory goes, so perhaps all we need is patience. By this logic, Mr. Erdogan's own economic success will inexorably bring an end to his authoritarian style of government.

But modernization theory has had little success in explaining the rise of democracy around the world. My research with Simon Johnson, James A. Robinson and Pierre Yared has shown, for example, that countries that have grown faster don't show any greater tendency to become democratic or to consolidate democratic institutions that already exist. A few cases where democracy has followed rapid growth, as in South Korea and Taiwan, did not occur automatically but as a result of a combative political process—and a far more violent set of confrontations between the military and protesters, trade unionists and students.

And it has little relevance to this week's protests in Turkey.

Even before the brutal suppression of the demonstrations, the belief that Turkey was on its way to becoming a mature democracy—a role model for the rest of the Middle East—had already become untenable.

As the A.K.P. consolidated its power, dissent was tolerated less and less. Judicial institutions lost the little independence they'd had, and an array of critics of the government, ranging from former high-ranking military officers to journalists, are now in jail, in most cases without having had a fair trial (According to the Committee to Protect Journalists, Turkey has now surpassed China for the number of jailed journalists.)

The bulwarks of democracy have not exactly distinguished themselves during the past week's events. There has been hardly any criticism of the prime minister from within his own party (except a mild rebuke from President Abdullah Gul).

The main opposition party, which was established by the Turkish republic's founding father, Mustafa Kemal Ataturk, still seems trapped in a time warp—focused solely on defending the nationalist, secularist ideology of the Turkish state.

And the Turkish news media still seems cowed into submission, so much so that it did not report much on how the small protests against a new shopping center on one of the few remaining parks in Istanbul turned into a spontaneous mass movement challenging Mr. Erdogan's authoritarianism. Indeed, while CNN International was reporting live from Taksim Square, the local channel, CNN Turk, which is partly owned by Turner Broadcasting, was airing a program on penguins.

Even so, what began as peaceful protests by a few hundred demonstrators in Taksim Square could define Turkish democracy for years to come—for two reasons.

First, democracy doesn't just take place at the polls, especially when the choices on the ballot are as unappealing as they have been in Turkey. British democracy came of age in the 19th century partly as a result of protests in the streets, which not only led to the enfranchisement of the previously disenfranchised but also to the formation of the Labour Party, offering new options to voters. Large numbers of people pouring into the street in several Turkish cities, even in the face of heavy-handed police action, may be Turkish democracy's coming-of-age moment.

Second, there is a real chance that these protests, and the political movements that they might spawn, will transcend the deep-rooted but stale political divisions of the last two decades, divisions captured pithily by Recep Tayyip Erdogan when he said in 1998: "In this country there is a segregation of Black Turks and White Turks. Your brother Tayyip belongs to the Black Turks."

In Turkey, these terms have nothing to do with skin color. "White Turks" are the well-educated, wealthy secular elites who see themselves as the defenders of Ataturk's legacy. They are often associated with government bureaucracy, the military and big businesses in major Turkish cities. "Black Turks" are those that the White Turks look down upon as poorly educated, lower class and trapped by their piety. Elites tend to view them as peasants or being unable to shake off their peasant heritage.

Although the Turkish military periodically used religion as a weapon in its struggle against the political left, particularly after the 1980 military coup, by the 1990s the most important challenge to the secular elite's rule came from religious conservative parties, who unabashedly represented the Black Turks.

In 1997, the military toppled a government led by the A.K.P.'s predecessor, the Welfare Party, which was subsequently shut down by the constitutional court. It similarly threatened the A.K.P. in 2007, with the Constitutional Court again following at its coattails and threatening to ban the party because its religious outlook violated the Turkish Constitution.

Particularly troubling for the secular elite was the fact that the wife of the new president, Mr. Gul, wore a head scarf, something banned in public spaces by the Constitution.

Since 1997, these divisions have defined Turkish politics. The military failed and the A.K.P. withstood the challenge. Turkey has become more democratic in the sense that the previously disenfranchised have become empowered. But it has not taken many steps toward liberal democracy. On the contrary, Turkish society has become more polarized between supporters of secular orthodoxy and the A.K.P., which, under Mr. Erdogan's leadership, has used its newly acquired power to exact revenge on the military, secular elites and its other critics with increasingly authoritarian certitude.

This week's protests are unlikely to topple the government or even force an about-face by the prime minister. Their import lies in their symbolism.

Suddenly, there is a diverse group of people pouring into the streets to demand not handouts or policy concessions but a voice in Turkish politics. The protesters are not hard-core opposition supporters wishing to turn the clock back to the secular orthodoxy of yore but young urbanites frustrated by the A.K.P.'s increasingly unresponsive monopoly on power.

As in 19th-century Britain, if the ballot box doesn't offer the right choices, democracy advances by direct action.

The danger in Turkey is that hard-liners in the A.K.P. will use these events to further divide society. They are already painting a picture in which the protests are an attempt to claw back the newly acquired powers of the previously disenfranchised, labeling the young men and women in the streets as alcoholics, looters and leftists.

These hard-liners have been aided by the Turkish news media, which, with a few exceptions, still obediently toes the party line. In the short run, they may well succeed, further polarizing Turkish politics and cementing the A.K.P.'s control over state institutions.

What makes these events a turning point, however, is that the discontent of a large segment of the Turkish public is now out in the open, and even if the Turkish media continues to ignore it, the knowledge of this discontent will spread.

The genie is out of the bottle. Neither it nor Turkish democracy can be put back.

DISCUSSION QUESTIONS

1) Fouad Ajami offers a general description of the Arab Spring. What are the causes of the Arab Spring, in his account? What is his prediction or expectation for where the Arab Spring will lead? Do you find his prediction about the Arab Spring is related to his understanding of its causes?

2) When considering the work by Aung Zaw, what might account for the move toward democratization in Myanmar? Did the authoritarian regime in Myanmar realize that a democratic wave is unfolding with the Arab Spring and worry that it would unseat them? Are the values and leadership of a particular leader the main cause? Is this about geopolitics and attempting to strengthen the regime's and country's position as China adopts a more muscular foreign policy? Which of these might you argue matters the most?

3) Do you believe there are instances when history, economic development, or other social changes have been enough to push democratization, even without understanding individual and group-level processes or using "proper names"? Is democratization better understood as coming from broad and general social forces beyond the control of any certain person or group of people? Or is it best understood as coming mainly from particular decisions by particular individuals or groups of people?

Authoritarianism

Like democracy and democratization, authoritarianism is of perennial interest in comparative political science. Scholars divide authoritarian regimes into numerous types and emphasize that authoritarianism is not simply the absence of elections but also the failure to protect political and civil rights to allow for (and, for some, to assure) citizen participation and to permit and even encourage debate about multiple points of view. Most polities in human history—from the agricultural revolution to the twentieth century—were authoritarian. As such, some scholars consider authoritarianism a kind of default and democracy and democratization as the relevant phenomena in need of explanation. But in the twenty-first century, with so many of the world's polities democratic and with the widespread perception (correct or incorrect) that polities will become democracies as they modernize, a number of scholars remain interested in explaining what is sometimes called authoritarian persistence.

This section has three readings, all of which deal in some way with arguments about authoritarian rule (or, in the last reading, at least for something like it) in the context of a democratizing world. The first is an extensive interview with Lee Kuan Yew conducted by Fareed Zakaria and published in *Foreign Affairs*. Lee Kuan Yew was the authoritarian leader of Singapore for several decades and is sometimes credited, rightly or wrongly, with that country's being an economic development success story during that same period. One of the interesting things about him, though, is that he was very well versed in social science and made theoretical arguments about the alleged appropriateness of certain types of regimes for certain types of cultures: indeed, he proposed that authoritarian regimes like his were the best available option for countries like Singapore (yes, this argument was conveniently self-serving).

The second reading, from *The Economist*, discusses another authoritarian leader who is sometimes given credit for economic success: Ethiopia's Meles Zenawi, who died in 2012. Cases like this raise important theoretical questions. On the one hand, some comparative politics theories suggest that economic development will, over the long run, cause democratization. If this is true, regimes like the one Meles founded will tend to be transitory, giving way to democratization. But other theories emphasize that one way to placate political constituencies is through ensuring economic opportunities and growth. This problem surfaces in analysts' efforts to predict the futures of a variety of regimes, including that of contemporary China. Apart from this, we can also consider the value of different outcomes. If Singapore and Ethiopia (or China) show that certain types of authoritarian rule may lead to economic success, how do we evaluate morally the trade-off between economic success and political freedom? To be clear, there is not conclusive evidence that either democracy or authoritarianism is better for economic development on average. Yet this question persists as an important one for the many social scientists who care about the moral implications of their research. There are important values at stake if it is even possible that there are tradeoffs between development and democracy.

The third reading in this section is by the Venezuelan journalist and intellectual Boris Muñoz. Contemporary Venezuela is often held up, alongside Russia, as an example of a hybrid or "competitive authoritarian" regime. In other words, many do not judge it to be a fully authoritarian regime, and relatively few political scientists think of it as a full democracy (though there are exceptions on each end of the spectrum). A "competitive authoritarian" regime, as analyzed by Steven Levitsky and Lucan Way, has notable authoritarian elements but continues to hold elections. This was true throughout the period of Hugo Chávez's leadership, and after his death in 2013 an election was held in which his protégé, Nicolas Maduro, narrowly defeated opposition politician Henrique Capriles (some of whose supporters allege the victory was fraudulent). The reading selection by Muñoz was written between Chávez's death and the election and begins with a brief discussion of Chávez's funeral. Muñoz stresses the adoration that many Venezuelans had for Chávez, what some have called a "cult of personality," and the way this plays out in the efforts of contemporary Chavistas to legitimate their political efforts. What do you make of this? What might it tell us, if anything, about how authoritarian and competitive authoritarian regimes remain in power?

Finally, we have a selection on the regime of Kim Jong Un in North Korea. While some of the other authoritarian regimes referenced in this section have prided themselves on a sort of "soft authoritarianism" that their leaders tout as more efficient or more participatory, the regime in North Korea has routinely been seen as one of the most dictatorial remaining on earth. Even leaders in highly autocratic governments, however, are not free to act however they please. This article by Victor Cha shows how the new, young leader must walk a tightrope between accommodating and asserting authority over the elites in North Korea (especially in the military) that could pose a threat to his power. And he must do so in the midst of pressures coming from many sources, including domestically (with many North Koreans increasingly becoming pro-market and having greater access to international communication) and from the United States and China. This suggests that even the toughest of authoritarian regimes faces internal challenges and is not simply the picture of unquestioned dominance that it may wish to project. In considering these pieces, consider: Do these different forms of authoritarianism imply different styles of leadership?

A Conversation with Lee Kuan Yew

FAREED ZAKARIA

Reprinted by permission of FOREIGN AFFAIRS, Volume 73, Number 2, March/April 1994. Copyright © 1994 by the Council on Foreign Relations, Inc. www.ForeignAffairs.com.

Singapore's Lee Kuan Yew has suggested that the "Western concepts" of democracy and human rights will not work in Asia. This is false: Asia has its own venerable traditions of democracy, the rule of law, and respect for the people. Asia's destiny is to improve Western concepts, not ignore them.

Meeting the Minister

"One of the asymmetries of history," wrote Henry Kissinger of Singapore's patriarch Lee Kuan Yew, "is the lack of correspondence between the abilities of some leaders and the power of their countries." Kissinger's one time boss, Richard Nixon, was even more flattering. He speculated that, had Lee lived in another time and another place, he might have "attained the world stature of a Churchill, a Disraeli, or a Gladstone." This tag line of a big man on a small stage has been attached to Lee since the 1970s. Today, however, his stage does not look quite so small. Singapore's per capita GNP is now higher than that of its erstwhile colonizer, Great Britain. It has the world's busiest port, is the third-largest oil refiner and a major center of global manufacturing and service industries. And this move from poverty to plenty has taken place within one generation. In 1965 Singapore ranked economically with Chile, Argentina and Mexico; today its per capita GNP is four or five times theirs.

Lee managed this miraculous transformation in Singapore's economy while maintaining tight political control over the country; Singapore's government can best be described as a "soft" authoritarian regime, and at times it has not been so soft. He was prime minister of Singapore from its independence in 1959 (it became part of a federation with Malaysia in 1963 but was expelled in 1965) until 1990, when he allowed his deputy to succeed him. He is now "Senior Minister" and still commands enormous influence and power in the country. Since his retirement, Lee has embarked on another career of sorts as a world-class pundit, speaking his mind

with impolitic frankness. And what is often on his mind is American-style democracy and its perils. He travels often to East Asian capitals from Beijing to Hanoi to Manila dispensing advice on how to achieve economic growth while retaining political stability and control. It is a formula that the governing elites of these countries are anxious to learn.

The rulers of former British colonies have been spared the embarrassment of building grandiose monuments to house their offices; they simply occupy the ones that the British built. So it is with Singapore. The president, prime minister and senior minister work out of Istana (palace), the old colonial governor's house, a gleaming white bungalow surrounded by luxuriant lawns. The interior is modern, light wood paneling and leather sofas. The atmosphere is hushed. I waited in a large anteroom for the "SM," which is how everybody refers to Lee. I did not wait long. The SM was standing in the middle of a large, sparsely furnished office. He is of medium build. His once-compact physique is now slightly shrunken. Still, he does not look 70.

Lee Kuan Yew is unlike any politician I have met. There were no smiles, no jokes, no bonhomie. He looked straight at me, he has an inexpressive face but an intense gaze, shook hands and motioned toward one of the room's pale blue leather sofas (I had already been told by his press secretary on which one to sit). After 30 awkward seconds, I realized that there would be no small talk. I pressed the record button on my machine.

> FZ: With the end of the Cold War, many Americans were surprised to hear growing criticism of their political and economic and social system from elites in East Asia, who were considered staunchly pro-American. What, in your view, is wrong with the American system?
>
> LKY: It is not my business to tell people what's wrong with their system. It is my business to

tell people not to foist their system indiscriminately on societies in which it will not work.

FZ: But you do not view the United States as a model for other countries?

LKY: As an East Asian looking at America, I find attractive and unattractive features. I like, for example, the free, easy and open relations between people regardless of social status, ethnicity or religion. And the things that I have always admired about America, as against the communist system, I still do: a certain openness in argument about what is good or bad for society; the accountability of public officials; none of the secrecy and terror that's part and parcel of communist government.

But as a total system, I find parts of it totally unacceptable: guns, drugs, violent crime, vagrancy, unbecoming behavior in public, in sum the breakdown of civil society. The expansion of the right of the individual to behave or misbehave as he pleases has come at the expense of orderly society. In the East the main object is to have a well-ordered society so that everybody can have maximum enjoyment of his freedoms. This freedom can only exist in an ordered state and not in a natural state of contention and anarchy.

Let me give you an example that encapsulates the whole difference between America and Singapore. America has a vicious drug problem. How does it solve it? It goes around the world helping other anti-narcotic agencies to try and stop the suppliers. It pays for helicopters, defoliating agents and so on. And when it is provoked, it captures the president of Panama and brings him to trial in Florida. Singapore does not have that option. We can't go to Burma and capture warlords there. What we can do is to pass a law which says that any customs officer or policeman who sees anybody in Singapore behaving suspiciously, leading him to suspect the person is under the influence of drugs, can require that man to have his urine tested. If the sample is found to contain drugs, the man immediately goes for treatment. In America if you did that it would be

an invasion of the individual's rights and you would be sued.

I was interested to read Colin Powell, when he was chairman of the Joint Chiefs of Staff, saying that the military followed our approach because when a recruit signs up he agrees that he can be tested. Now, I would have thought this kind of approach would be quite an effective way to deal with the terrible drug problem you have. But the idea of the inviolability of the individual has been turned into dogma. And yet nobody minds when the army goes and captures the president of another state and brings him to Florida and puts him in jail. I find that incomprehensible. And in any case this approach will not solve America's drug problem. Whereas Singapore's way, we may not solve it, but we will lessen it considerably, as we have done.

FZ: Would it be fair to say that you admired America more 25 years ago? What, in your view, went wrong?

LKY: Yes, things have changed. I would hazard a guess that it has a lot to do with the erosion of the moral underpinnings of a society and the diminution of personal responsibility. The liberal, intellectual tradition that developed after World War II claimed that human beings had arrived at this perfect state where everybody would be better off if they were allowed to do their own thing and flourish. It has not worked out, and I doubt if it will. Certain basics about human nature do not change. Man needs a certain moral sense of right and wrong. There is such a thing called evil, and it is not the result of being a victim of society. You are just an evil man, prone to do evil things, and you have to be stopped from doing them. Westerners have abandoned an ethical basis for society, believing that all problems are solvable by a good government, which we in the East never believed possible.

FZ: Is such a fundamental shift in culture irreversible?

LKY: No, it is a swing of the pendulum. I think it will swing back. I don't know how long it will take, but there's already a backlash in America against failed social policies that have resulted in people urinating in public, in aggressive begging in the streets, in social breakdown.

The Asian Model

FZ: You say that your real concern is that this system not be foisted on other societies because it will not work there. Is there another viable model for political and economic development? Is there an "Asian model"?

LKY: I don't think there is an Asian model as such. But Asian societies are unlike Western ones. The fundamental difference between Western concepts of society and government and East Asian concepts, when I say East Asians, I mean Korea, Japan, China, Vietnam, as distinct from Southeast Asia, which is a mix between the Sinic and the Indian, though Indian culture also emphasizes similar values, is that Eastern societies believe that the individual exists in the context of his family. He is not pristine and separate. The family is part of the extended family, and then friends and the wider society. The ruler or the government does not try to provide for a person what the family best provides.

In the West, especially after World War II, the government came to be seen as so successful that it could fulfill all the obligations that in less modern societies are fulfilled by the family. This approach encouraged alternative families, single mothers for instance, believing that government could provide the support to make up for the absent father. This is a bold, Huxleyan view of life, but one from which I as an East Asian shy away. I would be afraid to experiment with it. I'm not sure what the consequences are, and I don't like the consequences that I see in the West. You will find this view widely shared in East Asia. It's not that we don't have single mothers here. We are also caught in the same social problems of change when we educate our women and they become independent financially and no longer need to put up with unhappy marriages. But there is grave disquiet when we break away from tested norms, and the tested norm is the family unit. It is the building brick of society.

There is a little Chinese aphorism which encapsulates this idea: Xiushen qijia zhiguo pingtianxia. Xiushen means look after yourself, cultivate yourself, do everything to make yourself useful; Qijia, look after the family; Zhiguo, look after your country; Pingtianxia, all is peaceful under heaven. We have a whole people immersed in these beliefs. My granddaughter has the name Xiu-qi. My son picked out the first two words, instructing his daughter to cultivate herself and look after her family. It is the basic concept of our civilization. Governments will come, governments will go, but this endures. We start with self-reliance. In the West today it is the opposite. The government says give me a popular mandate and I will solve all society's problems.

FZ: What would you do instead to address America's problems?

LKY: What would I do if I were an American? First, you must have order in society. Guns, drugs and violent crime all go together, threatening social order. Then the schools; when you have violence in schools, you are not going to have education, so you've got to put that right. Then you have to educate rigorously and train a whole generation of skilled, intelligent, knowledgeable people who can be productive. I would start off with basics, working on the individual, looking at him within the context of his family, his friends, his society. But the Westerner says I'll fix things at the top. One magic formula, one grand plan. I will wave a wand and everything will work out. It's an interesting theory but not a proven method.

Back to Basics

FZ: You are very skeptical of government's ability to solve deeper social issues. But you're more confident, certainly than many Americans are, in the government's ability to promote economic growth and technological advancement. Isn't this a contradiction?

LKY: No. We have focused on basics in Singapore. We used the family to push economic growth, factoring the ambitions of a person and his family into our planning. We have tried, for example, to improve the lot of children through education. The government can create a setting in which people can live happily and succeed and express themselves, but finally it is what people do with their lives that determines economic success or failure. Again, we were fortunate we had this cultural backdrop, the belief in thrift, hard work, filial piety and loyalty in the extended family, and, most of all, the respect for scholarship and learning.

There is, of course, another reason for our success. We have been able to create economic growth because we facilitated certain changes while we moved from an agricultural society to an industrial society. We had the advantage of knowing what the end result should be by looking at the West and later Japan. We knew where we were, and we knew where we had to go. We said to ourselves, "Let's hasten, let's see if we can get there faster." But soon we will face a different situation. In the near future, all of us will get to the stage of Japan. Where do we go next? How do we hasten getting there when we don't know where we're going? That will be a new situation.

FZ: Some people say that the Asian model is too rigid to adapt well to change. The sociologist Mancur Olson argues that national decline is caused most fundamentally by sclerosis, the rigidity of interest groups, firms, labor, capital and the state. An American-type system that is very flexible, laissez-faire and constantly adapting is better suited to the emerging era of rapid change than a government-directed economic policy and a Confucian value system.

LKY: That is an optimistic and attractive philosophy of life, and I hope it will come true. But if you look at societies over the millennia you find certain basic patterns. American civilization from the Pilgrim fathers on is one of optimism and the growth of orderly government. History in China is of dynasties which have risen and fallen, of the waxing and waning of societies. And through all

that turbulence, the family, the extended family, the clan, has provided a kind of survival raft for the individual. Civilizations have collapsed, dynasties have been swept away by conquering hordes, but this life raft enables the civilization to carry on and get to its next phase.

Nobody here really believes that the government can provide in all circumstances. The government itself does not believe it. In the ultimate crisis, even in earthquakes and typhoons, it is your human relationships that will see you through. So the thesis you quote, that the government is always capable of reinventing itself in new shapes and forms, has not been proven in history. But the family and the way human relationships are structured, do increase the survival chances of its members. That has been tested over thousands of years in many different situations.

The Culture of Success

FZ: A key ingredient of national economic success in the past has been a culture of innovation and experimentation. During their rise to great wealth and power the centers of growth, Venice, Holland, Britain, the United States, all had an atmosphere of intellectual freedom in which new ideas, technologies, methods and products could emerge. In East Asian countries, however, the government frowns upon an open and free wheeling intellectual climate. Leaving aside any kind of human rights questions this raises, does it create a productivity problem?

LKY: Intellectually that sounds like a reasonable conclusion, but I'm not sure things will work out this way. The Japanese, for instance, have not been all that disadvantaged in creating new products. I think that if governments are aware of your thesis and of the need to test out new areas, to break out of existing formats, they can counter the trend. East Asians, who all share a tradition of strict discipline, respect for the teacher, no talking back to the teacher and rote learning, must make sure that there is this random intellectual search for new technologies and products. In any case, in a world where electronic communications are instantaneous, I do not see anyone lagging behind. Anything new that happens spreads quickly, whether it's superconductivity or some new life-style.

FZ: Would you agree with the World Bank report on East Asian economic success, which I interpret to have concluded that all the governments that succeeded got fundamentals right, encouraging savings and investment, keeping inflation low, providing high-quality education. The tinkering of industrial policies here and targeting sectors there was not as crucial an element in explaining these countries' extraordinary economic growth as were these basic factors.

LKY: I think the World Bank had a very difficult job. It had to write up these very, very complex series of situations. But there are cultural factors which have been lightly touched over, which deserved more weightage. This would have made it a more complex study and of less universal application, but it would have been more accurate, explaining the differences, for example, between the Philippines and Taiwan.

FZ: If culture is so important, then countries with very different cultures may not, in fact, succeed in the way that East Asia did by getting economic fundamentals right. Are you not hopeful for the countries around the world that are liberalizing their economies?

LKY: Getting the fundamentals right would help, but these societies will not succeed in the same way as East Asia did because certain driving forces will be absent. If you have a culture that doesn't place much value in learning and scholarship and hard work and thrift and deferment of present enjoyment for future gain, the going will be much slower.

But, you know, the World Bank report's conclusions are part of the culture of America and, by extension, of international institutions. It had to present its findings in a bland and universalizable way, which I find unsatisfying because it doesn't grapple with the real problems. It makes the hopeful assumption that all men are equal, that people all over the world are the same. They are not. Groups of people develop different characteristics when they have evolved for thousands of years separately. Genetics and history interact. The Native American Indian is genetically of the same stock as the Mongoloids of East Asia, the Chinese, the Koreans and the Japanese. But one group got cut off after the Bering Straits melted away. Without that land bridge they were totally isolated in America for thousands of years. The other, in East Asia, met successive invading forces from Central Asia and interacted with waves of people moving back and forth. The two groups may share certain characteristics, for instance if you measure the shape of their skulls and so on, but if you start testing them you find that they are different, most particularly in their neurological development, and their cultural values.

Now if you gloss over these kinds of issues because it is politically incorrect to study them, then you have laid a land mine for yourself. This is what leads to the disappointments with social policies, embarked upon in America with great enthusiasm and expectations, but which yield such meager results. There isn't a willingness to see things in their stark reality. But then I am not being politically correct.

FZ: Culture may be important, but it does change. The Asian "model" may prove to be a transitional phenomenon. After all, Western countries also went through a period in the eighteenth and nineteenth centuries when they were capitalist and had limited participatory democracy. Elites then worried, as you do today, that "too much" democracy and "too many" individual rights would destabilize social order. But as these societies modernized and as economic growth spread to all sections of society, things changed. Isn't East Asia changing because of a growing middle class that demands a say in its own future?

LKY: There is acute change in East Asia. We are agricultural societies that have industrialized within one or two generations. What happened in the West over 200 years or more is happening here in about 50 years or less. It is all crammed and crushed into a very tight time frame, so there are bound to be dislocations and malfunctions. If you look at the fast-growing countries, Korea, Thailand, Hong Kong, and Singapore, there's been one remarkable phenomenon: the rise of religion. Koreans have taken to Christianity in large numbers, I think some 25 percent. This is a country that was never colonized by a Christian nation. The old customs and religions, ancestor worship, shamanism, no longer completely satisfy. There is a quest for some higher explanations about man's purpose, about why we are here. This is associated with periods of great stress in society. You will find in Japan that every time it goes through a period of stress new sects crop up and new religions proliferate. In Taiwan, and also in Hong Kong and Singapore, you see a rise in the number of new temples; Confucianist temples, Taoist temples and many Christian sects.

We are all in the midst of very rapid change and at the same time we are all groping towards a destination which we hope will be identifiable with our past. We have left the past behind and there is an underlying unease that there will be nothing left of us which is part of the old. The Japanese have solved this problem to some extent. Japan has become an industrial society, while remaining essentially Japanese in its human relations. They have industrialized and shed some of their feudal values. The Taiwanese and the Koreans are trying to do the same. But whether these societies can preserve their core values and make this transition is a problem which they alone can solve. It is not something Americans can solve for them. Therefore, you will find people unreceptive to the idea that they be Westernized. Modernized, yes, in the sense that they have accepted the inevitability of science and technology and the change in the life-styles they bring.

FZ: But won't these economic and technological changes produce changes in the mind-sets of people?

LKY: It is not just mind-sets that would have to change but value systems. Let me give anecdotal evidence of this. Many Chinese families in Malaysia migrated in periods of stress, when there were race riots in Malaysia in the 1960s, and they settled in Australia and Canada. They did this for the sake of their children so that they would get a better education in the English language because then Malaysia was switching to Malay as its primary language. The children grew up, reached their late teens and left home. And suddenly the parents discovered the emptiness of the whole exercise. They had given their children a modern education in the English language and in the process lost their children altogether. That was a very sobering experience. Something less dramatic is happening in Singapore now because we are not bringing up our children in the same circumstances in which we grew up.

FZ: But these children are absorbing influences different from your generation. You say that knowledge, life-styles, culture all spread rapidly in this world. Will not the idea of democracy and individual rights also spread?

LKY: Let's not get into a debate on semantics. The system of government in China will change. It will change in Korea, Taiwan, Vietnam. It is changing in Singapore. But it will not end up like the American or British or French or German systems. What are we all seeking? A form of government that will be comfortable, because it meets our needs, is not oppressive, and maximizes our opportunities. And whether you have one-man, one-vote or some-men, one vote or other men, two votes, those are forms which should be worked out. I'm not intellectually convinced that one-man, one-vote is the best. We practice it because that's what the British bequeathed us and we haven't really found a need to challenge that. But I'm convinced, personally, that we would have a better system if we gave every man over the age of 40 who has a family two votes because he's likely to be more careful, voting also for his children. He is more likely to vote in a serious way than a capricious young man under 30.

But we haven't found it necessary yet. If it became necessary we should do it. At the same time, once a person gets beyond 65, then it is a problem. Between the ages of 40 and 60 is ideal, and at 60 they should go back to one vote, but that will be difficult to arrange.

Multicultural Schisms

FZ: Change is often most threatening when it occurs in multiethnic societies. You have been part of both a multiethnic state that failed and one that has succeeded. Malaysia was unwilling to allow what it saw as a Chinese city-state to be part of it and expelled Singapore from its federation in 1965. Singapore itself, however, exists peacefully as a multiethnic state. Is there a solution for those states that have ethnic and religious groups mixed within them?

LKY: Each state faces a different set of problems and I would be most reluctant to dish out general solutions. From my own experience, I would say, make haste slowly. Nobody likes to lose his ethnic, cultural, religious, even linguistic identity. To exist as one state you need to share certain attributes, have things in common. If you pressure-cook you are in for problems. If you go gently, but steadily, the logic of events will bring about not assimilation, but integration. If I had tried to foist the English language on the people of Singapore I would have faced rebellion all around. If I had tried to foist the Chinese language, I'd have had immediate revolt and disaster. But I offered every parent a choice of English and their mother tongue, in whatever order they chose. By their free choice, plus the rewards of the marketplace over a period of 30 years, we have ended up with English first and the mother tongue second. We have switched one university already established in the Chinese language from Chinese into English. Had this change been forced in five or ten years instead of being done over 30 years, and by free choice, it would have been a disaster.

FZ: This sounds like a live-and-let-live kind of approach. Many Western countries, particularly the United States and France, respectively, have traditionally attempted to assimilate people toward a national mainstream, with English and French as the national language, respectively. Today this approach is being questioned, as you know, with some minority groups in the United States and France arguing for "multiculturalism," which would allow distinct and unassimilated minority groups to coexist within the nation. How does this debate strike you as you read about it in Singapore?

LKY: You cannot have too many distinct components and be one nation. It makes interchangeability difficult. If you want complete separateness then you should not come to live in the host country. But there are circumstances where it is wise to leave things be. For instance, all races in Singapore are eligible for jobs and for many other things. But we put the Muslims in a slightly different category because they are extremely sensitive about their customs, especially diet. In such matters one has to find a middle path between uniformity and a certain freedom to be somewhat different. I think it is wise to leave alone questions of fundamental beliefs and give time to sort matters out.

FZ: So you would look at the French handling of their Muslim minorities and say "Go slow, don't push these people so hard."

LKY: I would not want to say that because the French having ruled Algeria for many years know the kind of problems that they are faced with. My approach would be, if some Muslim girl insists on coming to school with her headdress on and is prepared to put up with that discomfort, we should be prepared to put up with the strangeness. But if she joined the customs or immigration department where it would be confusing to the millions of people who stream through to have some customs officer looking different, she must wear the uniform. That approach has worked in Singapore so far.

Is Europe's Past Asia's Future?

FZ: Let me shift gears somewhat and ask you some questions about the international climate in East Asia. The part of the world you live in is experiencing the kind of growth that the West has experienced for the last 400 years. The West has not only been the world's great producer of wealth for four centuries, it has also been the world's great producer of war. Today East Asia is the locus of great and unsettling growth, with several newly rising powers close to each other, many with different political systems, historical animosities, border disputes, and all with ever-increasing quantities of arms. Should one look at this and ask whether Europe's past will be East Asia's future?

LKY: No, it's too simplistic. One reason why growth is likely to last for many years in East Asia, and this is just a guess, is that the peoples and the governments of East Asia have learned some powerful lessons about the viciousness and destructiveness of wars. Not only full-scale wars like in Korea, but guerrilla wars as in Vietnam, in Cambodia and in the jungles of Malaysia, Thailand, Indonesia and the Philippines. We all know that the more you engage in conflict, the poorer and the more desperate you become. Visit Cambodia and Vietnam; the world just passed them by. That lesson will live for a very long time, at least as long as this generation is alive.

FZ: The most unsettling change in an international system is the rise of a new great power. Can the rise of China be accommodated into the East Asian order? Isn't that kind of growth inevitably destabilizing?

LKY: I don't think we can speak in terms of just the East Asian order. The question is: Can the world develop a system in which a country the size of China becomes part of the management of international peace and stability? Sometime in the next 20 or 30 years the world, by which I mean the major powers, will have to agree among themselves how to manage peace and stability, how to create a system that is both viable and fair. Wars between small countries won't destroy the whole world, but will only destroy themselves. But big conflicts between big powers will destroy the world many times over. That's just too disastrous to contemplate.

At the end of the last war what they could foresee was the United Nations. The hope was that the permanent five would maintain the rule of law or gradually spread the rule of law in international relations. It did not come off because of Stalin and the Cold War. This is now a new phase. The great powers, by which I mean America, Western Europe as a group if they become a union, Japan, China and, in 20 to 30 years time, the Russian republic, have got to find a balance between themselves. I think the best way forward is through the United Nations. It already has 48 years of experience. It is imperfect, but what is the alternative? You can not have a consortium of five big powers lording it over the rest of mankind. They will not have the moral authority or legitimacy to do it. Are they going to divide the world into five spheres of influence? So they have to fall back on some multilateral framework and work out a set of rules that makes it viable. There may be conflicts of a minor nature, for instance between two Latin American countries or two small Southeast Asian countries; that doesn't really matter. Now if you have two big countries in South Asia like India and Pakistan and both with nuclear capabilities, then something has to be done. It is in that context that we have to find a place for China when it becomes a major economic and military power.

FZ: Is the Chinese regime stable? Is the growth that's going on there sustainable? Is the balancing act between economic reform and political control that Deng Xiaoping is trying to keep going sustainable after his death?

LKY: The regime in Beijing is more stable than any alternative government that can be formed in China. Let us assume that the students had carried the day at Tiananmen and they had formed a government. The same students who were at Tiananmen went to France and America. They've been quarreling with each other ever since. What kind of China would they have today? Something worse than the Soviet Union. China is a vast, disparate country; there is no alternative to strong central power.

FZ: Do you worry that the kind of rapid and unequal growth taking place in China might cause the country to break up?

LKY: First, the economy is growing everywhere, even in Sichuan, in the heart of the interior. Disparate growth rates are inevitable. It is the difference between, say, California before the recession and the Rust Belt. There will be enormous stresses because of the size of the country and the intractable nature of the problems, the poor infrastructure, the weak institutions, the wrong systems that they have installed, modeling themselves upon the Soviet system in Stalin's time. Given all those handicaps, I am amazed that they have got so far.

FZ: What about the other great East Asian power? If Japan continues on the current trajectory, should the world encourage the expansion of its political and military responsibilities and power?

LKY: No. I know that the present generation of Japanese leaders do not want to project power. I'm not sure what follows when leaders born after the war take charge. I doubt if there will be a sudden change. If Japan can carry on with its current policy, leaving security to the Americans and concentrating on the economic and the political, the world will be better off. And the Japanese are quite happy to do this. It is when America feels that it's too burdensome and not worth the candle to be present in East Asia to protect Japan that it will have to look after its own security. When Japan becomes a separate player, it is an extra joker in the pack of cards.

FZ: You've said recently that allowing Japan to send its forces abroad is like giving liquor to an alcoholic.

LKY: The Japanese have always had this cultural trait, that whatever they do they carry it to the nth degree. I think they know this. I have Japanese friends who have told me this. They admit that this is a problem with them.

FZ: What if Japan did follow the trajectory that most great powers have; that it was not content simply to be an economic superpower, "a bank with a flag" in a writer's phrase? What if they decided they wanted to have the ultimate mark of a great power, nuclear weapons? What should the world do?

LKY: If they decided on that the world will not be able to stop them. You are unable to stop North Korea. Nobody believes that an American government that could not sustain its mission in Somalia because of an ambush and one television snippet of a dead American pulled through the streets in Mogadishu could contemplate a strike on North Korean nuclear facilities like the Israeli strike on Iraq. Therefore it can only be sanctions in the U.N. Security Council. That requires that there be no vetoes. Similarly, if the Japanese decide to go nuclear, I don't believe you will be able to stop them. But they know that they face a nuclear power in China and in Russia, and so they would have to posture themselves in such a way as not to invite a preemptive strike. If they can avoid a preemptive strike then a balance will be established. Each will deter the others.

FZ: So it's the transition period that you are worried about.

LKY: I would prefer that the matter never arises and I believe so does the world. Whether the Japanese go down the military path will depend largely on America's strength and its willingness to be engaged.

Vive La Difference

FZ: Is there some contradiction here between your role as a politician and your new role as an intellectual, speaking out on all matters? As a politician you want America as a strong balancer in the region, a country that is feared and respected all over the world. As an intellectual, however, you choose to speak out forcefully against the American model in a way that has to undermine America's credibility abroad.

LKY: That's preposterous. The last thing I would want to do is to undermine her credibility. America has been unusual in the history of the world, being the sole possessor of power, the nuclear weapon, and the one and only government in the world unaffected by war damage whilst the others were in ruins. Any old and established nation would have ensured its supremacy for as long as it could. But America set out to put her defeated enemies on their feet, to ward off an evil force, the Soviet Union, brought about technological change by transferring technology generously and freely to Europeans and to Japanese, and enabled them to become her challengers within 30 years. By 1975 they were at her heels. That's unprecedented in history. There was a certain greatness of spirit born out of the fear of communism plus American idealism that brought that about. But that does not mean that we all admire everything about America.

Let me be frank; if we did not have the good points of the West to guide us, we wouldn't have got out of our backwardness. We would have been a backward economy with a backward society. But we do not want all of the West.

A Coda on Culture

The dominant theme throughout our conversation was culture. Lee returned again and again to his views on the importance of culture and the differences between Confucianism and Western values. In this respect, Lee is very much part of a trend. Culture is in. From business consultants to military strategists, people talk about culture as the deepest and most determinative aspect of human life.

I remain skeptical. If culture is destiny, what explains a culture's failure in one era and success in another? If Confucianism explains the economic boom in East Asia today, does it not also explain that region's stagnation for four centuries? In fact, when East Asia seemed immutably poor, many scholars, most famously Max Weber, made precisely that case, arguing that Confucian-based cultures discouraged all the attributes necessary for success in capitalism. Today scholars explain how Confucianism emphasizes the essential traits for economic dynamism. Were Latin American countries to succeed in the next few decades, we shall surely read encomiums to Latin culture. I suspect that since we cannot find one simple answer to why certain societies succeed at certain times, we examine successful societies and search within their cultures for the seeds of success. Cultures being complex, one finds in them what one wants.

What explains Lee Kuan Yew's fascination with culture? It is not something he was born with. Until his thirties he was called "Harry" Lee (and still is by family and friends). In the 1960s the British foreign secretary could say to him, "Harry, you're the best bloody Englishman east of the Suez." This is not a man untouched by the West. Part of his interest in cultural differences is surely that they provide a coherent defense against what he sees as Western democratic imperialism. But a deeper reason is revealed in something he said in our conversation: "We have left the past behind, and there is an underlying unease that there will be nothing left of us which is part of the old."

Cultures change. Under the impact of economic growth, technological change and social transformation, no culture has remained the same. Most of the attributes that Lee sees in Eastern cultures were once part of the West. Four hundred years of economic growth changed things. From the very beginning of England's economic boom, many Englishmen worried that as their country became rich it was losing its moral and ethical base. "Wealth accumulates and men decay," wrote Oliver Goldsmith in 1770. It is this "decay" that Lee is trying to stave off. He speaks of the anxious search for religion in East Asia today, and while he never says this, his own quest for a Confucian alternative to the West is part of this search.

But to be modern without becoming more Western is difficult; the two are not wholly separable. The West has left a mark on "the rest," and it is not simply a legacy of technology and material products. It is, perhaps most profoundly, in the realm of ideas. At the close of the interview Lee handed me three pages. This was, he explained, to emphasize how alien Confucian culture is to the West. The pages were from the book East Asia: Tradition and Transformation, by John Fairbank, an American scholar.

Ethiopia's Prime Minister: The Man Who Tried to Make Dictatorship Acceptable

THE ECONOMIST

The death of Meles Zenawi, Ethiopia's prime minister, on August 20th reveals much about the country he created. Details of his ill health remained a secret until the end. A short broadcast on state television, late by a day, informed Ethiopians that their "visionary leader" of the past 21 years was gone. He died of an unspecified "sudden infection" somewhere abroad. No further information was given. In the two months since the prime minister's last public appearance the only Ethiopian newspaper that reported his illness was pulped, its office closed, and its editor arrested. Further details of Mr Meles's death surfaced only when an EU official confirmed that he died in a Brussels hospital.

A towering figure on Africa's political scene, he leaves much uncertainty in his wake. Ethiopia, where power has changed hands only three times since the second world war, always by force, now faces a tricky transition period. Mr Meles's chosen successor is a placeholder at best. Most Ethiopians, whatever they thought of their prime minister, assumed he would be around to manage the succession. Instead he disappeared as unexpectedly as he had arrived. He was a young medical student in the 1970s when he joined the fight against the Derg, the Marxist junta that then ruled Ethiopia. He went into the bush as Legesse Zenawi and emerged as "Meles"—a *nom de guerre* he had taken in tribute to a murdered comrade.

Who exactly was he? As leader of the Tigrayan People's Liberation Front, an ethnic militia from the country's north, he presented himself to his countrymen as a severe, ruthless revolutionary; yet Westerners who spoke to him in his mountain hideouts found a clever, understated man who laid out, in precise English, plans to reform a feudal state. In 1991, after the fall of the last Derg leader, Mengistu Haile Mariam, the 36-year-old Mr Meles (pictured above) took power, becoming Africa's youngest leader. He had moral authority as a survivor of various famines. Western governments and publics, who became aware of Ethiopian hunger through the Band Aid and Live Aid charity concerts, gave freely. Mr Meles was often able to dictate terms under which donors could operate in Ethiopia and turned his country into Africa's biggest aid recipient.

Where others wasted development aid, Ethiopia put it to work. Over the past decade GDP has grown by 10.6% a year, according to the World Bank, double the average in the rest of sub-Saharan Africa. The share of Ethiopians living in extreme poverty—those on less than 60 cents a day—has fallen from 45% when Mr Meles took power to just under 30%. Lacking large-scale natural resources, the government has boosted manufacturing and agriculture. Exports have risen sharply. A string of hydroelectric dams now under construction is expected to give the economy a further boost in the coming years.

The flipside of the Meles record is authoritarianism. Before his departure he ensured that meaningful opposition was "already dead", says Zerihun Tesfaye, a human-rights activist. The ruling party controls all but one of the seats in parliament, after claiming 99.6% of the vote in the 2010 elections. It abandoned a brief flirtation with more open politics after a vote five years previously, when the opposition did better than expected. The regime subsequently rewired the state from the village up, dismantling independent organisations from teachers' unions to human-rights groups and binding foreign-financed programmes with tight new rules. Opposition parties were banned and their leaders jailed or driven into exile; the press was muzzled.

Internationally, Mr Meles made friends with America, allowing it to base unarmed drones at a remote airfield. He also liked to act as a regional policeman. His troops repeatedly entered neighbouring Somalia (they are slowly handing over conquered territory to an African Union peacekeeping force). Hostilities have at times flared along the border with Eritrea. Mr Meles cowed his smaller neighbour and persuaded the world to see it as a rogue state. This in turn helped him restrain nationalists at home. In his absence, hardliners on both sides may reach for arms once again.

The nature of power in Mr Meles's Ethiopia has remained surprisingly opaque. On the surface, the ruling Ethiopian People's Revolutionary Democratic Front is a broad grouping encompassing all of the country's ethnic factions. Like the liberal constitution, it is largely a sham. Real power rests with an inner circle of Mr Meles's comrades. They all come from his home area, Tigray, which accounts for only 7% of Ethiopia's 82m people. His acting successor is an exception. Haile Mariam Desalegn, the foreign minister, is from the south. His prominence raises hopes that the long dominance of the Habesha, the Christian highlanders of the Amhara and Tigray regions, may be diluted. But few think he has enough standing to exert real control.

Power will be wielded by Tigrayans such as Getachew Assefa, the head of the intelligence service; Abay Tsehaye, the director-general of the Ethiopian sugar corporation; and Mr Meles's widow, Azeb Mesfin. An MP, she heads a sprawling conglomerate known as EFFORT, which began as a reconstruction fund for Tigray but now has a host of investments. It is unclear whether any of the Tigrayans will seek the leadership of the ruling party or be content to wield control from the sidelines. A struggle among this elite would be a big threat to stability.

In the Shadow of Chávez

BORIS MUÑOZ

A month ago, I attended the epic funeral of Hugo Chávez. What amazed me most were the huge crowds of Venezuelans, above all women from the lowest rungs of society, who were ardently—and melodramatically—devoted to the cult of his personality. It didn't matter that his death had been foreseeable, nor that those in charge of the government had deliberately kept millions of Venezuelans misinformed about the true state of the President's health. The sea of people who had been waiting for hour upon hour had a single aim: to see Chávez for the last time, to see the face of the man who had wooed them and won them by giving them a political identity, by giving direction to their desires and resentments. Now they swore their loyalty to him beyond death. It seemed evident to me that a new religion had been born—a religion whose prophet was Hugo Chávez.

I interviewed several average *Chavistas* during the funeral and wasn't surprised by their adoration for Chávez. But I was struck by the similarity of their responses. I asked Luz Marina Laya, an outgoing and committed militant, what Chávez meant to her. Tearfully, she replied that Chávez was her father, her brother, her lover, her husband, and her protector. On July 1, 2012, during the opening act of Chávez's final electoral campaign, I'd put the same question to America Carvallo, a woman in her mid-fifties wearing a red T-shirt. Her response was almost identical. "He's my brother, my husband, my friend, my mother, and my father," she said. "I love him, and all I want is for God to give him good health."

This kind of dèjà vu was not limited to the funeral; it has pervaded the Presidential election to replace Chávez, which ends Sunday. Memories of the last Presidential election are still fresh and the cult of Chávez's personality is sponsored by the state and indirectly supported by the opposition. Nicolás Maduro, the government candidate proclaims, "I am the son of Chávez!", while Henrique Capriles, the opposition leader, says "Maduro is *not* Chávez."

Apart from this, the most notable aspect of the campaign has been the offensive, vicious, and sexist language. Chávez used to bully his opponents and disparage them, but he wrapped his attacks in an entertaining and grandiose flood of words on his strategic objectives in defense of the revolution. This time, the attacks have been direct and barefaced.

Many Venezuelans say they miss Chávez's presence in the campaign. One can inherit political machinery, political rhetoric, and a political party, and win elections by doing so, but a leader's charisma, popularity, and strategic vision are not transferable.

Like Chávez did in the last election, Maduro has called Capriles an oligarch and a Nazi—a particularly hurtful epithet for Capriles, whose great-grandparents were both killed in the Holocaust. But he has also mounted an attack on the sexual orientation of Capriles—a forty-year-old bachelor—insinuating that he's a closeted homosexual, which has aroused the fury of the L.G.B.T. community. Unlike the last campaign, when Capriles did all he could to avoid confronting Chávez, this time he has accepted the fight. A lesson he learned from that campaign was that political ends can't be separated from the means employed to reach them. In fact, he has gone on the offensive, continuously denouncing the abuses of power and poor government under *Chavismo*. The campaign has, as a result, been marked by the near-total absence of substantive proposals for change.

One leitmotif among Chavistas has been that even a dead Chávez would win the elections by a landslide. No one doubted this a month ago. Maduro was the candidate of the multitudes who mourn for Chávez. He wagered that his identification with Chávez would attract the popular vote, and bring Chávez's party to him. This strategy will likely end up as a winning one, but it has had downsides. Maduro tries hard to fill his predecessor's shoes, but it has become clear that the differences between the leader and his apostles are overwhelming. Compared with Chávez, a consummate showman, a master of oratory and manipulation, Maduro seems like the sorcerer's apprentice. The comparisons have worn him down rather than strengthened him.

Luis Vicente León, the president of Datanálisis, one of the country's most reliable polling companies, says Maduro is still the favorite, but Capriles has been gaining ground. "The present situation is completely different from what the surveys showed a month ago," León says. "When Chávez died, it didn't matter if his heir was good or bad. All the people's feelings of adoration were transferred to Maduro. Those feelings have weakened. Maduro had decided not to be himself but to be the representative of Chávez's legacy here on earth, but there was a limit to that strategy. Capriles forced Maduro to stop being Chávez."

On October 5th, two days before the last Presidential election, I asked León what the result would be, and he did not hesitate to say that Chávez would win by eleven percentage points. Chávez won by ten points. On Thursday, three days before the current election, I asked him the same thing. He told me that the gap between Capriles and Maduro was now only six points and narrowing. The acting President was still the favorite, but of Capriles, León said, "If he wins it will be a surprise, but not a miracle anymore".

The Venezuelan economy is marching over a cliff. The murder rate was already one of the highest in the world, and the number of murders was up by fourteen per cent last year. (The rate grew by nine per cent.) There are shortages of electricity, food, and medicines, and the country is divided in two. Margarita López Maya, a historian of Venezuelan social movements and left wing activist, sees a pattern similar to the one that led to the social explosion that took place in 1989, known as the Caracazo, which was brutally repressed and left more than three hundred dead. "The fall in the standard of living is frightening. My husband, a faculty professor, took his car for a routine maintenance and had to pay the equivalent of three months' salary. On Sunday we'll know if many people whose conditions of life have deteriorated dramatically are going to vote for Maduro because of their debt to Chávez, or if they'll abstain."

There is a small chance that Capriles could pull off the upset. If he does win, though, it would likely be by a very narrow margin, and he would find himself in an almost impossible situation, with the

National Assembly, the Supreme Court, and twenty out of twenty-three state governors against him, as well as many other parts of the government. "This would force him to look for ways to widen his popular support by opening up to Chavista ideas and try to move towards a hybrid model that combines elements of *Chavismo* with some proposals of the opposition", says López Maya.

If, as is more likely, *Chavismo* wins, it will need to ask itself if it can gradually open up to the other half of the country without abandoning the social ideals that inspired Chávez's vague twenty-first-century socialism, and if it can improve its style of government, which so far has been dysfunctional and inefficient. "The winning margin will be decisive not only in relation to the opposition, but internally," León says. "If Maduro manages to maintain or improve on Chávez's margin of ten points, he'll consolidate his leadership. If it's smaller and Capriles catches up on him, the problems inside *Chavismo* that were hidden because of the need to survive a transition without Chávez will come to the fore."

What's at stake is not just the choice between *Chavismo* and change or between two men, but between a viable society and one in permanent conflict. The winner, whoever he is, will have to struggle with the spectre of a violent social crisis.

Next of Kim: North Korea, One Year Later

VICTOR CHA

Reprinted by permission of FOREIGN AFFAIRS, December 18, 2012. Copyright © 2012 by the Council on Foreign Relations, Inc. www.ForeignAffairs.com.

One year ago, the chubby and blubbering soon-to-be leader of the Democratic People's Republic of Korea was seen walking alongside the hearse that carried his dead father, Kim Jong Il. Kim Jong Un was young, inexperienced, unqualified, and bereft of any of the larger-than-life myths that had sustained his father's and grandfather's rules. And yet, just days later, he assumed power in the only communist dynasty in the world.

Today, the junior Kim can be seen riding high in Pyongyang. And last week, he became the first Korean to launch a domestically designed satellite into orbit on the back of a domestically designed rocket. But more broadly, some analysts see him as pushing his own version of reform. His new ways might not exactly be Gangnam style, but they are undeniably a break from the past. He promulgates high heels and miniskirts for women and commissions amusement parks and (pirated) Walt Disney productions for children. Never too busy to ride rollercoasters and frolic with school kids, the prince of Pyongyang also found time to take on a wife, Ri Sol-Ju, whom the *New York Times* compared to the British Duchess Kate Middleton.

Optimists look to these changes and to Kim's years of Swiss schooling—during which he took courses on democratic governance, wolfed down pizza, and came to idolize NBA stars—and declare that North Korea is ready for reform. This past spring, I participated in track-two meetings in New York at which North Korean officials sought out executives from Coca-Cola and Kentucky Fried Chicken to discuss opening branches in Pyongyang. Rumors that the regime is hatching a new economic policy only fuel speculation that Kim is "distanc[ing] himself from the regime of his father and grandfather," as one article in *The Telegraph* had it. Some onlookers even predict China-like reforms in Rason (a city near the Russian border) and Hwanggumpyong Island (an island near the Chinese border) that would create the next Hong Kong or Shenzhen, where low taxes, high returns, and reduced government intervention reign free.

Weathered North Korea watchers, however, will remember that similar predictions were made in 1994, when the 52-year-old Kim Jong Il took over after his 82-year-old father died. The journalist Selig Harrison believed that North Korea was signaling a coming transformation by sending officials abroad to learn about market economics. Likening the Kim regime to the Communist Party in China, Harrison remarked that "as Pyongyang gradually liberalizes its economy and opens up to the outside world," the ruling regime and the North Korean political system as a whole will transform. But believers in the irresistibility of Disney, Dior, and Coke have short memories.

Back from the Brink

North Korea's political system, helmed by a young and unproven leader, faces severe challenges. The regime will not change because the West hopes that it will.

For optimists in the United States, North Korea's quiescence as the country's leadership changed this past year confirmed that Kim was on the right path. Last week's rocket launch from a snowy facility in the northwest corner of the country poured ice water on those expectations. And with presidential elections in the United States last month and in South Korea this month, Pyongyang is unlikely to be finished. A study I undertook at the Center for Strategic and International Studies found that Pyongyang has usually done something provocative within an average of 16–18 weeks of every South Korean election since 1992. For example, within four weeks of Lee Myung-bak taking the South Korean presidency in 2008, North Korea expelled all South Koreans from the joint industrial complex at Kaesong and tested two missiles. Pyongyang's election antics are not just reserved for other Koreans. In early 2009, U.S. President Barack Obama was welcomed into office with ballistic-missile and nuclear tests. Last week's successful rocket launch is thus only the first in a series of provocations that the Obama administration is likely to see.

Why? Because even an authoritarian dictator must justify his or her rule to the "selectorate," as the Georgetown professor Daniel Byman and the Dartmouth professor Jennifer Lind have written. Otherwise, they could "find a better deal from a rival leader." The current Kim's grandfather, Kim Il Sung, had revolutionary credentials as a guerilla fighter against the Japanese. And Kim Jong Il had a decade of training and preparation for the job. Without a day of military service, Kim Jong Un was

grafted to the top of the power structure in his late twenties. Kim's regime is thus only as strong as his ability to prove to the elites that he is worthy. If he does not affirm his ability to actually do something—say a third and successful nuclear test—he will struggle to justify his rule.

The danger, however, is that decelerating from such a crisis this time will not be easy. In the past, the United States often provided the exit ramp. Based on my research of U.S.–North Korean negotiations since 1984, within an average five months of a provocation, Washington was usually back at the bargaining table. This diplomacy has often been for the express purpose of ratcheting down a crisis. So, after the October 2006 nuclear test, the George W. Bush administration returned to negotiations in January 2007 and reached a deal with the North Koreans the following month. But the Obama administration, having been burned thrice (first by the April-May 2009 missile and nuclear tests, then again in April 2012 by another missile test, and yet once more last week by a third missile test) is not interested in such diplomacy but rather in "strategic patience," or not negotiating with North Korea until it commits to denuclearization.

Perhaps that explains the Obama administration's relatively muted response to last week's missile test. The White House's bland condemnation of the test was a stark contrast to its stern announcement of a red line against the Syrian regime using chemical weapons, especially since last week's missile test indicated that North Korea's weapons program has come a long way in the last year. By successfully launching a payload into orbit, North Korea joined only China and Russia as non-allied countries that could potentially reach the United States with an intercontinental ballistic missile. It is probably just a few years before the country is able to load those missiles with a nuclear weapon.

Like the United States, South Koreans are fed up with negotiations. After North Korea torpedoed a South Korean navy ship and shelled one of its islands in 2010, the South Korean government and public are no longer willing to preach patience and stability, as they had been doing during the previous decade-long "Sunshine policy" toward North Korea. It is an open secret that South Korea has rewritten its rules of military engagement with its northern adversary. Seoul is now prepared to retaliate to the next military act, not just by returning fire but also by going after North Korean support systems and command structures. This escalation would not even require high-level political approval. In interviews with top officials, it was apparent that the military leadership could determine the steps to be taken based on the situation on the ground. Meanwhile, South Korea's newly-elected president, Park Geun-hye, has evinced a mild interest in more engagement with Pyongyang. But if Pyongyang tries to test the new leader, it will be very difficult for her to turn the other cheek.

Chinese Diplomacy

China might be ready to step in where the United States and South Korea have demurred. Beijing's preferred solution to North Korean rambunctiousness has always been to make it more like China (or Vietnam)—that is, to push a slow process of economic reform that would get North Korea out of its attention-getting cycle of provocation and crisis. But despite all the economic assistance and food Beijing showers on its communist brother, Pyongyang bites the hand that feeds it. Recent high-level meetings between Chinese officials and Kim were preludes to more economic deals between the two countries. They might even presage a visit by Kim to Beijing to meet the newly ensconced Xi Jinping. But the day after the meeting with the Chinese, North Korea announced its rocket launch, which just goes to show that China can neither restrain Pyongyang nor reform North Korean leadership, no matter how much economic assistance it provides or how many bureaucrats it offers to train.

After all, every time Kim's father, Kim Jong Il, made a visit to China, his Chinese interlocutors urged him to tour factories and cities to see the benefits of capitalism with communist characteristics. Over a decade, Kim willingly walked through facilities that manufactured fiber optics, computers, telephones, lasers, and computer software. With each visit, Chinese and Western journalists and scholars proclaimed a new chapter in North Korea's economic transformation that would inevitably make it more peaceful. And each time, they

were proved wrong. Kim invariably made the trips to appease his Chinese hosts (and to receive the requisite aid packages) but had no intention of changing. And all the while, he forged ahead with his ballistic-missile, chemical weapons, and nuclear programs.

China's long-term strategy remains to institute top-down economic reform in North Korea. But faced with short-term failures, China resorted to trying to bribe Pyongyang into returning to the six-party talks and holding off missile and nuclear tests. As last week's test showed, though, this is not sustainable either, so China has recently adopted a medium-term coping mechanism: engage with North Korea economically but solely for the benefit of Chinese economic interests, not as part of a reform agenda.

This medium-term solution is evident in the slew of mining contracts and further agreements to excavate coal, minerals, and other resources from North Korea to fuel China's two poor inland provinces, Jilin and Liaoning. In 2005, China and North Korea cooperated to build a "commercial corridor" associated with the Greater Tumen Initiative, which would connect Jilin Province to the seaport in Rajin, North Korea. China subsequently leased Rajin for ten years in 2010. In 2011, Chinese and North Korean trade reached $6 billion, according to Scott Snyder, a senior fellow for Korea studies and the director of the Program on U.S.-Korea Policy at the Council on Foreign Relations. Meanwhile, in the same year, total Chinese investment in North Korea reached $98.3 million. That might sound like a lot, but this number is dwarfed by Chinese investments in South Korea ($1.2 billion), Vietnam ($437 million), and Mongolia ($890.7 million). In the end, Pyongyang's restrictions and inability to make rational economic decisions have confounded China's hope of seeing North Korean economic reform and peace. Only when the Kim regime decides to prize wealth and growth more than power will this vision be realized.

Hermit No More

Even as the nuclear and missile programs continue to grow unimpeded, the domestic situation inside the dark country seems unsettled. Presumably, there is some degree of infighting within the North Korean government, which resulted in the surprise sacking in July 2012 of Ri Yong-ho, the country's top military general. In fact, all of the military generals who walked with Kim aside his father's hearse last December are gone. Some interpret these unceremonious departures as evidence that the reform-minded Kim is trying to usurp power from the hardline military. Others suggest that Kim, in a move to assert his authority, wanted to signal that he is fully able to silence rivals who challenge his power. More likely, Kim wants to strengthen his own patronage network by reclaiming some of the money that the military, presumably including Ri, was making through lucrative business activities awarded to them by Kim's father. This means that there are some very unhappy military generals in North Korea today.

Perhaps to befriend the military, Kim continues to pay lip service to his father's military-first (*songun chongch'i*) brand of rule. But he appears to have complemented this with a fundamentalist version of his grandfather's *juche*, or self-reliance, ideology of the Cold War. It could be that the bankruptcy of his father's rule compelled him to find a better idea to justify the family's continued rule. Fundamentalist *juche* ideology, or what I call "neojucheism," appeals because it reminds North Koreans of an era of relative economic development and affluence, when production levels outpaced those of the rival South, and Chinese and Soviet money poured into the country. *Juche* fundamentalism was, and will be, a time of deep ideological indoctrination, mass mobilization, and rejection of foreign influences. Indeed, Kim has made himself the physical reincarnation of his grandfather down to the Mao suit, protruding stomach, cropped hairdo, and hearty laugh.

But even as the regime's ideology is growing more hard-line, the society that Kim inherited is moving in a diametrically opposed direction. The biggest difference between the hermit kingdom of 1994, when Kim Jong Il took over, and the one of 2012 is the development of a market mentality among the people—something that grew out of terrible food shortages. Official and unofficial markets sprung up as people struggled to cope with the

breakdown of the government's ration system. A study by the Peterson Institute for International Economics' Marcus Noland and his colleagues Stephen Haggard and Erik Weeks, found that recent defectors admitted that at least 50 percent of total food they consumed in North Korea came from sources apart from the government. That creates an independence of mind that is dangerous in a society such as North Korea's.

Other elements of modernity are starting to seep in, as well. Over one million North Koreans use cell phones, and more than 4,000 crawl the Web. Daily NK, one of the biggest new sites, attracts over 150,00 hits online per month for its timely insider information on North Korean issues. Thanks to expanded cell-phone access, North Korean "citizen journalists" operating between the Chinese-North Korean border can transmit bits of information more effectively both within the country and worldwide.

The peculiar part about these advancements in communication technology is that most of them are legal. The North Korean government promotes, to an extent, cell-phone use because it holds a 25 percent stake in Koryolink (the North Korean branch of the Egyptian telecommunications company Orascom Telecom). With the number of subscribers to Koryolink steadily rising, mostly in Pyongyang, phones are quickly finding a permanent place in daily life.

Where does all this lead? Toward a dead end for Kim, I think, and perhaps a nightmare loose-nukes scenario for the United States. The new leadership is exercising a more rigid ideology that seeks greater control over an increasingly independent-minded society and over disgruntled elements of the military. Meanwhile, its nuclear-bomb- and ICBM-making programs continue. All that is not sustainable. If Kim tried true reform and an opening North Korean society, however, he would immediately create a spiral of expectations that the regime would not be able to control. The young and untested leadership will try to navigate between these two perils. But it may prove too difficult. And if it does, Obama may find his pivot to Asia absorbed by a new crisis on the Korean peninsula.

DISCUSSION QUESTIONS

1) Lee Kuan Yew is critical of efforts of the some states to promote "their" conceptions of democracy for other countries. He claims that different cultural traditions have different development paths and find best expression in different political institutions. Is this good analysis or just a self-serving argument of an authoritarian leader?

2) The first three readings in this section all discuss leaders and regimes that blur the conceptual boundaries of authoritarianism in certain ways. The fourth reading discusses a straightforwardly and fully authoritarian regime. What accounts for the difference? What do these different authoritarian regimes tell us about the concept of authoritarianism more generally?

3) The reading by Boris Muñoz discusses the late Hugo Chávez, who was repeatedly elected but whose regime had notably authoritarian features. Can a political regime be both democratic and authoritarian? How might we analyze the proliferation of regimes that mix democratic and authoritarian elements?

Constitutions and Constitutional Design

Ever since the first political units were formed, people have debated the best principles and rules for political organization, and these have often been codified in constitutions. In ancient Greece, the philosopher Aristotle examined the constitutions of different city-states in his efforts to formulate the ideal designs for government. The United States has retained its original Constitution since its ratification in 1788, yet debates have persisted ever since about the power of different actors in the Constitution's design. Besides the relative power of the legislature and the executive, one of the biggest constitutional questions (in the United States and elsewhere) has been how much power the judiciary should assert in interpreting the constitution versus how much the judiciary should defer to elected officials. Another major question is how much power belongs to the central government and how much belongs to the states or other subnational units. These questions of constitutional design are present in most countries in the world today.

Using the United States as an example, in the first reading in this section Paul Gewirtz and Chad Golder ask questions about how far judges go in interpreting laws. In particular, they ask which types of judges are the most "activist." Their analysis is based on the frequency with which Supreme Court justices vote to overturn legislation that has been passed by Congress and signed into law by presidents. For many years conservatives argued that liberal justices were "legislating from the bench," substituting judicial rulings for legislative statute. Gewirtz and Golder, however, challenge that with intriguing findings about which justices are most activist. Though the piece is from 2005, it certainly has many implications for current questions of judicial review and judicial activism, in the U.S. Supreme Court and beyond. The piece also shows the importance of debating what measures and indicators analysts should use when dealing with slippery (but important) concepts like "judicial activism."

Questions of constitutional design go far beyond the United States, of course. In many countries around the world today, the basic design and structure of the constitution is still in flux. One country where this has proved to be very important in recent years is Iraq. In the wake of the country's long war in the 2000s, political leaders in Iraq and around the world debated whether Iraq should become a federal polity. On the one hand, federalism can accommodate different identity groups—protecting minority rights, for instance—and help stabilize divided countries. On the other hand, federalism is seen by some as a recipe for cementing divisions and further exacerbating tensions. In their article, Sean Kane, Joost Hiltermann, and Raad Alkadiri explore the potential for a federal system in Iraq, making use of some of the key theoretical distinctions between "coming together" and "holding together" federalism, as well as symmetrical vs. asymmetrical federalism.

Federalism is also posited to have effects on economies. A line of thinking in the study of federalism is that this can come from a sort of "healthy competition" between states to become more economically competitive. It also holds that centralized economic planning (which India had for many decades prior to entering into a period of decentralization beginning in the 1990s) tends to be quite inefficient and is best replaced by more nimble and responsive decision making closer to the local level. In India in recent years, some states have performed especially well in economic terms, and Ruchir Sharma attributes this (at least in part) to the country's different states taking the lead in promoting economic growth, rather than the central government. In reading this piece, consider how Sharma thinks a federal constitutional design—with power decentralized to the states—benefits the overall economy. Since this debate has not resulted decisively in favor of federalism, consider also if there are contrary circumstances when centralizing economic and political authority would be preferable.

These pieces—in different country contexts and in different ways—show how debates over constitutional design and constitutional interpretation are not simply relegated to history: they are current and pressing issues in global politics today.

So Who Are the Activists?

PAUL GEWIRTZ AND CHAD GOLDER

When Democrats or Republicans seek to criticize judges or judicial nominees, they often resort to the same language. They say that the judge is "activist." But the word "activist" is rarely defined. Often it simply means that the judge makes decisions with which the critic disagrees.

In order to move beyond this labeling game, we've identified one reasonably objective and quantifiable measure of a judge's activism, and we've used it to assess the records of the justices on the current Supreme Court.

Here is the question we asked: How often has each justice voted to strike down a law passed by Congress?

Declaring an act of Congress unconstitutional is the boldest thing a judge can do. That's because Congress, as an elected legislative body representing the entire nation, makes decisions that can be presumed to possess a high degree of democratic legitimacy. In an 1867 decision, the Supreme Court itself described striking down Congressional legislation as an act "of great delicacy, and only to be performed where the repugnancy is clear." Until 1991, the court struck down an average of about one Congressional statute every two years. Between 1791 and 1858, only two such invalidations occurred.

Of course, calling Congressional legislation into question is not necessarily a bad thing. If a law is unconstitutional, the court has a responsibility to strike it down. But a marked pattern of invalidating Congressional laws certainly seems like one reasonable definition of judicial activism.

Since the Supreme Court assumed its current composition in 1994, by our count it has upheld or struck down 64 Congressional provisions. That legislation has concerned Social Security, church and state, and campaign finance, among many other issues. We examined the court's decisions in these cases and looked at how each justice voted,

regardless of whether he or she concurred with the majority or dissented.

We found that justices vary widely in their inclination to strike down Congressional laws. Justice Clarence Thomas, appointed by President George H. W. Bush, was the most inclined, voting to invalidate 65.63 percent of those laws; Justice Stephen Breyer, appointed by President Bill Clinton, was the least, voting to invalidate 28.13 percent. The tally for all the justices appears below.

Thomas 65.63%
Kennedy 64.06%
Scalia 56.25%
Rehnquist 46.88%
O'Connor 46.77%
Souter 42.19%
Stevens 39.34%
Ginsburg 39.06%
Breyer 28.13%

One conclusion our data suggests is that those justices often considered more "liberal"—Justices Breyer, Ruth Bader Ginsburg, David Souter and John Paul Stevens—vote least frequently to overturn Congressional statutes, while those often labeled "conservative" vote more frequently to do so. At least by this measure (others are possible, of course), the latter group is the most activist.

To say that a justice is activist under this definition is not itself negative. Because striking down Congressional legislation is sometimes justified, some activism is necessary and proper. We can decide whether a particular degree of activism is appropriate only by assessing the merits of a judge's particular decisions and the judge's underlying constitutional views, which may inspire more or fewer invalidations.

Our data no doubt reflects such differences among the justices' constitutional views. But it even more clearly illustrates the varying degrees to which justices would actually intervene in the democratic work of Congress. And in so doing, the data probably demonstrates differences in temperament regarding intervention or restraint.

These differences in the degree of intervention and in temperament tell us far more about "judicial activism" than we commonly understand from the term's use as a mere epithet. As the discussion of Justice Sandra Day O'Connor's replacement begins, we hope that debates about "activist judges" will include indicators like these.

Correction

Because of an editing error, this article misstated the date the court started. Its first official business began in 1790, not 1791.

Iraq's Federalism Quandary

SEAN KANE, JOOST R. HILTERMANN, AND RAAD ALKADIRI

"Iraq's Federalism Quandary" by Sean Kane, Joost R. Hiltermann, Raad Alkadiri, March/April 2012. Reprinted by permission of *The National Interest*.

With U.S. combat troops out of Iraq and that country facing an uncertain future, many challenges hover over the lands of old Mesopotamia. The most ominous is the unsettled struggle over power, territory and resources among the country's political elites. While often described in straightforward ethnic and sectarian terms, this strife has gone through many phases. Various alliances have come together and broken apart as the power struggle has shifted from a sectarian street war to heightened tensions between Baghdad and the Kurdistan Regional Government (KRG) in Erbil. Most recently, the main axis of confrontation has been between Prime Minister Nouri al-Maliki's Shia-led government and its putative governing partner, the mostly Sunni Iraqiya list.

One constant that complicates this maelstrom is the unresolved question of what kind of federal structure the new nation should have—essentially, the power-sharing arrangement between those who rule Baghdad, the autonomous government in Erbil and the country's provincial leaders.

Within this puzzle reside a number of interlocking quandaries. For example, it is grudgingly accepted that the Kurds in northern Iraq should be able to retain the level of autonomy acquired after the Gulf War in 1991. But the details of this arrangement remain in dispute, and it raises some difficult questions: Would Iraq remain viable as a country if other provinces were to pursue similar autonomy? Even in the context of the Kurdistan region, can revenue-sharing arrangements that respect both Kurdish autonomy and Baghdad's basic sovereign prerogatives be crafted? Would those same arrangements work for oil-rich Basra in Iraq's South or gas-rich Anbar in its West?

These are not dry, structural matters. They drive deeply into emotionally held convictions on all sides. Iraq's new constitution describes the country as a federal state, with significant grants of autonomy to Iraqi Kurdistan as well as potentially to future regions throughout the country. But the word federalism remains one of the most charged in the Iraqi political lexicon.

For Kurds, federalism has almost acquired the status of a religious belief system because it is tied to their century-old quest for their own state. But for many Iraqi Arabs, federalism is seen as synonymous with partition. Especially among Iraqi nationalists, there is fear that if the Kurdish federalist vision is implemented, it would bring about what Peter Galbraith, a controversial and influential advisor to the KRG, called "the end of Iraq."

So far, this fundamental question of governance has generated little more than stalemate. Agreement between the federal government and the KRG on the final contours of their relationship has proved elusive. This stalemate is most consequential in the realm of oil and gas development, which will generate an estimated $1 trillion in revenue over the coming decade. The KRG has proposed a revenue-sharing regimen that not only would protect Kurdistan's share of the pie but also would reduce the federal government to little more than a cash clearinghouse that disburses oil and gas revenue around the country. Not surprisingly, this proposal is totally unacceptable to Maliki's regime. In the meantime, the KRG moved defiantly to sign contracts with more than twenty-five international oil companies, including, most recently, the world's largest, ExxonMobil. Baghdad has rejected the contracts on grounds that they require its approval. For good measure, it also blacklisted the companies that signed them (but has yet to decide what approach to take toward Exxon, which already has contracts in the South).

Meanwhile, the deadlock between Baghdad and Erbil has complicated efforts to establish a workable relationship between the state and Iraq's other provinces. Given the strong association between federalism and the Kurds' ultimate desire for statehood, almost any exploration of greater local autonomy by the provinces raises suspicions of a partitionist agenda.

In the current debate, the federalism dispute has come full circle. During the writing of the 2005 constitution—a period of intense civil strife—a powerful group of Shia Islamists openly championed the Kurdish-inspired model of ethnosectarian federalism as a hedge against the return of a Sunni strongman such as Saddam Hussein. Now, however, with U.S. troops gone, Iraq's Sunni-majority provinces worry about an unchecked and autocratic Shia-led government in Baghdad. Despite their emotional attachment to the notion of a centralized Iraq, leading national Sunni politicians and local leaders have now challenged Baghdad by issuing symbolic declarations of provincial autonomy.

All this friction raises questions about whether the constitution contains intrinsic flaws that prevent accommodation. It is based on the idea that federalism should be symmetrical, meaning that levels of autonomy should be equivalent for all regional governments. And therein lies the conundrum. When the constitution was written, it was unrealistic to expect

the Kurds to retreat from the self-governance they achieved through their long struggle and blood investment during the Saddam years. Their post-1991 Gulf War autonomy became the effective floor for regional authority in the constitution. But if the rest of Iraq were to get this one-size-fits-all style of autonomy, the survival not only of the central government but of the country itself could be threatened. Hence Baghdad's hard line with Erbil and fierce response to any new regional initiatives.

We believe that rather than pursuing the principle of symmetrical federalism, Iraq should instead pursue a deliberately asymmetrical federal model under which the level of autonomy granted to the KRG would be exclusive. Such a model would recognize the unique oil-contracting abilities of the KRG while also safeguarding Baghdad's fiscal and monetary powers as well as authority over oil contracting elsewhere.

According to this concept, Baghdad could negotiate with the provincial governments over precisely what level of autonomy they should enjoy. No longer would the Kurdistan example serve to complicate these separate discussions, and Baghdad would be freed from its current fears that this federalism conundrum threatens to turn Iraq into a mere agglomeration of competing regional entities.

Some might argue that the prospects are dim for implementing such a system at any point soon. To be sure, Iraq faces a number of daunting immediate challenges that in turn have spawned two disparate responses. One is that the only way to keep Iraq together is to fully implement the federal model in the constitution and give Sunnis, Shia and Kurds each the authority to run their own regional affairs—a notion known as soft partition by its American proponents. The other view is that federalism is the worst possible solution for Iraq's current woes, as it would lead to division and sectarian war.

We believe neither represents a solution. Those who favor the first option should consider the sobering mix of violent protests, arrests and mobilization of state security forces that occurred after the diverse Sunni-Shia-Kurdish province of Diyala sought to declare itself an autonomous region in December 2011. What then might happen if identity-based federalism were attempted on a nationwide scale? Likewise, those who advocate delaying a discussion of federalism until more propitious times need to explain how growing discontent with Baghdad's governance in non-Kurdish Iraq is to be kept from boiling over in the interim.

In the current strained environment, a system of asymmetric federalism may be the most practical solution for the problems that Iraq faces because it most accurately reflects the country's enduring ethnic and political realities. No other model is likely to enable the country to reach an acceptable solution for Kurdistan while at the same time ensuring that the central government in Baghdad is viable enough to function. This is not to say that it will guarantee that Iraq comes together into a smoothly functioning democracy. The country's constitutional flaws are symptoms of the tensions and animosities embedded in the polity, not their source. But it seems clear that the current federal concept retards efforts to resolve the high-stakes competition for power and resources. Removing that barrier could enhance prospects for resolving these conflicts in a reasonably amicable way.

Asymmetrical federalism is not a novel concept. It has been employed in several countries around the world to recognize diversity and manage internal conflict. The theoretical case for asymmetrical federalism in Iraq should begin with an examination of two main stylized models of federalism: "coming together" and "holding together."

A coming-together model arises when a group of formerly independent or self-governing units join to form a new country. Classic examples include the United States, Australia and the UAE, which formerly consisted of seven independent sheikhdoms. Not surprisingly, those accustomed to ruling themselves are reluctant to abandon power to new national governments. Thus, these coming-together federations are relatively decentralized, with checks on the authority of the central government and the provinces running their own affairs. They also tend to be relatively symmetrical, with all provinces enjoying more or less the same privileges vis-à-vis the center.

In contrast, the holding-together model is usually an attempt to maintain the territorial integrity of an existing state. It often occurs in the case of formerly unitary countries that face ethnically or territorially based secessionist threats. In many cases, attempts are made to reconcile these groups through a grant of special autonomy. The result can be an asymmetrical structure, where the potential breakaway province enjoys heightened self-government compared to other territories in the union. While few countries are purely symmetrical, asymmetrical federations are distinguished by the deliberate nature of these special arrangements, which are protected in laws or the constitution. Recently, in the case of Banda Aceh and Indonesia, asymmetrical arrangements helped end a long-running internal conflict. In other countries, such as Spain, these arrangements have been used to forestall wider conflict by granting cultural and administrative autonomy to Basque and Catalan communities.

The puzzle of Iraq's 2005 constitution is that it introduced a coming-together symmetrical model of federalism rather than building on the clear asymmetrical foundation of the Kurdish safe haven established after the 1991 Gulf War. An examination of the recent history of devolution in Iraq suggests that a holding-together asymmetrical model may better promote stability by serving the interests of all parties.

The genesis of Iraq's new federal system lies in the aftermath of the 1991 Gulf War, when exile groups stepped out from the regime's shadow of fear to plot its demise. They were a motley collection of secularists and Islamists, Arabs and Kurds, all with their own visions of a post-Saddam Iraq.

The Kurds had long aimed to build on an autonomy agreement negotiated with the Baathists in the 1970s that was never implemented. Motivated by their desire for a Kurdish state and the fresh horrors of a genocidal Iraqi Army campaign against them in the late 1980s, Kurds in the post-Saddam era pushed for something more extensive: an ethnically based confederation that would afford the Kurds maximum autonomy over their own affairs. The Kurds' partners in opposition had not given the idea of federalism much thought, but many agreed.

A central ally to the Kurds in this quest was a party then known as the Supreme Council for the Islamic Revolution in Iraq (SCIRI). SCIRI was a

Shia Islamist party established by the Iranians in 1982 during the Iran-Iraq War that was dedicated to overthrowing Saddam's regime. It saw decentralization as both the best guarantee against a return to dictatorship and a good way to protect Shia interests in the new state. In 2007, SCIRI renamed itself the Islamic Supreme Council of Iraq (ISCI), deemphasizing its historical ties to Iran's revolutionary regime.

ISCI and the Kurds' calculations on federalism were not solely about identity. The Kurds saw in federalism the freedom to develop their local oil assets, which would allow them the ability to run their own affairs without being financially dependent on Baghdad. Meanwhile, the Shia region in southern Iraq that ISCI was to propose was not coincidentally home to the majority of Iraq's vast oil reserves.

The United States, following its overthrow of Saddam's regime in 2003, made no secret of its own preference for a decentralized Iraq, sharing with the opposition the view that this would prevent the return of dictatorship. From the start, the term used was federalism. With their close ties to the Bush administration, the Kurds and certain ISCI leaders returning from exile had a head start that allowed them to leave an outsized imprint on the new state structure. The areas outside the Kurdistan region, which had yet to produce homegrown parties, were not positioned to give strong expression to their populations' wills.

Yet resistance to federalism began almost right away. Iraqi nationalists, many with links to the former regime, championed the state's paramount unity but struggled to articulate a practical alternative to the previous, now-discredited centralization. They were joined by what remained of Iraq's secular elite and important parts of the Shia clerical leadership. Moreover, some Shia Islamist political leaders outside ISCI, now well on their way to gaining significant power in Baghdad, sought to protect their new domain and began to suggest that Iraqis were not yet ready for federalism.

Notwithstanding these objections, the Kurds proved the best organized of the parties that came to the table to draft the new permanent constitution; they also benefited from their strong ties to the U.S. officials who midwifed the new text. The Kurds' goal

was to maximize their autonomy, even emphasizing that Iraq's union was voluntary and could be reconsidered if Baghdad did not fully respect guarantees to the Kurds in the new constitution. They also promoted the sectarian regionalization of Arab Iraq to ensure that Baghdad would never regain the power to threaten Kurds.

As the drafting process unfolded, those opposed to federalism were so weak and divided that the Kurds and ISCI pushed through language establishing the formation of federal regions with equivalent powers to the Kurdistan region. With Iraq's sectarian civil conflict brewing, ISCI tabled the proposal for the creation of an oil-rich, nine-governorate "super-region" in the Shia South that it aimed to govern and protect against insurgents operating in the Sunni heartland west and north of Baghdad.

The result was the 2005 constitution, which prescribes a federal system with two exceptional characteristics: It hollows out the national government through radical devolution to federal regions that can mostly ignore Baghdad on many important matters, including most importantly oil and gas management and revenue sharing. It also provides minimal barriers to prevent the provinces outside of Iraqi Kurdistan from forming new autonomous regions, either standing alone or in conjunction with other provinces, with no limit on their size or number.

From the start, these features raised sharp fears regarding the viability and unity of the new state, prompting a near-unanimous rejection of the new charter by the Sunni Arab community in the October 2005 constitutional referendum. In recent years, the Sunnis have been increasingly joined in their objections by most of the newly empowered Shia Islamist parties, which have grown accustomed to ruling Baghdad. Even ISCI, the principal Arab proponent of Kurdish-style federalism in the rest of Iraq, appears to have shelved its project for a Shia super-region in the face of popular opposition. A Kurdish constitutional veto, however, has so far prevented any meaningful reconsideration of Iraq's new federal architecture.

At the cusp of the U.S. troop withdrawal in late 2011, Iraq found itself in a peculiar situation. The majority of its political class outside the Kurdistan region, including the most powerful actors in Baghdad, has publicly objected to the constitution's basic structure. Yet an early review of the constitution in 2007, intended to broaden its appeal, quickly foundered. Partially this is because the review committee took a symmetrical approach. It proposed to adjust the balance of power not just between Baghdad and any future regions but also to bring the Kurdistan region into line with a more centralized state structure. The latter crossed a clear Kurdish red line, prompting the veto threat that killed the amendment process. No clear avenue now exists on how to address this short circuit.

After six years of experience with the implementation of the constitution, two things have become clear. First, the type of countrywide sectarian regionalization advocated by the Kurds and ISCI remains unpopular outside Kurdistan. Second, there is rising discontent in the provinces with Baghdad's poor and nonresponsive governance. Especially over the last year, there appears to be a growing sentiment similar to that expressed by the governor of Nineveh, Atheel al-Nujaifi: the people of his province support giving the provinces greater power instead of creating independent regions, but if Baghdad does not respond, they might go down the latter path.

The stalemate between Baghdad and Erbil has hampered any response to these grievances. The Kurdistan region can veto any reconsideration of Iraq's state structure—and the controversy over the Kurdish model of federalism tars any calls for devolution of authority and greater local control outside Kurdistan as promoting partition. Maliki has pointedly reacted to interest in decentralization, saying that the country is not ready for federalism in its western, central or southern regions and that differences should be addressed through common action on administrative deficits rather than by "division or secession."

Yet in the past year, calls for new regions have grown louder as political disputes in the center contribute to more troubled governance. Meanwhile, a growing sense of political marginalization from Baghdad and victimization by government-controlled security forces continues to amplify interest in decentralization in the country's predominantly Sunni West and Northwest.

Unsurprisingly, Kurdish leaders have sought to embrace renewed interest in decentralization as supporting their view of the Iraqi state, but there are key distinctions. The most obvious is the absence of an ethnic agenda. Calls for decentralization in predominantly Arab provinces are driven primarily by functional rather than ethnic motives: better government and more effective distribution of resources are the principal goals, rather than the creation of multiprovince autonomous cantons as a precursor to possible independence. Indeed, most Arab proponents of decentralization frequently distinguish their federalism projects from those of Kurdistan.

Decentralization appears to enjoy strong support in the southern oil-producing provinces of Basra, Maysan and Dhi Qar. The difference between the contribution to state revenues by Iraq's richest oil province, Basra, and the development funds it receives through the federal budget has driven local leaders there to campaign repeatedly to establish the province as a separate federal region. Rumblings in support of decentralization have also been heard from Basra's neighbors, with occasional talk of creating a three-province, oil-rich region. Meanwhile, in south-central Iraq, the Wasit Provincial Council has reportedly made a formal request to hold a regional referendum, and the Shia holy provinces of Najaf and Karbala have considered forming regions out of a desire for greater local control of the lucrative religious-pilgrimage trade.

But grassroots support for regionalization has not yet been sufficient to spur administrative change. Basra leaders failed in their 2008 attempt to secure popular support for a referendum on establishing the province as a region. Their most recent effort, in July 2011, was tellingly headlined in the Iraqi press as Basra "demands secession." At the same time, the party that holds the reins of power in Baghdad, Prime Minister Maliki's State of Law coalition, has neutralized southern proponents of local decentralization and tabled individual requests by Basra and Wasit to organize local referendums on becoming regions.

The most recent manifestations of support for autonomous regions in Iraq's predominantly Sunni provinces are somewhat different, born of a pervasive sense of alienation and sectarian discrimination by Baghdad. Pro-federalism sentiment in the oil-rich Shia South may create huge uncertainty over the country's economic future, but sectarian-tinged moves by Sunni-majority provinces to seek regional status and Baghdad's strong response have left Iraq on a political knife-edge.

These tensions came to a dramatic head in October 2011 when, following a wave of arrests of alleged conspirators in a Baathist coup plot, the provincial government of Salahuddin, a governorate north of Baghdad, symbolically voted to become an autonomous region. Other Sunni-majority provinces, including Nineveh and Anbar, quickly said they were prepared to follow suit if Baghdad did not do a better job of responding to their demands.

The provincial government in Diyala, a mixed Sunni-Shia-Kurd province in northeastern Iraq, went a step further. In December 2011, it adopted its own symbolic declaration of autonomy. The blowback was troubling. Baghdad-controlled security forces were quickly mobilized to the province, thousands of Shia demonstrators stormed the provincial government headquarters, unidentified armed groups blocked major highways and members of the mainly Sunni political bloc that sponsored the measure fled the province ahead of arrest warrants. Almost simultaneously, serious disputes erupted between Maliki and two of the most prominent national Sunni politicians who had supported Salahuddin's and Diyala's calls for federalism. One of them, Vice President Tariq al-Hashimi, fled to the Kurdistan region to escape his own arrest warrant for alleged involvement in assassination plots. The other, a deputy prime minister, has had his cabinet participation frozen.

Some national-level proponents of decentralization for these provinces may indeed have the more pernicious agenda that Baghdad attributes to them: using federalism as a way to destroy Iraq's new political order, with the hope that a new, Sunni-nationalist-dominated state can emerge from the embers. But in the midst of this controversy, it is important to recall that the driving local motive in Salahuddin and Diyala was not separation. Salahuddin's council in fact emphasized that

it wanted to remain part of a "united Iraq." There also have been no explicit calls for the creation of a multiprovince Sunni region. Instead, provincial leaders in Salahuddin, Diyala, Anbar and Nineveh are looking at a single-province-as-region model, precisely to avoid accusations that they seek to destroy Iraqi unity.

Moreover, there is no consistent popular support for federalism in these provinces. In fact, powerful local tribes in Anbar have organized public protests against the idea of transforming their province into a region. Local opinion polls show frustration with the central government but no desire for Kurdish-style autonomy. Respondents consistently favor Baghdad's control over oil revenues to protect national unity, but they also want greater local administration of basic services and reconstruction.

To fully appreciate how an asymmetrical model could address this impasse, consider how centralized administration of the governorates by Baghdad works at present. Governors and provincial councils have limited direct budgets, no control over local public-sector hiring and no formal say over projects undertaken by federal ministries within their provinces. In many cases, the bulk of the security forces operating in the governorates report directly to the prime minister's office, and access to the minority share of capital-investment funds given to provincial councils requires a laborious series of approvals from multiple ministries in Baghdad.

In our view, the complaints of the Arab provinces of Iraq could be addressed through more empowered local administration, greater local say over security and greater distribution of oil revenues. And this in fact is close to what the heads of Iraq's fifteen provincial councils outside the Kurdistan region laid out in a joint letter to Prime Minster Maliki last October, when they asked for more functional revenue sharing and a greater local say on both public-sector hiring and environmental and customs policy.

Finally, it is important to recognize that this is a markedly different prescription from the relationship between the federal government and the Kurdistan region. The gulf between the centralization endured by the provinces and the virtual autonomy enjoyed by the Kurdistan region leaves ample room for an asymmetrical model to raise the status of the provinces without approaching the kind of regionalization seen as a threat to national unity.

Iraq's Kurds still dream of their own state, but for now their fortunes remain tied to Baghdad. Mostly because of their own restive Kurdish minorities, neighboring countries will simply not countenance an independent Kurdistan. In the meantime, nationalist Iraqis resent what they see as the Kurds' influence over the constitution aimed at furthering their independence by hollowing out the Iraqi state. Absent a reset, this set of affairs is a recipe for what could be a perpetual cycle of recrimination and internal strife.

Some Iraqi nationalists may be starting to conclude privately that Erbil is more trouble than it is worth in terms of the country's territorial integrity. But all must accept that whatever Kurdish nationalists may dream, both sides are stuck with each other for the time being. After decades of bloody armed struggle, it took the cataclysmic 2003 U.S. invasion for the Kurdistan region's autonomy to be enshrined in the Iraqi constitution. A crisis of similar magnitude would be required for the Middle East's century-old, post-Ottoman order to be shattered and international borders redrawn.

Short of apocalyptic regional war, reexamining the federalism question appears to be necessary for Iraq to move toward some degree of stability. The straightforward way would be a redrafting of the constitution with authority of the Kurdistan region and other provinces delineated in separate chapters. But Iraqi politics are much messier than that ideal. In 2010, the country spent more than nine months forming a still-incomplete coalition government—it is unlikely the same parties could successfully undertake a comprehensive constitutional overhaul.

A possible asymmetric solution must identify key areas of dispute and recast the debate to affirm the KRG's autonomy without applying the same concept to other provinces and eviscerating Baghdad's sovereignty. An elevated administrative status for the provinces could be negotiated among Arab parties and local leaders. Given the difficulties in wholesale revision of the constitution, this change would come via legislative and political means rather than a constitutional amendment.

This represents a second-best outcome but is realistically as far as the envelope can be pushed under present circumstances. Initial understandings could then be codified in the constitution once circumstances permit. Indeed, any progress must present benefits compelling enough to challenge the status quo. In other words, each of the three levels of government described in the constitution—provincial, regional and national—would need to see clear benefits from an asymmetrical system for the idea to gain traction.

The path to pursuing this complex trifecta is perhaps through a bilateral deal between Baghdad and Erbil on oil and revenue sharing, followed by constitutional amendments that remove the threat of Kurdish-style regionalization elsewhere in Iraq, especially by Iraq's main wealth producer, oil-rich Basra. In order to accept these arrangements and put aside their current constitutional right to form autonomous regions, the governorates should quickly receive tangible administrative empowerment from Baghdad. The concrete proposals included in last October's joint letter by the heads of Iraq's fifteen provincial councils could form the basis of these latter talks.

Oil has been at the heart of the federalism dispute from the beginning. At present, with a standoff over legislation governing oversight of the hydrocarbon sector, a deal between Baghdad and Erbil on oil matters feels a long way off. But there are potential trade-offs that could improve confidence between the two sides and lay the groundwork for a more stable, asymmetrical federal system.

In its essence, such a deal would entail the federal government guaranteeing the KRG an automatic share of oil revenues, authority to sign oil contracts, and access to the oil- and gas-export infrastructure necessary to develop a long-term platform for self-governance. (The KRG is currently unable to export the oil it produces and its day-to-day operational funding is subject to the vagaries of Baghdad's annual budgetary process.) In return, the KRG would recognize the center's paramount authority on oil revenue handling and setting national oil- and gas-contracting standards. Kurdish leaders also would need to agree that these arrangements apply only to the Kurdistan region and undertake not to oppose laws or constitutional amendments that consolidate Baghdad's oil and fiscal powers elsewhere.

Several factors could potentially make such a deal attractive to both sides. In the absence of an independent pipeline network to neighboring states, Kurdish hydrocarbon exports are dependent on infrastructure controlled by Baghdad. The KRG could build its own pipelines, but the Kurdish region is landlocked and can only export through Iran and Turkey. Both countries are wary of an independent Iraqi Kurdistan as a model that could inspire their own restive Kurdish minorities. A more promising option is a negotiated deal, where Kurdish exports could be guaranteed unfettered flow through the national Baghdad-controlled pipelines in return for the KRG conducting all crude sales through the federal government, with revenue collection through the federal treasury. This meets Kurdish export needs and recognizes Baghdad's role in selling and collecting oil revenues.

Second, the present nationwide revenue-sharing scheme is a source of leverage for Baghdad. The next decade's projected oil exports from central and southern Iraq will dwarf the best-case scenario for Kurdish production. In draft legislation, the KRG has sought to protect its share of this growing national revenue and control over how to spend it. But it has irritated Baghdad by insisting that spending authority be symmetrically decentralized across the rest of Iraq, which would leave the federal government close to penniless and hence powerless. Baghdad should offer a clear choice: Kurdistan can receive a guaranteed automatic share of national oil revenue, but only if it accepts legal arrangements that protect the central government's fiscal power outside of Kurdistan. Alternatively, the Kurdistan region could become financially self-reliant, controlling all revenue and taxes collected within its boundaries, including from oil and gas—but give up any grants from the federal budget.

Finally, on the issue of oil-contracting authority, the KRG and the federal government should consider a compromise where Erbil gradually standardizes its oil-contract terms with Baghdad's. In return, Baghdad would need to acknowledge the

KRG's autonomous licensing authority and stop blocking international investment in Kurdistan's oil fields. Erbil would also recognize Baghdad's right to oversee oil contracting outside the Kurdistan region, allowing Arab Iraqis to determine amongst themselves the federal government's role in supervising southern oil and gas contracts.

Both Kurds and Shia Islamists intended for the new constitution to promote decentralization. Indeed, given the starting point, a highly centralized Saddam-era state, the KRG achieved remarkable success in introducing a federal structure that contains the basic features of a coming-together model: highly decentralized with existing and future federal regions granted the same powers. A chain reaction toward this outcome might even be initiated were a single additional province—perhaps oil-rich Basra—to successfully grasp the chalice of regional status.

Yet Iraq is not a set of former colonies or emirates coming together to form a new country. It is a ninety-year-old, historically centralized state that has grappled for decades with the latent Kurdish desire for independence. Moreover, Iraq's oil and gas is geographically distributed in a way that highlights the country's ethnic and sectarian fault lines. In this context, full local control of oil resources—a feature of symmetrical, coming-together federations such as the United States, Canada and the UAE—could be dangerously destabilizing in Iraq, leading to large regional wealth disparities. And radical decentralization is not popular among Iraq's Arab majority—even as Sunni areas chafe under the perceived excesses of the new order.

The incentives generated by the 2005 constitution force Baghdad and Erbil to make a strategic choice. Under the charter's most radical option, Kurdistan would establish some form of self-sufficient autarky. This would be a poor outcome for all involved. The KRG would need to raise capital for export pipelines, persuade hostile neighbors to accept Kurdish hydrocarbon exports and rely on its own comparatively meager revenues to fund its regional administration. In Baghdad, preoccupation with Arab-Kurdish tensions would stunt development of the state. In addition, with Erbil continuing to block constitutional changes, Baghdad could one day be gutted by new autonomy movements in oil-rich Basra or gas-rich Anbar. In contrast, by isolating and containing the dispute between Baghdad and Erbil, an asymmetrical model would reinforce Iraqi unity and free the rest of the country to choose alternative governance arrangements on their own merits. This could at least provide a framework to consider the grievances of provincial leaders and perhaps defuse the potentially grave crisis sparked by angered Sunnis' symbolic declarations of autonomy.

In short, Iraq is a textbook candidate for a holding-together, asymmetrical model of federalism. Merely elucidating the concept will not lead to its implementation. But doing so may be a basis for reframing the debate to facilitate a workable and lasting solution to Iraq's foundational issues.

The Rise of the Rest of India: How States Have Become the Engines of Growth

RUCHIR SHARMA

Reprinted by permission of FOREIGN AFFAIRS, Volume 92, Number 5, September/October 2013. Copyright © 2013 by the Council on Foreign Relations, Inc. www.ForeignAffairs.com.

When Nitish Kumar became chief minister of the dirt-poor Indian state of Bihar in 2005, kidnapping was said to be the leading industry in the capital city of Patna. People searching for stolen cars were advised to check the driveway of a leading politician, who reportedly commandeered vehicles for "election duty." Although known for his soft-spoken manner, Kumar cracked down hard. He straightened out the crooked police, ordering them to move aggressively against all criminals, from the daylight robbers to the corrupt high officials. He set up a new fast-track court to speed the miscreants to jail. As Biharis gained the courage to go out on the street, even after dark, Kumar set about energizing a landlocked economy with few outlets for manufactured exports. He focused on improving the yields of Bihar's fertile soil and ushered in a construction boom. Within a few years, a state once described by the writer V. S. Naipaul as "the place where civilization ends" had built one of the fastest-growing state economies in India. And Kumar was recognized as a leader in the new generation of dynamic chief ministers who are remaking the economic map and future of India.

This generation includes the socialite turned statesman Naveen Patnaik in Orissa, the spell-binding orator Narendra Modi in Gujarat, the self-effacing Raman Singh in Chhattisgarh, and the quiet personalities of Sheila Dikshit in Delhi and Shivraj Singh Chauhan in Madhya Pradesh. As a result of their economic successes, these leaders have each won consecutive reelection bids; India now has six chief ministers who have returned to office for at least three terms in a row, a feat unheard of in a generation. Kumar and Patnaik represent ambitious regional parties that are ready to compete with the country's two dominant political forces: the ruling Indian National Congress and the opposition Bharatiya Janata Party, or BJP. But the best known among these chief ministers is Modi, who now looks poised to run as the prime ministerial candidate of the BJP in the next national elections, set for May 2014.

That these chief ministers have managed the double feat of economic success and political longevity belies the conventional wisdom about India's doldrums. After a decade of strong economic growth, during which India was hailed as democracy's answer to China, the bad news is back: New Delhi seems politically paralyzed in the face of the global economic slump. India's GDP growth rate has fallen from near double digits to five percent, and the capital has been buried in scandalous headlines about corruption, power outages, and incompetent police.

Things do look bad in New Delhi, but the capital is not the whole of India. Think of the country as a continent, like Europe. After all, it is made up of 28 states, the largest of which, Uttar Pradesh, has more than 200 million people. India has 34 officially recognized languages, and only 40 percent of Indians speak a dialect of its first language, Hindi. There is as much variation in the political and economic culture among India's states as there is within Europe; Bihar and Gujarat are as different as Germany and Greece. Drive a hundred miles between any two states in India, and everything from the names of the leading political parties to the kind of hair tonic sold in the stores can change completely. For all the talk of India's booming young population, nine of its major states have fertility rates below the replacement level.

As India's most dynamic states post rapid and sustainable growth rates, the country is rediscovering its natural fabric as a nation of strong regions. States still growing at or near double-digit rates represent India's secret weapon for competing with the other major emerging markets, from China to Brazil, Indonesia to Mexico. The only hitch is that despite the chief ministers' high popularity in their home states, many of them are pushing rapid development with an autocrat's haste. Nevertheless, if India is to come back as a success story among the emerging markets, New Delhi should find ways to encourage the rise of its breakout states and the spread of their success to India's other states.

New Roads for Votes

Until recently, India's state chief ministers did not have the power or much incentive to push economic development. Before its independence, in 1947, India was divided into hundreds of major, minor, and princely states with varying degrees of autonomy, including, in some cases, the power to raise taxes. After independence, the country's new political leadership worked to centralize power, both to stave off the very real threat of secessionist movements and to address the nation's deep poverty through Soviet-style central planning. The Indian public was so grateful to the Congress party for liberating them from British rule that it was willing to tolerate the desperately inadequate economic growth of only three percent a year that resulted from central planning. For decades, the Congress party, and the Nehru-Gandhi dynasty that rules it, was able to cash in on the liberation dividend come election day.

But times changed. Chronic slow growth made it difficult for India to earn the foreign currency it needed to pay for imports, leading to an economic crisis in 1991. In response, the Congress party began to unwind the stifling bureaucracy known as "the license raj," which gave the central planners the authority to decide who could manufacture what products, in what quantities, and in which areas of the country. The easing of these restrictions freed entrepreneurial businesspeople and state officials alike to begin looking for ways to meet the rising aspirations of the consumer classes. It was in the early 1990s, too, that the advent of satellite television and the Internet exposed Indians to the economic booms in China and other developing nations and fed their dreams for a richer life.

The fall of the license raj and the devolution of powers to the states came at the right time. Before, chief ministers had built their political support by positioning themselves as champions of religion and caste, the touchstones of Indian identity. Even into the late 1980s, it was commonplace for lower castes to be refused entry to the same buses, temples, or even police stations occupied by members of the upper castes. For this huge mass of voters who weren't allowed on the public bus, developing the roads was a secondary priority. State politicians focused on building caste-based coalitions, but with shaky results. Because India is divided among several thousand subcastes, many of which exist in only one state, caste coalitions are inherently fragile and short-lived. In the 1980s and 1990s, nearly three out of every four state governments lasted only one term, which made economically ineffectual state governments even weaker.

Starting in the mid-1990s, state politicians realized that they could build more enduring bases of support if they used their newfound economic clout to cater to voters' rising economic aspirations. One of the first to do this was N. Chandrababu Naidu, who came to power in Andhra Pradesh in 1995.

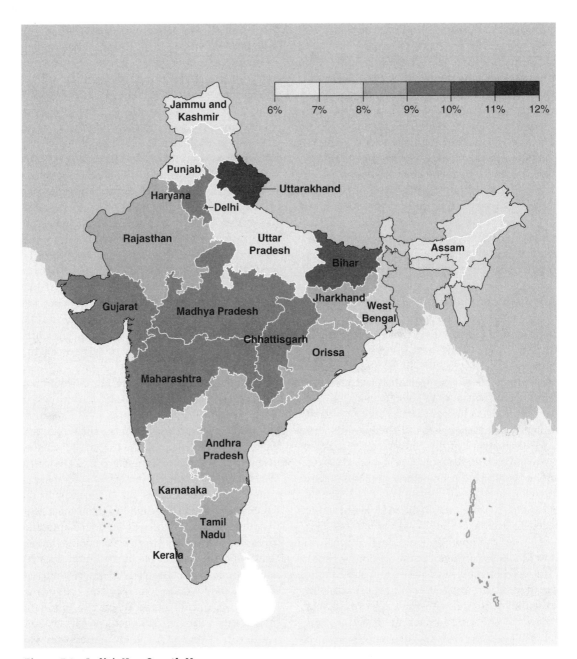

Figure 7.1   India's New Growth Map

The Country's 20 Largest Economies and Their Average GDP Growth Rates, 2007–12

Source: Indian Planning Commission

Note: Although Delhi is a federally administered union territory, it is headed by a chief minister, as states are.

He focused so heavily on reviving the state's blighted cities that he was voted out by the rural majority after nine years in power. But by then, others were getting the balance right as voters elsewhere looked to their state's chief minister for economic leadership. That is why, since 1999, voter turnout has been declining at the national level but rising at the state level. And those state governments that have lived up to voters' expectations have been rewarded: in the 30 state elections since 2007, 50 percent of the incumbent chief ministers have won reelection, compared with just 25 percent in the preceding three decades; nearly 66 percent of those reelected had delivered five years of growth that was faster than the national average.

Today, caste and religion still matter, but in many states, economic competence matters more. Kumar's career in Bihar embodies this evolution in state politics. Kumar rose as a champion of his own Kurmi caste, which is concentrated in Bihar and represents around two percent of the state's population. He had spent much of his career building a caste coalition that included the Kurmis and Bihar's other marginal castes, before turning to development issues in his run for the chief minister's office.

Regional parties and the BJP have gained strength at the expense of the ruling Congress party by showing that they have a closer connection to the aspirations of local people. In the 1960s, the chief ministers of India's ten largest states were all from the Congress party. That number has fallen steadily and is now just two. The decline of the Congress party has led, in turn, to weaker and more divided governments in New Delhi but stronger and more lasting governments in the states, run by regional parties such as Kumar's Janata Dal (United) and Patnaik's Biju Janata Dal and by the BJP under leaders such as Modi and Chauhan. These durable state governments may provide the political push India needs to delegate even more power to the states.

Autocratic Growth

The new generation of state leaders sets itself apart from the genteel Brahmans of the Congress party, who have dominated Indian politics for decades and have never been comfortable promoting what they see as crass commerce. The new state leaders,

eager to compete, are younger, too. In contrast to the aging New Delhi elite, headed by an 80-year-old prime minister and a cabinet with an average age of 65, in the last five years, the average age of a state chief minister at election has been 56. This relative youth matches the country's demographics; the average age of the population is expected to decrease for another three decades. And younger voters, impatient for India to catch up with the rest of the world, have sent clear signals to the state chief ministers that they expect competence, not just political handouts.

In their hunger for economic performance, Indians have proved tolerant of creeping authoritarianism. Several of the new state ministers emerged from feudal provincial cultures to lead parties built on promoting a single strong figurehead. Most of these men and women are unmarried, an unusual trend in India's culture, which suggests a relentless focus on self and career. Several have set up personal television channels to promote their own achievements. One went so far as to erect monuments to herself while in office; Kumar has been accused of violating civil rights in his crackdown on Bihar's crime.

Even Patnaik, who came to office with little political experience, surprised many with his Machiavellian knack for sidelining rivals in Orissa. The son of a two-time chief minister, Patnaik spent much of his life abroad as a socialite and writer and had never held a regular job before he came home and won a seat in parliament in 1997, and then the chief minister's post in 2000. Patnaik quickly impressed the state's elite by assembling a team of accomplished technocrats to push forward a reformist economic policy, working to control runaway spending and encourage industrial growth. Today, Orissa's deficit stands at less than two percent of its GDP, the state's growth has averaged close to double-digit rates throughout his term, and this relatively small state of 20 million people is one of the top state destinations for foreign companies investing in India. Like other savvy chief ministers, Patnaik is focused on exploiting his state's local advantages: in Orissa, that means mines to produce iron ore and bauxite and steel plants to refine those metals.

Modi is the most controversial of the new chief ministers, because his aggressive push to develop and industrialize Gujarat has earned the state a reputation as the upcoming China of India. The sun sets red over the newly constructed highway that leads into Gujarat's commercial capital, Ahmadabad, one of the fastest-growing cities in the world. Factories sprout from the farmland just outside town, in scenes evocative of southern China. Today, Gujarat generates about 40 percent of its income from industry, compared with 15 percent nationwide. Modi is widely admired by businesspeople for his efforts to attract investors, but he is loathed by human rights activists, who consider him a Hindu chauvinist because of his alleged complicity in the deadly 2002 riots against the state's Muslim minority. With opposition politicians whispering that Gujaratis live in fear of challenging the state boss, Modi embodies the inherent tension surrounding the rise of can-do autocrats in a developing country with a strong democratic tradition.

The fact remains, however, that Modi, like many of the new generation, is highly popular, and this popularity allows him, and the others, to push painful but necessary decisions, such as hiking electricity tariffs and cutting state subsidies. Indeed, since 2005, state budget deficits have declined to 2.5 percent of state GDP on average, whereas the federal deficit is rising and now stands at five percent of national GDP. New Delhi lacks the support to push unpopular cuts.

At the state level in India, there is no European-style contest between the free market and government power. On one side, there is the socialist tradition of the Congress party, in which patrons argue over who has done more to help the poor. On the other side, there is the new breed, also peddling populism but with a more practical focus on building roads, schools, and other infrastructure that generates growth.

It is not at all clear, however, that any of the bold, autocratic chief ministers can be a good fit to lead the whole country. Since independence, the most successful prime ministers have had weak regional roots but strong nationwide appeal, starting with India's founding father, Jawaharlal Nehru of the National Congress. Successful chief ministers have

typically failed to reach the prime minister's office because the political formula that works in one state tends to be a liability in others. Until recently, for all his popularity in Gujarat, Modi had shown little more drawing power outside his home state than, say, Angela Merkel enjoys outside Germany. Now, Modi's run for national office will depend on a growing feeling among middle-class Indians that the political paralysis in New Delhi runs so deep that the country's rebound depends on a return to strongman rule.

But Indians should recognize that it doesn't take an autocrat to deliver growth. Since 1980 in emerging markets, democratic and authoritarian regimes have been equally likely to deliver GDP growth averaging more than five percent for a decade. What it does take is good governance, and there is no reason why democrats cannot push growth in India, as Dikshit has proved in Delhi and Chauhan has demonstrated in Madhya Pradesh.

Backward States Forward

Even if one of these formidable regional leaders cannot, in the end, secure the national throne, they have already redrawn the economic map of India. In the 1990s, the first states to benefit from the fall of the license raj were the rich ones of the southern and western coasts, particularly Gujarat, Maharashtra, and Tamil Nadu, which already had strong industrial bases. But in the last decade, the center of rapid growth has shifted northward and inland, to the states of Bihar, Chhattisgarh, Madhya Pradesh, Orissa, and others. The average growth rate of these northern states jumped from 2.2 percent in the 1990s to 9.1 percent over the past decade, while India's national growth rate gained just two percentage points.

The rise of the north is nothing less than a revolution. For decades, much of the country's elite looked at the stagnant poverty there and concluded that these states were fast-breeding, overpopulated regions that were somehow culturally ill suited to economic development. Today, although some of the northern states are growing faster than the national economy, southern elites tend to dismiss this success as a result of "the base effect," the idea that it is easier for an economy to grow fast from a low per capita income level. But this is starting to look like an excuse for poor leadership in the south. For one thing, the rich southern states of India are seeing their growth slow down at much lower income levels than the rich southern provinces of China, which grew rapidly for many decades, not just one. Good leadership produces good economic results: Modi has proved that even a relatively rich state such as Gujarat can grow at a double-digit pace for more than a decade. Meanwhile, in the absence of strong leadership, southern states such as Andhra Pradesh and Karnataka have seen their growth slow.

A recent analysis by Credit Suisse confirmed the connection between strong state leadership and solid economic performance. The report found that most of the periods of rapid state GDP growth in India over the last 20 years came when a competent regional party leader was at the helm. In only one instance, in Maharashtra in the mid-1990s, when Sharad Pawar was chief minister, was that leader a Congress party member. The culture of the Congress party, so steeped in the personalities of the Gandhis and the socialist instincts of Nehru, discourages the rise of new leaders and only reluctantly embraces market competition. Increasingly, businesses recognize which states understand economic reform and are steering their investments accordingly.

Beyond the north-south power shift, some Indians see the transfer of power from New Delhi to the states as a symptom of national decline. They shouldn't. Weak central governments are common in other major democracies, particularly in those, like India, that merged once-autonomous principalities into a unified state. In Germany, coalition rule does not spell anarchy, and it doesn't have to in India, either. The rise of India's states could just as easily be read as a sign of national maturity: a tacit recognition among voters that the country will not fall apart just because its states can control their own economies.

Power to the Regions

To revive India's competitiveness in the global economy, New Delhi should step aside and allow the rising states to reclaim even more economic decision-making power from the center. Some chief ministers are already contesting the right of the national Environment Ministry to regulate the height of high-rise buildings in various cities. Others are challenging New Delhi's authority to manage the distribution of coal supplies to power plants.

Still more question the rationality of the so-called centrally sponsored schemes, a throwback to socialist central planning. These projects are hatched in the capital, with funds disbursed by the central Planning Commission, which often sets uniform targets that don't account for the stark socioeconomic differences among the county's states. The newest scheme would expand the government's heavily centralized food-distribution network, promising subsidized grain to two out of every three Indians at an annual cost to New Delhi of at least $20 billion. Another scheme promotes universal enrollment in primary school, a largely redundant goal in those states, such as Kerala, where enrollment levels are already high. Similarly, the National Rural Health Mission, a program to improve health care in the countryside, does not account for states' varying levels of malnutrition. Left to their own devices, India's new state leaders would be able to mold social policies in ways that suited regional conditions.

New Delhi appears ready to step back, recognizing what one of India's foremost state leaders, N. T. Rama Rao, once said: "The center is a myth and the state is a reality." The government recently resolved a major controversy over whether to allow international retailers such as Walmart and Tesco to open stores in India by kicking the decision down to the state level. The Planning Commission has proposed allowing states more flexibility in how they spend federal funds, and the newly constituted Finance Commission is looking at ways to devolve more power to the states. In a symbolic gesture, in the National Development Council, where state and federal officials coordinate economic policy, plans are afoot to change the seating arrangement so that the state leaders sit alongside the central leaders instead of looking up to the New Delhi VIPs from seats in the gallery.

New Delhi should go even further: the latest opinion polls suggest that the upcoming general elections could spell a major Congress party defeat. Some of the seats that the party could lose are likely to go to the BJP, but the polls suggest that even more will go to the ascendant regional parties, such as Kumar's Janata Dal (United) and Patnaik's Biju Janata Dal. There is even growing talk that the next government might be led by a coalition of regional parties. That does not, however, mean that one of the better-known or more controversial state leaders will become prime minister. Often in India, the backroom negotiations to build a coalition government lead to the choice of a compromise candidate or an accidental prime minister, such as the current one, Manmohan Singh. Singh got the job in 2004 only after the leader of his coalition, Sonia Gandhi, unexpectedly turned it down and nominated him instead.

As a rising force, the regional parties represent hope: they are young, energetic, focused on economic development, and very much in sync with the practical aspirations of the youthful majority. The next elections will see a generational shift, with 125 million new voters raising the likely turnout to more than 500 million. This is a post-liberalization generation: all the new voters will be too young to remember the darkest days of caste discrimination or the worst absurdities of the license raj, and they are likely to push the outcome in favor of younger leaders who understand their economic aspirations. If a combination of state leaders spurs India to embrace its natural federal structure and delegate more economic power to the states, it could well put the country on the path to a comeback.

DISCUSSION QUESTIONS

1) According to Gewirtz and Golder, who are the judicial activists on the U.S. Supreme Court? How do they measure whether a given justice is an activist or not? Judicial activism often has a negative connotation, but are there ways of defending its practice or the decisions of the more activist judges. Are there alternative ways of measuring "judicial activism" that might change the ranking of these justices?

2) What are the arguments for how federalism might help stabilize a country like Iraq? Conversely, in what ways could federalism—or dividing and separating power—destabilize a country? Where do Hiltermann, Kane, and Alkadiri seem to come down on this debate? What are the implications for applying the lessons of one country's experience to another country's reality? Does Iraq suggest that the best and most effective institutional designs can work most anywhere? Or that the effectiveness of a given institutional design depends almost entirely on context? Or something in between?

3) In what ways does decentralization seem to be contributing to development in at least some of India's states? In what sense might we say some states the "laboratories" of economic growth and political development? Can you envision any downsides to decentralizing power to states, provinces, or localities in India or other countries?

Legislatures

Legislatures are key governing bodies in most every political system, even in those countries where they are relatively weak when compared with a dominant executive, such as a strong president. Legislatures can be described by what they do, or at least what they are *supposed* to do. They are expected to represent the citizenry, deliberate on substantive ideas for public policy, and pass laws that will reflect a thoughtful response to their deliberations. Not every legislature works in an ideal fashion, however. In fact, many of the leading debates about legislatures today are about *dysfunction*. Some legislatures seem to perform poorly at representing the interests of the populace, at least when the citizenry at large is asked about legislative performance. Legislatures may not pass the laws that a majority would prefer, or perhaps they will not exercise sufficient independence from powerful lobbies and "special interest groups."

This leads to questions about how legislatures function. What makes for an effective process of representation? Or what makes legislatures do things that might not be in the "public interest" or the "good of the country," broadly construed? Several pieces in this section illustrate these issues. In the first reading in this section, Cameron Abadi raises questions about how well (or poorly) legislatures work in parliamentary systems. The second reading, a selection from *The Economist*, notes the propensity for legislatures in certain countries to become little more than "rubber stamps" that do the bidding of the executive branch. This is not to suggest that every legislature is a disaster, of course. Rather, it is to say that the proper functioning of legislatures is a much-debated phenomenon, often motivated by the concern that legislatures in the real world do not always work the way they are presumed to in introductory textbooks (except ours, of course).

Political scientists also frequently debate the relative merits of different electoral systems for legislatures, and two pieces here show how much this debate matters for the "real world." The electoral system in a given country is a crucial feature that shapes the actions of legislatures because it affects how legislators make their decisions; electoral rules provide incentives for politicians to respond to constituents (say, in their home district) or to the leaders of the political parties to which they belong. Since politicians are often presumed to be ambitious about getting (re)elected or moving up the political ladder, their behavior (their votes and actions) is shaped at least partly by these rules, though politicians are also informed by their ideologies and individual backgrounds. Broadly speaking, the two main forms of electoral rules are *district-based* systems and *proportional representation* (or PR) systems. In the former, voters generally select candidates and legislators to represent a geographic constituency; as a result, legislators often vote in accordance with the preferences and interests of voters in that district. In most PR systems, voters vote for parties (not individual candidates) and the party leaders have say in determining how high a given politician will be on the party's "list" to be a legislator, depending on how many votes and seats the party receives. This gives much more leverage to party leadership, and tends to make politicians more responsive to the party than to a given geographic district.

But what are the consequences of these and other electoral systems? For many years, advocates of PR and district-based systems have debated the pros and cons of each. While districts may seem most intuitive to those raised on such systems (because each voter has "their" representative from "their" area), the argument for PR has often revolved around making parties coherent and disciplined, which commits them to a given program, platform, or set of policies. This may make parties as a whole more accountable for their political beliefs, and voters more capable of deciding on the merits which parties deserve to govern. This debate continues to the present, with one of its current applications being to the Middle East and North Africa after the Arab Spring of 2011. Two "competing" pieces illustrate how contemporary this debate is. Timothy Meisburger argues in favor of single-member district systems, especially in the divided and heterogenous societies of the Arab world, on the grounds that these systems can challenge entrenched elites and reduce extremism. Andrew Reynolds and John M. Carey (who wrote a prior piece to which Meisburger is responding) reply that PR is preferable on these same counts. Both use countries such as Tunisia and Egypt to test and debate their respective claims. In conclusion, the selections here show that legislatures are not simply assemblies that process the preferences of the majority and turn them into law. They are rather complex creatures, filled with often ambitious individuals and characterized by rules and patterns that condition the behavior of politicians.

As with other sections, these debates are not resolved once and for all. This can be frustrating as a student first approaches the discussion seeking "the right answer." On the other hand, the fact that these debates remain open is precisely why they are worth considering in detail: the relative merits of different institutional arrangements are not just matters of fact, they are rather points of debate to which every informed person (scholar, student, citizen, or all of the above) can contribute.

Parliamentary Funk

CAMERON ABADI

The debt-ceiling negotiations going on in Washington right now have not, to put it mildly, cast the collected membership of the U.S. Congress in the most flattering possible light. In theory, members of Congress are meant to serve as enlightened representatives of their local districts, virtuous stewards of the common good. But the last several weeks have offered instead a portrait of shallow partisans willing to risk global economic catastrophe for the sake of indulging their personal vanity and furthering their own agendas, and a legislature unable to accomplish even the most basic of tasks.

Sadly, the United States is not the only country suffering from its lawmakers in this fashion. Legislative gridlock is commonplace—as are the partisanship and vanity at its root—in governments around the world. At least the United States can blame the creakiness of its institutions on the fact that they were designed some 200 years ago: Most other countries don't have nearly such a convenient excuse—and, yet, they act just as shamelessly.

Belgium

Think America's divided government is a hassle? Try not having a government at all. Belgium has lacked a functioning parliamentary majority for more than a year, ever since its last national election on June 13, 2010. Negotiations to form a new majority have broken down eight times over the past 400 days, as the country earned the dubious distinction of entering the Guinness World Records for the longest period of time without a government. The major Belgian parties aren't just talking past one another; they don't even share the same native language—and that's a big part of the problem. Belgium's Flemish-speaking region wants to secure more financial autonomy, the better to enjoy the rewards of its economic success, but the country's French-speaking territories, dependent as they are on Flemish tax receipts to maintain their welfare provisions, have refused.

In the absence of any majority in Parliament, previous Prime Minister Yves Leterme has continued to preside over cabinet meetings, though proposals for ambitious legislation have been put on hold indefinitely. That's not to say, however, that Belgians necessarily notice any disruption in their daily lives. Many state functions, from education to welfare, are already administered at the regional, rather than the federal, level. Leterme's caretaker government, meanwhile, did succeed in serving its pre-scheduled six-month stint as president of the European Council in 2010. And in 2011, Belgium managed to send four fighter jets and 150 military personnel to enforce the no-fly zone over Libya.

Apparently, the reason that Parliament has yet to call for a new election is for fear that the international community (and bond markets) will judge the country incapable of solving its problems (though one would have thought that train had long ago left the station). Presiding over the stalemate, and tirelessly goading all parties to reach a final resolution, is the lonely King Albert II—among the few symbols of national identity, apart from frites, that enjoys broad recognition throughout the country.

Iraq

With political and sectarian violence still common throughout their country, Iraqi parliamentarians could perhaps be forgiven some measure of cynicism about the democratic process. Still, the zero-sum strategies of sectarian parties have managed repeatedly to nearly push the country's entire parliamentary system off the brink, and calls for election boycotts by Sunni parties have been common in Iraq's short democratic history. Sunni threats to boycott the 2005 parliamentary elections proved especially detrimental to the political atmosphere, fanning the flames of the ongoing low-level sectarian civil war.

Sunni parties called for boycotts again in 2010, after Shiite parties pushed to disqualify hundreds of Sunni candidates because of their alleged affiliations with the Baath Party. With sectarian tensions primed by that show of Shiite power, the parliamentary election on March 7, 2010, produced a stalemate. After nine months of threats and aggrieved posturing—and cajoling interventions by the United States—the legislative body finally confirmed a new government with incumbent Prime Minister Nouri al-Maliki at its head in December 2010.

Little significant legislation has passed since then, though the parliament did agree this month to formally blame the United States for continuing violence along Iraq's borders. But Iraq has yet to pass an oil revenue-sharing law, something that could tamp down major sectarian strife. The parliament also has yet to address the status of the semiautonomous Kurdistan region, a subject of dispute that may also eventually spark a civil war.

Japan

If Japan's parliament has seemed slow in responding to the disaster at Fukushima Daiichi nuclear power plant, that's partly by design. Although the national parliament is meant in theory to serve as the country's highest lawmaking body, in reality it's subordinate to a branch of government largely invisible to the public: the elite civil service, made up of senior ministry bureaucrats who basically write policy before it's perfunctorily debated and rubber-stamped into law by parliament.

Conditioned in deference, the parliament has little redress apart from withdrawing its formal support of the government and forcing the selection of a new prime minister or a new round of elections. Unsurprisingly, Japan has had five prime ministers in the past five years, but little in the way of major legislation, despite the fact that a major debt crisis seems to be looming on the horizon, with gross government debt soaring to over 200 percent of GDP this year.

In the case of the meltdown of Fukushima's nuclear reactors this year, the toothlessness of Japan's parliament was starkly exposed, as lawmakers were unable to compel bureaucrats in the government or in the Tepco power utility to give truthful testimony about the extent of damage to the reactors and the threat of exposure to dangerous radioactivity.

Afghanistan

The Afghan parliament is among the few structural checks on the power of President Hamid Karzai, but that's not to say it's a particularly effective one: Its independence has repeatedly come under attack by Karzai and his allies.

In June, Karzai appointed a tribunal to re-examine the results from the most recent parliamentary elections. One week later, the court revoked 62 seats, 25 percent of the number awarded the previous September. Members of parliament made a symbolic show of protest by slapping their desks in unison, but most held their tongues for fear of earning Karzai's ill favor. One Karzai ally appointed to a newly open seat who did feel compelled to refute allegations that the tribunal acted unjustly compared the process to the U.S. Supreme Court's intervention in the disputed 2000 presidential contest between George W. Bush and Al Gore.

Karzai's own belief that he needn't defend the legality of the tribunal process signals a waning national confidence in the parliament. That may make it harder for Kabul and Washington to eventually reach a political settlement to end the ongoing war, as it might confirm the Taliban's suspicions that the only way to effectively oppose Karzai is through military, rather than peaceful, means.

Taiwan

With a system designed to produce divided government—the executive and legislative branches are elected independently of one another—Taiwan's gridlocked status quo may sound familiar to Americans. But those original sins are exacerbated by the hyperpartisan politics of this relatively new democracy. The main "blue" and "green" party coalitions don't just oppose one another—they despise each other. Indeed, they have a greater tradition of engaging in fistfights in the halls of government than cooperating on policy.

Taiwan's eight years of divided government during the previous decade produced an utter and acrimonious political stalemate. At the time of the Asian financial crisis in 2000, the Taiwanese government was paralyzed and generally acknowledged to have acquitted itself poorly in its attempts at crisis management. As much of the region was working furiously to maintain good standing with the international bond markets, Taiwan's parliament was busy trying to impeach President Chen Shui-Bian because of a disagreement over energy policy.

Taipei currently has both branches of government under the control of a single party, but polls show that this may change in the parliamentary and presidential elections scheduled for 2012.

What Makes a Rubber Stamp?

THE ECONOMIST

© The Economist Newspaper Limited, London (March 5, 2012).

Each year in early March, Beijing welcomes not only the sense of spring's imminent arrival, but also the thousands of out-of-town delegates who descend on the capital for the once-yearly full session of the National People's Congress (NPC), China's version of a national legislature. It is a time of year when the weather in Beijing might yet go any which way. But not the NPC session, which is a closely scripted and tightly controlled event featuring much pageantry and precious little drama.

The orderly proceedings and the pre-arranged outcomes are predictable. So too are the frequent invocations of the term "rubber-stamp" to describe the NPC, as well as heated complaints about that term from Chinese officials and other supporters of the system.

Like many western media outlets, *The Economist* has been a frequent "rubber-stamper" in its coverage of the NPC over the years. So too have many Chinese-language media, for that matter, including some of China's own outlets.

Yet many in China take the term as an insult, feeling that it belittles the institutions and procedures by which the nation makes its laws.

Not long after the close of the 2010 NPC, your correspondent moderated a panel at Beijing's Renmin University, where one of the panellists veered off topic to criticise western media for their biased coverage of China. The panellist, Yang Rui, a popular and often truculent host of a political talk show on state-run China Central Television (CCTV), said he found the "rubber-stamp" comparison particularly galling. When, he asked, would the foreign media finally stop using the term "rubber-stamp" to describe China's parliament?

The answer to that question should be obvious: when it finally rejects something put before it.

Among the matters the nearly 3,000 legislative delegates get to vote on are the approval of new laws, "work reports" delivered by senior officials, and new appointees to top government posts. Unanimous votes were once common. Multiple Chinese reports have noted with interest the first occasion on which a delegate cast a "no" vote, in 1988. They also reported that in 1982, when three delegates offered the first abstentions in NPC history, a reporter's request to report this unusual development truthfully was greeted with approval by Deng Xiaoping.

Since then things have gotten slightly more interesting. In 1992, the NPC caused something of a stir when only 1,767 delegates, two-thirds of the total, voted to approve the massive and massively controversial Three Gorges Dam project. There were 177 votes against, 644 votes to abstain, and 25 delegates who failed to vote at all.

In other cases where reports or candidates are approved by less than 75%, it is seen as a clear rebuke to the leadership.

None of this is to say that the NPC is entirely irrelevant. In important ways, the NPC—as an institution—has become more interesting than its ritual-laden yearly sessions would indicate. Its full-time professional staff has grown in size and professionalism. In the course of drafting legislation, it has taken great strides in reaching out to social stakeholders and soliciting their input. Often it even pushes back against the Communist party leadership by insisting on substantial revisions to draft laws before moving them along.

In these ways, the NPC plays a meaningful and increasingly important role in China's governance. And there are some political scientists, Chinese and foreign alike, who reckon that China's system may evolve in ways that give the legislature genuine independence and substantial power in decades to come.

Nor should the frequent reference to the rubber-stamp tendencies of today's NPC be taken to suggest that empty political theatre is unique to China's institutions. After all, in less than half a year America's two major political parties will each hold elaborate, multi-day nominating conventions, full of over-wrought pomp, ceremony and ritual. Barring any departure from what has been standing practice for decades, all this will culminate with a grand theatrical set piece of a vote with a preordained outcome.

Indeed, many people will use terms like "rubber-stamp" and "coronation" to describe these conventions, in Charlotte, North Carolina and Tampa, Florida. Nobody will get angry about it. And why should they? After all, there is another, even more powerful force in Washington that provides actual checks and balances to the political power of the executive branch. That one bears the mark of another well-worn stamp: Gridlock.

Getting Majoritarianism Right

TIMOTHY M. MEISBURGER

Meisburger, Timothy M. "Getting Majoritarianism Right." *Journal of Democracy* 23:1 (2012), 155–163. © 2012 National Endowment for Democracy and The Johns Hopkins University Press. Reprinted with permission of Johns Hopkins University Press.

In their essay in the October 2011 issue of this journal, John Carey and Andrew Reynolds capably outline existing electoral systems in the Middle East and North Africa (MENA) and propose reforms in countries that have either begun a democratic transition or shown signs that such a transition may lie ahead.[1] Through their essay runs a vein of implicit or explicit support for the idea that electoral systems based on proportional representation (PR) of political parties will be best for whatever democracies may emerge in the MENA region, while majoritarian systems are more conducive to authoritarianism.

I would like to challenge these assumptions by suggesting that, in the special case of developing or emerging democracies, PR may not be the most appropriate system, and that in many cases majoritarian or plurality systems may do a better job of ensuring effective representation and promoting democratization.

Experience shows that effective democracies do not emerge overnight. Democratization is a process, not an event, and can take several generations. At different stages, it may require different electoral systems. PR may be a good choice for the mature democracies of northern Europe, which already have such key PR prerequisites as parties with clear ideological profiles, well-defined platforms, and democratic internal-governance rules. An emerging democracy, by contrast, might be better off with a system that is more flexible than PR and hence more likely to aid the development of democratic attitudes and the emergence of fully democratic parties and states.

Under PR, each voter is primarily choosing a party, with seats in the legislature awarded to parties based on their respective vote shares. There are two main types of PR, closed list and open list. In a closed-list system, a party puts forward a slate of, for example, ten candidates for a parliament of ten seats. In this case the "quota" for winning a seat is 10 percent of the vote. If the party receives 30 percent, the top three candidates on its list are elected. An open list works the same way, except that voters can also record a preference for a particular candidate on the list, so that the three elected may not necessarily be the top three on the list. Proponents of the open list say that voters are better represented through this system, while critics of PR point out that parties still decide who will be on the list, and that representatives still owe their main allegiance to party leaders rather than voters.[2] Under majoritarian or plurality systems, voters are primarily choosing candidates. Whichever candidate receives the most votes gains office, and votes for losing candidates are "discards" leading to no representation. Often referred to as first-past-the-post or winner-take-all, the plurality rule most commonly is combined with the single-member district (SMD) system, in which candidates vie for a single seat representing a particular geographic area. It is also possible to use majoritarian or plurality voting in multimember districts, though the practice is uncommon.

In most developing democracies, political ideology is not very important. People in developing countries seldom fit comfortably along the sort of left-right spectrum that is familiar to observers of European or European-descended polities. In emerging democracies, where political ideology is less important as an organizing principle, parties often form around preexisting social cleavages—including differences of religion, ethnicity, tribe, language, or culture—and PR-based systems can have the unfortunate effect of sharpening rather than dulling such splits. [3]

When parties are organized along lines of ethnicity or religion, as they are in Bosnia, parts of Africa, and much of the Muslim world, they are by definition exclusionary. You are inside or outside the group based on characteristics that you did not choose and cannot change. Under PR systems, the most successful party leaders are those who best represent their group's interests through patronage and protection, rather than those with a broader focus on the general public welfare. Party leaders have no incentive to reach across ethnic or religious lines for votes; rather, to maintain their power it is often in their interest to perpetuate such cleavages. In Bosnia, this has been taken to such extremes that ethnic cleavage is embedded in the fabric of the constitution, and PR inhibits interethnic cooperation.

As an election system, PR is designed to provide proportional representation for ideologies and *parties* in government, rather than representation for a particular region. It is well suited to smaller countries with populations that are more or less homogeneous (one thinks of Northern Europe) and with patterns of political contention that feature ideology rather than geography (such that a typical voter would rather be represented by someone ideologically congenial from across the country than by a near neighbor from a rival party). In other developed democracies with less homogeneous populations and where political affiliation does not always fit comfortably on the familiar left-right spectrum, PR has been less successful.

The democratic assumptions underlying PR are that all people will be represented in government through their respective parties, and that party members will share common ideas about most local and national issues. Unfortunately, in most developing democracies—and in the MENA region—parties are dysfunctional if they exist at all. When parties are dysfunctional or lack internal democracy or fail to faithfully represent their constituents' interests for some other reason, the quality of representation in PR systems can sink very low. This, in turn, brings a danger that ordinary citizens will become disillusioned with democracy. Consequently, a party-based election system that requires functional and democratic parties may be ill suited to the Middle East, where most parties are in the early stages of democratic development.

In Tunisia, the MENA country generally rated as most likely to transition successfully to democracy, there are no long-established ideologically based *democratic* parties. The only established parties are the previous (undemocratic) ruling party and a few sham parties set up under the prior regime to provide an illusion of democracy. A party-based election in this environment, where most or all parties lack clear ideologies (the exception being the Islamist parties) or policy positions, will feature the existing undemocratic and unrepresentative parties, plus a handful of hastily established parties created by commercial, political, and military elites to protect their respective interests under the new "rules of the game." By advocating a party-based election system before legitimate parties have had the opportunity to develop, we may inadvertently empower parties that have little or no democratic legitimacy.

Another drawback of PR systems in emerging democracies is that representative accountability is primarily upward to party leaders rather than downward to constituents. Because party leaders decide which candidates to put on the party's list in each district (and, under closed-list PR, also each candidate's ranking on the list), representatives owe their position to the party leadership rather than their own constituents. This is not a problem if parties are internally democratic, allowing voters to express their aspirations through the party, but one of the most common problems encountered with parties in developing democracies is their lack of internal democracy.

In a number of countries that introduced PR in the early or mid-1990s, including Cambodia, Serbia, and South Africa, democratic development has been limited. In Egypt and Tunisia, where entrenched elites are likely to capture most parties, adoption of PR is likely to diminish voter influence and the quality of political representation, thereby potentially stoking public anger and instability. Should voters come to feel that they lack political efficacy in the new dispensation, their disillusionment could boost the appeal of radical or extreme alternatives.

The Danger of Extremism

Because PR allows even small minorities to get into government, it may provide a handhold for extremist parties. In a plurality system, a party with a small following that lives scattered among the rest of the populace will have little chance of winning seats. Plurality-rule politics is about chasing the "moderate middle," not appealing to intense subgroups. Under PR, extremists have much better prospects of gaining a share of power, perhaps including access to government funding for campaigns and advertising. Well-known examples of this include the rise of the Freedom Party in 1980s Austria, and the National Socialists in Weimar Germany.[4] In established democracies, PR contributes to party proliferation and weak coalition governments. Not only the Weimar Republic, but also

Italy between 1946 and 1993 and Israel today are oft-cited examples. In the Israeli case, critics argue that the need to include hard-liners in the ruling coalition has hindered negotiations with the Palestinians.[5]

In majoritarian systems, parties must exert a broad appeal to be successful, and thus they pursue the median voter. The current lack of such a dynamic in the MENA region is glaring. If Egypt's elections are held under a straight PR system (as Carey and Reynolds advocate), there will be dozens of poorly organized new parties competing against the former ruling party and the Muslim Brotherhood. Only a few of the new parties (led by prominent personalities) can expect to win even 4 or 5 percent of the vote and, with it, a few seats. The Brotherhood, which polls suggest has the support of about a fifth of the electorate, will win at least a fifth of the seats, and probably be the largest single bloc on a political landscape populated by dozens of small new parties.

By contrast, a majoritarian election held in an emerging democracy is likely to install in office a collection of prominent individuals (local notables) rather than a specific party. In this system, candidates prosper by broadening rather than narrowing and intensifying their appeal. In an Egypt with plurality elections, to use a hypothetical example, the Brotherhood's 20 percent support would hand it only a few races (especially if the system featured two rounds or a distribution-of-preferences device such as the alternative vote). And those Brotherhood candidates who were elected would form a party caucus significantly more moderate than the one that would emerge under PR. For in the latter system party leaders choose candidates who display ideological purity and personal or party loyalty, and who may be counted on to maintain a solid front once in office. In a majoritarian system the same representatives would have needed to shift toward the moderate middle to get elected, and they would owe their primary allegiance to constituents rather than party bosses.

One of proportional representation's selling points is that it fosters the development of stronger parties. That is true, but the catch is that PR does not necessarily promote *democratic* parties. In Egypt, Tunisia, and other countries that lack established parties, PR may prevent the formation of democratic parties by empowering existing elites. These will have the money and clout to form parties quickly and campaign effectively, but will have little or no incentive to let the system ever become more inclusive and democratic. Representatives beholden to party leaders rather than voters will lack the independent democratic legitimacy needed to break party discipline and form cross-party alliances that might better represent constituent interests. Leaders have so much power under this arrangement that challengers to them find it hard to emerge and gain traction.

In countries without established parties, the wiser path is to foster the creation of democratic parties rather than to strengthen existing undemocratic parties in hopes that they will eventually become democratic. The best choice for producing democratic parties in a transitional country may be an SMD system where candidates run as individuals, regardless of their party affiliation. Since elections will not be party-based, each legislator will have equal power, and each will be free to form whatever alliances seem best for constituent interests. Over time, democratic factions and parties may develop organically as interest groups form, interact, and coalesce. The class of party potentates (not to mention the single strongman) that is PR's trademark is less likely to appear, as SMD disperses power equally among representatives whereas PR concentrates power in the hands of a few party leaders.

PR and Representation

Advocates of PR often present it as being more representative than other systems, but this is generally not the case in developing democracies. True, women or minorities can easily be added to a party list, but because their accountability is to leaders rather than constituents, they lack the independence required to effectively support constituent interests. For example, female representatives in PR systems are prevented by party discipline from forming cross-party alliances with other female representatives to advance issues of specific interest to women. In PR systems, representation is seen as an ascriptive property (based on ideology, ethnicity, religion,

tribe, or gender) rather than as a process. Consequently, in many PR countries entrenched elites like to point to token minority members in their parties or governments as proof of "representation," regardless of the tokens' actual desire or ability to look out for the interests of those whom they are supposedly "representing."

Although it may be slightly more complicated to ensure representation for minority or disadvantaged groups in majoritarian systems, there are means available to accomplish that goal (including smaller districts, gerrymandering, and reserved seats) that also preserve representative independence and enhance accountability. Small district sizes lower entry barriers for women and minorities because fewer resources are required to run in the election than would be needed in a large multimember district. Also, a legislature drawn from small single-member districts with a residency requirement for candidates is more likely to be representative of the general population, and much less likely to be dominated by capital-based economic or political elites, rather than a legislature drawn from large multimember districts (as in a PR system).

Proponents of PR also assert that it results in fewer wasted votes and more representation. Since even small parties can expect to win a few seats, most voters will be able to point to a party elected with their support. In a first-past-the-post system, PR-friendly critics assert, even a mathematical majority of the vote may be "wasted" by being dispersed among candidates who fail to gain office. But this criticism assumes that if your candidate is not elected, you are unrepresented in government—a basic misunderstanding of geographical representation. It is like saying "You voted for pizza, everyone else voted for Chinese food, so you get no dinner." Representatives in geographical districts do their best to represent all of their constituents, or they do not get reelected.

In their section on Tunisia, Carey and Reynolds support closed-list PR for the transition: "At the constitution-making moment," they assert, "the inclusiveness of electoral rules must be a top priority." At the same time, they acknowledge that the "inclusiveness" provided by closed-list PR is achieved by sacrificing accountability, and suggest that this be fixed later by changing to a system that promotes greater accountability. But changing an established electoral system is extremely difficult, particularly when the change involves making legislators more accountable.

In the early 1990s, Reynolds, Arend Lijphart, and Jørgen Elklit strongly supported a PR system for South Africa after its transition from apartheid; but by 2000, even they had realized that the lack of geographical representation had seriously compromised accountability in a polity where the leaders of the dominant African National Congress essentially have de facto power to appoint most of the national legislature.[6] Although the need for reform in South Africa is widely acknowledged, there is little incentive for those now in charge to weaken their power by altering the system, and to date there has been no reform. This is not an isolated case. Scholars have shown that it is much more common for consolidating democracies to switch from SMD to PR or a mixed system, than it is to go in the other direction.[7] Unsurprisingly, party leaders tend to support a change to PR because it enhances their power, and to resist a change to SMD because it diminishes their power.

PR and Conflict

Is PR a good choice for postconflict countries, as is often said? Friends of MENA-region democracy should approach this claim with caution. Although it is true that in several countries suffering from long-term conflict PR has been a key element in consociational[8] power-sharing agreements that ended the conflict, high-level power-sharing between the elites at the top of warring factions has seldom resulted in an improvement in democracy for the average person, who often ends up trading one set of authoritarian leaders for another.

Sometimes the only way to stop a war may require guaranteeing unsavory characters a protected place in government, and in such cases, PR may be the best option. But in many cases where there were several possible options during the fluid time around transitions, PR has been recommended and adopted with little discussion about whether it would be best over the long term. Rather than reaching first for PR, constitution drafters in the Middle

East and those proffering advice would be well-advised to examine other options and carefully consider whether the short-term stability provided by elite power-sharing is going to be worth the long-term loss of democratic accountability.

A more appropriate system than PR for the developing democracies of the Middle East may be the simple SMD system. It is easy to understand and, because the district size is small, voters will be in closer touch with each representative. Accountability and transparency are enhanced rather than diminished, and research has shown that enhanced accountability yields more responsive and less corrupt government, helping to prevent disillusionment with democracy once the initial euphoria of a postauthoritarian transition has passed. Proportional systems, by contrast, require large multi-member districts, diluting accountability and transparency and distancing representatives from their constituents.

The smaller districts of SMD also mean that fewer resources are required to run for office than are needed in a typical large multimember district, easing participation by disadvantaged groups. Unlike PR systems, where power is concentrated in party leaders or even (as in Cambodia) a single person, SMD elections are less party-based. Each legislator will have been individually elected and have the same power as his or her colleagues, and each legislator will have the freedom to form cross-party alliances if and when it seems these will best serve constituent interests. Because party affiliation is looser to begin with, there is a greater chance that democratic and responsive parties will develop over time.

While SMD promotes more moderate parties and candidates than PR, if several candidates are running for a single seat, the more liberal and centrist candidates could split the vote and allow an extremist candidate from a disciplined party to win a seat with a relatively small plurality. In countries where this is a concern, the possibility of extremist candidates being elected can be further reduced through the adoption of a two-round or alternative-vote SMD system, which would require a winning candidate to garner a majority—not just a plurality—of the votes or preferences in the district.

The choice of an electoral system must not be taken lightly. Experience shows that it is a key step in the constitutional development of emerging democracies. The choice can have a significant effect not only on the long-term quality of a country's democracy, but also on the underlying political stability of the country itself. No system should be selected without extensive public discussion of the various options and their implications. Most countries have few people familiar with different electoral systems. Far too often in transitional or developing settings, the choice of a system is the work of a lamentably small group of people who then enshrine their decision in a constitution adopted after a sketchy public debate held in a context where few have a full grasp of the long-term significance of electoral-system design. Electoral experts and their supporters have a moral obligation to help ensure that ordinary voters in emerging democracies can develop that grasp in a timely way. Above all, this means doing all that can be done to insist that the process for choosing an electoral system must go forward in a way that is deliberative, open, and consultative rather than rushed, closed, and untransparent.

NOTES

1. John M. Carey and Andrew Reynolds. "Comparing the Arab Revolts: The Impact of Election Systems," *Journal of Democracy* 22 (October 2011): 36–47.

2. For an explanation of how, even under an open-list arrangement, party leaders exert overweening power over who becomes a legislator, see Maja Sahadžiæ, "The Electoral System of Bosnia and Herzegovina: A Short Review of Political Matter and/or Technical Perplexion," *Contemporary Issues* 2, no.1 (2009): 61–78.

3. Donald Horowitz, *Ethnic Groups in Conflict* (Berkeley: University of California Press, 1985).

4. The Weimar Republic's system of no-threshold, national-list PR allowed Adolf Hitler's National Socialists, in their breakout election in 1930, to go from 12 seats in the 491-member Reichstag to 107 seats in an enlarged (577-member) body. Under first-past-the- post rules, the Social Democrats would have doubled their seats rather than declined from 153 to 143, and the National Socialists would have actually lost seats. See Dieter K. Buse and Juergen C. Doerr, eds., *Modern Germany: An Encyclopedia of History, People, and Culture, 1871–1990* (2 vols., New York: Garland, 1998), 2, p. 192.

5. For an example of this argument, see Seth Freedman, "Look to Israel for a Case Study in Proportional Representation's Flaws," *Guardian,* 29 April 2010, available at www.guardian.co.uk/commentisfree/2010/apr/29/israel-proportional-representation.

6. See the October 2002 report of the Electoral Institute for the Sustainability of Democracy in Africa, "South Africa: Proportional Representation: Pros and Cons," available at www.eisa.org.za/WEP/sou3.htm.

7. Andrew Reynolds, *Designing Democracy in a Dangerous World* (New York: Oxford University Press, 2011), p. 76.

8. "Consociational Democracy Means Government by Elite Cartel Designed to Turn a Democracy with a Fragmented Culture into a Stable Democracy." Arend Lijphart, "Consociational Democracy," *World Politics* 21 (January 1969): 216.

Getting Elections Wrong

ANDREW REYNOLDS AND JOHN M. CAREY

Reynolds, Andrew, and John M. Carey. "Getting Elections Wrong." *Journal of Democracy* 23:1 (2012), 164–168. © 2012 National Endowment for Democracy and The Johns Hopkins University Press. Reprinted with permission of Johns Hopkins University Press.

We agree with Timothy M. Meisburger that the choice of an electoral system is a key step in the constitutional development of an emerging democracy. Beyond this, there is little in his essay with which we can concur. Meisburger's advocacy of majoritarian (chiefly first-past-the-post) electoral systems for the fragile polities of the Arab world rests on a weak foundation, both in the criticisms that he launches against proportional representation (PR) and in the claims that he makes on behalf of single-member-district (SMD) elections.

In a nutshell, Meisburger accuses PR of being bad for democracy. He argues that PR systems sharpen and politicize differences of ethnicity and culture, that PR has been less successful than SMD elections in heterogeneous societies in the developed world, that PR empowers existing elites and unsavory elements in democratizing states, and that majoritarian systems do a better job of ensuring effective representation. In our estimation, the weight of the evidence—from nations actually going through democratic change, as well as from the scholarly literature that tries to understand such change—points to just the opposite conclusions. The evidence that we have from a series of waves of democratization is that majoritarian election systems can be deeply problematic, and that proportional systems, while not solving all the problems by any means, are a better option in most contexts.

Meisburger is particularly concerned by the lack of strong party systems in the Arab world, stipulating that "parties with clear ideological profiles, well-defined platforms, and democratic internal-governance rules" are "key prerequisites" for democracy to function under PR. If these are lacking, he claims, SMD elections are better, for they are supposedly "more flexible than PR and hence more likely to aid the development of democratic attitudes and the emergence of fully democratic parties and states." Meisburger makes sweeping statements about bad outcomes "in many PR countries," but rarely points to specifics. He nods at times to Northern Europe as a region where PR is appropriate, but ignores its success in many other environments.

Make no mistake, we think parties in the style of Northern Europe's, complete with detailed platforms and well-established procedures designed to guarantee internal democracy, are lovely. Were they to develop in the Arab world, we would be pleased. But setting Danish parties up as a necessary precondition for workable PR is a distraction, not a serious argument. Nor does it comport with the successful experiences of many newly established PR democracies from Southern Europe in the 1970s to Latin America in the 1980s and Eastern Europe as well as parts of sub-Saharan Africa in the 1990s.

Meisburger's insistence that fully developed party systems must precede PR echoes the arguments of autocrats (Yoweri Museveni of Uganda and King Abdullah of Jordan, to name two) who fear PR as a threat to current elites and resist it publicly on the grounds that parties in their countries are too young or corrupt, or that party politics is simply culturally unfamiliar and inappropriate. Meisburger clearly does not share their autocratic motives, but we are not sure on what basis he thinks SMD elections do better than PR at fostering democratic attitudes and party development. The SMD experiences of nineteenth-century Latin America or postindependence sub-Saharan Africa seem inauspicious to say the least. Unfortunately, we cannot evaluate the historical basis of Meisburger's claim because he does not provide any.

For Meisburger, a chief virtue of SMD elections is the link that they forge between voters and individual representatives. We concur that politicians' accountability to citizens matters, but maintain that in post-conflict situations, it must be married to substantial proportionality—preferably in moderate-sized districts with open lists. We are adamant that individualism must not come at the cost of abandoning collective accountability altogether, as Meisburger's antiparty position would have it. There are no vibrant democracies, new or old, with purely individualized and nonpartisan forms of electoral competition. There are many cases where the electoral system is designed to preclude or suppress parties and to privilege independent candidates. The most notable modern examples are Afghanistan, the Gulf states, Jordan, and Saudi Arabia. In these cases "no-party" elections are thin veils meant to hide electoral authoritarianism and executive dominance.

Some of Meisburger's claims for the virtues of SMDs go beyond contradicting the empirical evidence and contradict his own claims elsewhere in his essay. He asserts first that PR works only when politics is structured around the kinds of coherent ideologies that the Arab world lacks, and then appeals to the logic of the median-voter theorem to contend that SMD will encourage a more moderate Arab politics. But the median-voter theorem plainly hinges on competition along a dominant *ideological* dimension.[1] What is the dimension along which Meisburger thinks SMD competition will find a "median" if he also believes that "in most developing democracies, political ideology is not very important"?

In our view, the broader Middle East has too many complex dimensions of conflict for median-voter logic to take hold. But this does not mean that ideology is lacking or insignificant. On the contrary, the first thing that a visitor notices in Egypt, Libya, or Tunisia is the enormous importance of competing views about how best to organize state and society—in other words, ideologies. Politics in those places is more than just a tribal scramble for power, and is colored by questions of political economy, regionalism, nationalism, and religiosity. Do Arabs want parties? It depends on whom you ask. Old-regime holdovers do not, but many others do. Meisburger rightly acknowledges that in the Arab world

majoritarian systems will preclude virtually all women and minorities from representation. He agrees with us that list PR provides a space for women and minorities to be elected, but argues that such elected representatives are just "tokens" beholden to party bosses. There is a grain of truth to the point that MPs from reserved seats can be weakly attached to the group they purport to represent, but there is a wealth of empirical evidence showing that many women and minorities elected by special mechanisms, or indeed through simple PR lists, can have a significant and positive impact on gender and minority rights.[2] Because Meisburger refuses to countenance proportionality as a means of achieving balanced representation, he proposes to fall back on the dubious practice (common in the United States) of rigging district boundaries in order to artificially create "majority-minority" districts.

PR in Tunisia and Egypt

The case of Tunisia tells strongly against Meisburger's objections to PR. In 2009, elections under a mixed but mostly majoritarian system handed President Ben Ali's ruling party every contested seat in the sham legislature. After Ben Ali's fall, Tunisians understandably felt that including all significant voices in their new parliament was the *sine qua non* of successful democratization, so they chose to use PR in moderatesized districts. That system worked exceptionally well in the 23 October 2011 Constituent Assembly elections—undoubtedly far better than the old (or any new) majoritarian system would have.

Hizb al-Nahda (Renaissance Party), a Muslim Brotherhood–inspired Islamist formation, was the plurality winner in every one of the 27 geographical constituencies within Tunisia, as well as the half-dozen constituencies for Tunisians voting from abroad.[3] Of course, had Tunisia relied on SMDs to fill the 217-seat Assembly, there would have been many more, smaller districts with individual contests. Support for candidates other than al-Nahda's would likely have been concentrated enough for some non-Islamists to win. Yet the results from Tunisia strongly suggest that, had the elections been held under majoritarian rules, al- Nahda could have won 90 percent or more of the seats instead of the 41 percent (only slightly above its vote share) that it actually did win. It outpaced all its rivals, but it still needs to form a coalition with smaller partners. In Tunisia, PR has allowed multiple alliances to win Constituent Assembly seats, and prevented complete one-party control.

Tunisia in 2011 is reminiscent of South Africa in 1994. The success of South Africa's transition to democracy rested on the inclusiveness of its first PR-based election system. South Africans from Nelson Mandela on down argued that the spirit of respect and of allowing everyone a voice that was so crucial to that first postapartheid government was underpinned by a strongly proportional election system. Without it, black and white minority voices would have been silenced and things could have taken a very dire turn. Meisburger notes that in the early 1990s, one of us strongly supported a PR system for South Africa, but he goes on to say that "by 2000, even [Reynolds] had realized that the lack of geographical representation had seriously compromised accountability." Meisburger's error speaks to more than his lack of familiarity with the literature. In fact, Reynolds had warned from the very beginning that large-district, closed-list PR was problematic for South Africa. In a book published in 1993 (even before the first elections) and again in the pages of this journal in 1995, he urged a more accountable form of smaller-district, open-list PR for that country. The more general point, which we feel Meisburger misses throughout, is that one need not sacrifice the crucial benefits of proportionality on the altar of close geographic representation.[4]

Meisburger speculates that PR elections in Egypt would hand the Muslim Brotherhood something like a fifth to a quarter of seats, whereas SMD elections would produce an assembly of individualistic "local notables." Given that Meisburger acknowledges the Brotherhood as the largest, best-organized party throughout Egypt, it is unclear why he does not expect that its candidates would win almost all the seats if elections were held under SMD. As the biggest single force in the country, competing in district after district against fragmented opposition, the Brothers could readily be expected to win a solid majority. In any event,

Meisburger prefers the "local notables" outcome, confident that the notables would lead Egypt more responsibly than a majority coalition that either: 1) included the Brotherhood's 20 to 25 percent plus representatives from other parties and movements totaling an additional 25 to 30 percent of seats, or 2) consisted of *non*-Brotherhood representatives totaling more than 50 percent in a disparate coalition that left the Brotherhood in opposition.

Our own recommendations are not based on a preference for the Brotherhood to win or lose or join or not join a government. We leave those matters to Egyptian voters. But we do favor electoral rules that award representation to parties and alliances in accord with the level of support that they enjoy among voters. In environments where there is great uncertainty among leaders and voters about the relative strength of different movements and alliances, SMD elections are likely to produce severe anomalies between votes and seats. Some groups that win narrow victories will reap vastly outsized seat bonuses. Other groups that lose narrowly will wind up with sizeable vote totals but no seats. The fortunate winners will be in a position to consolidate power, rewriting constitutions to lock in their early gains. PR, by contrast, lowers the stakes of that first free election and thus makes free elections likelier to continue. It will tend to produce constituent assemblies that are more balanced if less decisive— at least initially, until majority coalitions can form. These seem like reasonable tradeoffs, and as we have stressed, choosing an electoral system inevitably means making tradeoffs.

NOTES

1. Duncan Black, "On the Rationale of Group Decision-Making," *Journal of Political Economy* 56 (February 1948): 23–34; Anthony Downs, *An Economic Theory of Democracy* (New York: Harper, 1957).

2. See, for example, Sarah Childs and Mona Lena Krook, "Critical Mass Theory and Women's Political Representation," *Political Studies* 56 (October 2008): 725–736; and Andrew Reynolds, *Designing Democracy in a*

Dangerous World (New York: Oxford University Press, 2011), ch. 6.

3. In one district, Sidi Bouzid, another list won but suffered partial disqualification when the electoral commission sanctioned it for illegal campaigning.

4. Andrew Reynolds, *Voting for a New South Africa* (Cape Town: Maskew Miller Longman, 1993) and "Constitutional Engineering in Southern Africa," *Journal of Democracy* 6 (April 1995): 93–94.

DISCUSSION QUESTIONS

1) The pieces by Cameron Abadi and *The Economist* highlight some of the ways that parliaments fail to function well in practice. Are there any reasons to prefer the parliamentary system of government to a "Congress"-type system as found in the United States? If so, what would these be?

2) Why does Timothy Meisburger favor single-member district electoral systems? What are the theoretical grounds for his preferring this type of election? What is his empirical evidence for them working better than the alternative? Does this logic seem intuitive? Prior to reading the reply by Carey and Roberts (if you will do so), could you offer any critique yourself of Meisburger's argument?

3) John Carey and Andrew Roberts are critical of Timothy Meisburger's argument in favor of single-member district electoral systems? Why do these authors favor proportional representation (PR)? Again, what are the theoretical grounds and what is the empirical evidence for preferring PR?

Executives

Politics is very often associated with executives. Presidents and prime ministers are among the first things we think of when we think of "politics." Some countries have directly-elected executives (usually called presidents), while others have chief executives that are selected by a parliament or legislature. In the latter, it is more common that executive leaders (often called prime ministers, but also premiers, chancellors, or other titles) have to sustain the support of a coalition of parties in order to remain in power. When a prime minister can have his/her government toppled by a vote of no confidence in the parliament, the task of managing the governing coalition becomes paramount.

The selection of readings here outlines several of the features of how executives operate. One of the lessons that seems to cut across these readings is that most presidents and prime ministers are not simply able to dominate their political systems however they want. This is true in advanced, industrialized democracies and in so-called developing countries alike. Executive leaders such as presidents and prime ministers may often be the most powerful single individuals in their respective polities, but this does not mean unfettered power. As you read these items, consider the constraints on the actions of different leaders or the limitations to their power. This is clearer in some cases than in others, of course. But limitations on presidents happen even in Russia, where President Vladimir Putin has amassed considerably more power than presidents in most other countries. In this case, the view expressed by Vladimir Frolov is that even Putin will inexorably run into political difficulties in the long run from exercising leadership in a centralized, top-down fashion.

Another country where the "supreme leader" is reputed to be exceedingly powerful is Iran. This is a fascinating country for studying the executive, because the elected president has a degree of power that is circumscribed by the top clerics in the powerful Guardian Council; these leading religious figures review and rule upon the laws passed by the legislature and oversee the actions of the president. This is what leads many observers to consider Iran a "theocracy." But here again, even the supreme leader Ayatollah Ali Khamenei is limited by broader forces in the society. The tensions between the presidency and the clerics again show what powers executives have as well as the ways in which they are limited.

We might expect executive leaders to be even more "limited" in their powers when we get to robust democracies. In parliamentary systems such as India, we indeed find that prime ministers may exert authority but are subject to the support of legislators and the electorate. Executives are not simply in charge of politics: their actions and decisions are shaped by events as much as they shape them in turn. In countries such as India, where many parties elect legislators, it is often necessary for even the top vote-getting parties to seek partners in order to gain enough legislative seats to form a governing coalition. The drama of forming and sustaining a coalition is a major feature of politics in such systems, as the piece by Eswaran Sridharan shows. In recent years, the Congress Party has increasingly seen its political support slowly erode due to a number of governing challenges, including weaker economic growth, greater corruption, and challenges in foreign policy. Notice how this article describes both the electoral politics of India and the broader issues that are likely to shape elections in the country.

Putin's Leadership Trap

VLADIMIR FROLOV

The Moscow Times, by Vladimir Frolov, 14 April 2013.

When elected president in 2000, Vladimir Putin's first order of business seemed straightforward: strengthen the Russian state and bring it back from oligarchic control and regional warlordism. Consolidation was in order.

There were two ways to achieve that.

One way was taking a low view of human nature and would have required rebuilding formal political institutions to increase their capacity for checking power-grabbing appetites of politicians. This would have meant an emphasis on formal rules and procedures and their strict observance by all levels of government. Transparent rules and their unbiased enforcement would have guarded the state against destructive influences. Free and fair elections and equal justice under the law would have been central to the regime's legitimacy.

The alternative way was to build a highly personalized system of power that relies heavily on personal relationships and shadowy deals enforced through a selective application of informal and constantly changing rules. This required making the presidency, with the multiple security agencies at its disposal, politically dominant, while consistently gutting the power and legitimacy of all other state institutions. Elections would have to be tightly managed to guard against unplanned outcomes.

To be fair, Putin in 2000 was facing a situation where some institutions did not work, while others were captured by groups openly hostile to him. He viewed the institutions he did not personally control as likely threats to his rule.

He set out to use what Alyona Ledeneva of University College in London and author of the forthcoming book "Can Russia Modernize?" calls "informal governance"—personal networks and relationships, friends and loyalists in key positions and street-gang bargaining—to achieve the desired outcomes that could not be obtained through formal channels.

But what was initially intended as stop-gap measures to enact badly needed reforms, quickly acquired a logic of expanding the president's power through arbitrary, informal rules.

This logic views supreme power as flowing down from the popular elected leader to other political institutions who aspire to legitimacy while serving as little more than decorations. With decisions taken at the very top and objectives secured through informal instruments of governance, public institutions could simply imitate their constitutional functions.

Thus, the parliament does not legislate on its own but only adopts those initiatives that have been supported or introduced by the presidential administration, reducing the legislators' role to a rubber-stamp formality. Putin's 2010 off-the-cuff remark that he had thought of disbanding the State Duma at the height of the economic crisis in 2009 to expedite his anti-crisis measures demonstrates that public institutions are expendable if they stand in his way.

The end result: Inefficiency permeates state institutions. Unused, or undermined, formal institutions become weak and atrophy. They bleed competent workers. People shun them as they seek to serve their needs through informal networks of governance.

The country falls into what Ledeneva calls the "modernization trap of informality," or, simply put, when there are no effective people you can trust to run the country. The informal networks become unmanageable, loyalties corrupted, results diminished, and the nation's long-term vision is undermined.

Today, Putin is trying to make his system of informal governance more efficient. The war on corruption, the "nationalization of the elites," the People's Front are all tools to boost the projection of his power through informal instruments. The People's Front, for example, has the grim potential for supplanting all formal political institutions by creating a pretense of direct popular rule by an attentive national leader. The trap of informality becomes inescapable.

Why Rouhani Won—And Why Khamenei Let Him

The Ahmadinejad Era Comes to an Auspicious End

SUZANNE MALONEY

Reprinted by permission of FOREIGN AFFAIRS, June 16, 2013. Copyright © 2013 by the Council on Foreign Relations Inc. www.ForeignAffairs.com.

Four years ago, after the dubious reelection of Iranian President Mahmoud Ahmadinejad, the Iranian streets were filled with protestors demanding to know what had happened to their votes. This weekend, the voters finally got their answer—and, once more, they filled the country's streets. This time, though, they were celebrating as the government confirmed that Hassan Rouhani, the presidential candidate who had campaigned on promises of reform and reopening to the world, had won an overwhelming victory.

The election of Rouhani, a centrist cleric who has been close to Iran's apex of power since the 1979 revolution, is an improbably auspicious end to the Ahmadinejad era. Rouhani is a blunt pragmatist with plenty of experience maneuvering within Iran's theocratic system. He is far too sensible to indulge in a power grab à la Ahmadinejad. And, as a cleric, he assuages the fears of the Islamic Republic's religious class. He embraced reformist rhetoric during the campaign, but will not deviate too far from the system's principles, the foremost of which is the primacy of the Supreme Leader. Meanwhile, Rouhani's focus on the economic costs of Ahmadinejad's mismanagement resonates with the regime's traditionalists as well as with a population battered by a decade of intensifying hardship and repression. All in all, the new president might benefit from a broader base of support than any in Iran's postrevolutionary history, which will be an important asset as he seeks to navigate the country out of isolation and economic crisis.

Going into the election, a Rouhani victory seemed unlikely. The conservatives' favored candidate was said to be Saeed Jalili, a pious and prim bureaucrat who was appointed as lead nuclear negotiator six years ago. Jalili's chief qualifications for the post were his status as a "living martyr" (he lost a leg in the war with Iraq), his discolored forehead (from dutiful prayer), and his cultivation of Ayatollah Ali Khamenei over the past ten years. It is easy to understand why Jalili was seen as leading the pack; he is basically an improved version of Ahmadinejad, a younger generation hard-liner who boasts total commitment to the ideals of the revolution but who, given his limited national profile, would be perfectly subservient to Khamenei.

By contrast, Rouhani initially drummed up minimal excitement within Iran and even less attention outside the country, despite the implicit imprimatur of Ali Akbar Hashemi Rafsanjani, Iran's foremost power broker. Because the clergy is so unpopular in Iran at the moment, and because the hard-liners disparaged Rouhani's track record on the nuclear issue almost non-stop, his prospects seemed dim. Further, in the unlikely event that his campaign did gain steam, it seemed, hard-liners would have no qualms about doing whatever it took to neutralize a potential threat.

In retrospect, though, it is easy to see that Rouhani had a number of things going for him. First, his campaign was sharper than many gave it credit for. He pushed against the regime's red lines, for example, by promising to release political prisoners. And, in a clear reference to Mir Hossein Mousavi and Mehdi

Karroubi, two reformist candidates who were detained after the 2009 vote, he said that he would free all those who remain under house arrest as well. Rouhani sparred heatedly with Jalili's campaign chief and bypassed state media by releasing a compelling video that highlighted his experience during the war with Iraq (he was on the Supreme Defense Council, was a member of the High Council for Supporting War, and was commander of the Iran Air Defense Force, among other roles) and on nuclear negotiations (he was Iran's top nuclear negotiator from 2003 to 2005). His aggressive campaign caught the attention of a disaffected Iranian population, who eventually began to throng his rallies.

Rouhani also benefitted from an unprecedented alliance between Iran's embattled reform movement and the center-right faction to which Rouhani, as well as Rafsanjani, are generally understood to belong. The division between the two factions dates back to the earliest years of the revolution. It became more entrenched after the reformists gained power in 1997, when Mohammad Khatami, the reformist standard-bearer, was elected president in a major upset. By joining with the center-right now, the reformists got a path out of the political desert in which they have languished since the end of Khatami's presidency. By joining with the reformists, Rouhani got a powerful get-out-the-vote effort and the withdrawal from the race of Mohammad Reza Aref, the sole approved reformist candidate. By contrast, the conservative camp remained divided, never coalescing around a single candidate. Had it managed to do so, it could have at least forced the election into a run-off.

Of course, Rouhani's most powerful advantage was the bitter unhappiness of the Iranian people, who have witnessed the implosion of their currency, the return of austerity measures not seen since the Iran-Iraq War, and the erosion of their basic rights and freedoms over the past eight years. The fact that they were willing to hope again, even after the crushing disappointment of 2009 election, underscores a remarkable commitment to peaceful change and to democratic institutions.

All this might explain the massive turnout on election day and Rouhani's overwhelming popular victory. It does not explain, though, why Khamenei avoided the chicanery that plagued the 2009 vote and why he let the result stand.

One explanation is that the Ayatollah simply miscalculated and found himself, once again, overtaken by events when Rouhani's candidacy surged with little forewarning. Indeed, it is likely that Khamenei really did expect Iranians to vote for the conservatives. After all, the conservatives have held all the cards in Iran since 2005; they dominate its institutions and dictate the terms of the debate. With the leading reformists imprisoned or in exile, no one expected that the forces of change could be revived so powerfully. When his expectations proved off base last Friday, Khamenei could have simply opted not to risk a repeat of 2009.

There is another possibility, however, and one that better explains Khamenei's strangely permissive attitude toward Rouhani's edgy campaign and toward the extraordinary debate that took place between the eight remaining presidential candidates on state television only a week before the election. In that discussion, an exchange about general foreign policy issues morphed unexpectedly into a mutiny on the nuclear issue. One candidate, Ali Akbar Velayati, a scion of the regime's conservative base, attacked Jalili for failing to strike a nuclear deal and for permitting U.S.-backed sanctions on Iran to increase.

The amazingly candid discussion that followed Velayati's charge betrayed the Iranian establishment's awareness of the regime's increasing vulnerability. It could only be understood as an intervention—one initiated by the regime's most stalwart supporters and intended to rescue the system by acknowledging its precarious straits and appealing for pragmatism (rather than Jalili's dogmatism). The discussion was also an acknowledgement that the sanctions-induced miseries of the Iranian public can no longer be soothed with nuclear pageantry or even appeals to religious nationalism.

It is therefore possible to imagine that Khamenei's unexpected munificence, including his last-minute appeal for every Iranian—even those who don't support the Islamic Republic—to vote, was planned. In this case, those who see Rouhani's election as a replay of the shocking political upset that Khatami pulled off in 1997 are off base. Instead, Rouhani's election is an echo of Khamenei's sudden shift in 1988 and 1989, when he charged Rafsanjani, a pragmatist, with ending the war with Iraq, and then helped Rafsanjani win the presidency so that he could spearhead the post-war reconstruction program. Now, as then, Khamenei is not bent on infinite sacrifice. Perhaps allowing Rouhani's victory is his way of empowering a conciliator to repair Iran's frayed relations with the world and find some resolution to the nuclear dispute that enables the country to revive oil exports and resume normal trade.

That does not mean, of course, that Rouhani has an easy road ahead. He must wrangle the support of the hard-liners and lock in at least continued tacit backing from Khamenei. In doing so, he will have to overcome a decade of resentment. During his stint leading nuclear talks, Rouhani made the sole serious concession that the Islamic Republic has ever offered on its nuclear ambitions: a multi-year suspension of its enrichment activities that was ended just before Ahmadinejad took office.

The move won Rouhani the unending fury of the hard-liners, including Khamenei, who approved the deal but has publicly inveighed against Rouhani's nuclear diplomacy as recently as last summer. Today, however, many Iranians—including, apparently, many within the establishment—find his ability to craft a viable deal with the world on the nuclear issue appealing. His election thus suggests that a historic shift in Iran's approach to the world and to the nuclear standoff could be in the offing. Still, to overcome old antipathies among the conservatives and to advance his agenda for change within Iran's Machiavellian political culture, Rouhani will need the clear and unwavering support of Khamenei, something that the Supreme Leader has only accorded to one president during his 25-year tenure: Ahmadinejad, in his first term.

For Washington, meanwhile, the election offered stark confirmation that its strategy is working, at least to a point. The outcome confirmed that political will for a nuclear deal exists within the Islamic Republic. Even with a more moderate president at the helm, however, the nuclear issue will not be readily resolved, and Iran's divided political sphere is as difficult as ever. To overcome the deep-seated (and not entirely unjustified) paranoia of its ultimate decision-maker, the United States will need to be patient. It will need to understand, for example, that Rouhani will need to demonstrate to Iranians that he can produce tangible rewards for diplomatic overtures. That means that Washington should be prepared to offer significant sanctions relief in exchange for any concessions on the nuclear issue. Washington will also have to understand that Rouhani may face real constraints in seeking to solve the nuclear dispute without exacerbating the mistrust of the hard-liners. And all the while, the Obama administration will have to proceed cautiously, since appearing too effusive will diminish Rouhani's domestic standing.

In other words, the path out of isolation and economic crisis is perilous, but Iran's new president, who has sometimes been dubbed "the sheikh of diplomacy," may just be the right man at the right moment to walk it.

Drift and Confusion Reign in Indian Politics

ESWARAN SRIDHARAN

"Drift and Confusion Reign in Indian Politics" by Eswaran Sridharan. Reprinted with permission from *Current History* magazine. (Vol. 112, Issue 753, April 2013). © 2013 Current History, Inc.

As India heads into an election year, its politics seems characterized by confusion and drift. The Congress Party–led United Progressive Alliance (UPA) government, which began its second term in 2009 (hereafter referred to as UPA II), appears adrift on all fronts. Indeed, the party is in danger of losing its governing position in the next national election, which is due in the spring of 2014, with a new government to be sworn in by May 22 of that year.

It is not certain if the Congress will put forward heir apparent Rahul Gandhi as its prime ministerial candidate. Gandhi, the newly appointed party vice president, is the 42-year-old son of the party's president, Sonia Gandhi, and the scion of the Nehru-Gandhi family that has dominated Congress and Indian politics since independence.

It is not even certain if the election will be held next year, rather than advanced to some date in 2013. The latter is possible if the Congress Party thinks it could benefit from holding an early election, as its main rival, the Bharatiya Janata Party (BJP), miscalculated in 2004. An election this year also is possible if either or both of the Congress's supporters from outside the governing coalition—the left-of-center Samajwadi Party and the Scheduled Caste (formerly "untouchable")–based Bahujan Samaj Party, both based in India's largest state, Uttar Pradesh—decide to withdraw support, depriving the UPA II of its legislative majority.

State assembly elections in India are a pointer to the prospects of parties in subsequent national elections, and the Congress Party's performance in the state elections of 2012 was none too impressive. It lost Punjab to Akali Dal, a Sikh party allied with the BJP; won back the small states of Uttarakhand and Himachal Pradesh from the BJP; lost tiny Goa to the BJP; retained tiny Arunachal Pradesh and Manipur; and lost Gujarat to the BJP, headed in that state by the BJP's likely prime ministerial candidate, the controversial Narendra Modi. In India's largest state, Uttar Pradesh, the Congress finished a poor fourth in the assembly elections, quite unlike its second-place showing in the state in the 2009 national election.

The current year will see assembly elections in as many as eight states, and possibly a ninth (Jharkhand). The small states of Nagaland, Meghalaya, and Tripura in the northeast already held elections in February. (The Congress won only Meghalaya; the Left Front won Tripura, and a regional party won Nagaland.) Mizoram, also in the northeast, will vote in November. Meanwhile, five straight Congress-BJP contests will take place in the two-party states of Karnataka, Rajasthan, Madhya Pradesh, Chhattisgarh, and Delhi (technically a federal territory, not a state, but with more lower house seats than several small states).

These state, assembly elections, particularly the five Congress-BJP contests, are straws in the wind indicating shifts in public approval between the UPA II coalition and the BJP-led coalition, the National Democratic Alliance (NDA). At the moment, the governing coalition's electoral strength remains anything but certain.

The Growth Deficit

Nor does the state of the economy or its prospects in the coming 12 months appear to augur well for the Congress and its allies. Today, at the start of fiscal year 2013–14 (April to March), the Indian economy is in its worst shape since the governing coalition came to power in May 2004—and chances for a significant recovery before a 2014 election seem poor. After three years of over 9 percent annual GDP growth in fiscal 2005–08, and a slight slowdown (to 6.5 percent in 2008–09, and 8.6 percent in 2009–10) due to the international financial crisis and subsequent global downturn, the economy recovered to a 9 percent-plus growth rate again in 2010–11. Yet the rate slid to 6.4 percent in 2011–12. Estimates for 2012–13 are down to 5 percent.

In a country where a third of the inhabitants are under age 15, and 54 percent are under 25, and where only 18 percent of college-age citizens are enrolled in higher education, huge numbers enter the labor market every year. A significantly higher growth rate—together with a composition of growth that generates jobs for a largely unskilled or low-skilled labor force—is necessary to contain unemployment to socially and politically manageable levels, compared with developed economies with a demographic composition weighted toward older age groups. More rapid growth is required, too, to bring in the tax revenues that are needed to support the social programs that most political parties perceive as necessary to win public support—particularly in rural areas, where the majority of Indians live, and among the poor and disadvantaged social groups.

It is doubtful if the strategy employed to win the 2009 election by the Congress in its UPA I (2004–09) avatar will work for 2014. UPA I rode on the back of cumulative economic reforms by earlier Congress, United Front, and BJP-led governments. The reforms released growth impulses by raising the savings and investment rates (from 23 percent before liberalization to the mid-30s), and encouraged entrepreneurship by deregulation and trade liberalization.

UPA I was also helped by the global economic boom of 2002–08. The 9 percent-plus growth of 2005–08, with growth slowing just slightly in the election year 2008–09, allowed a massive expansion of social programs aimed at the poor and rural areas. In particular, the 2005 National Rural Employment Guarantee Act assured 100 days of wage work for at least one member of a rural family. It also allowed a waiver of farmers' loans from public financial institutions in the year before the 2009 election. In addition, some popular governance reforms, such as the 2005 Right to Information Act, significantly improved transparency in government.

Dwindling Options

As of now, however, there is little fiscal space for a growth boost led by public infrastructure investment, or for expanded antipoverty or public employment programs. The finance minister is under pressure to bring the fiscal deficit down. The 2013–14 budget tries to stimulate the economy based on heroic assumptions about tax revenue and public enterprise divestment revenues, in turn based on assumptions of 6.1 to 6.7 percent growth, and thereby a reduction of the fiscal deficit from 5.2 percent to 4.8 percent of GDP despite a rise in spending. These expectations are unlikely to materialize. Inflation, in the high single digits for over two years, has eased slightly after monetary tightening over most of the past two years. But monetary easing could stoke inflation again. And in India, inflation, particularly of food prices, can be fatal in an election. Therefore, the government has few policy options.

Part of the domestic reason for the growth slow-down is that the investment rate is down to about 31 percent of GDP, from 35-plus percent before. Some of this is due to delays in land acquisition for new projects, particularly mining projects that displace tribal people from forest areas, as well as to fear of public agitation by rural residents who lose precious farmland to such projects. Improved laws and policy implementation on these fronts could boost investment in infrastructure and industry and revive the growth momentum. However, second-generation market-oriented reforms such as labor market liberalization or privatization of public enterprises—which will help boost long-term growth and employment—will not be politically possible in an election year.

The Congress Party was lucky in the 2009 national election. On its own it won the second highest number of seats (21 out of 80) in the large state of Uttar Pradesh, and with its allies won 25 out of 42 seats in West Bengal, a state that had been dominated by the Left Front (communist) parties since 1977. The Congress seems most unlikely to be able to repeat its feats in Uttar Pradesh in 2014, going by its dismal performance in the state assembly elections in 2012, or in West Bengal, where its partner, and the largest coalition partner in UPA II, the Trinamool Congress, has left the coalition.

Likewise, its prospects are highly uncertain in the large southern state of Andhra Pradesh, where the party has split and the splinter faction won most of the local elections in 2012. In the southern state of Tamil Nadu, the Congress's alliance partner Dravida Munnetra Kazhagam (DMK) seems in a weak position. DMK lost power in the state assembly in 2011, and remains divided by internal rivalries deriving from a succession battle.

The Search for a Majority

In short, there is hardly a state where the Congress can confidently assume victory—even though it is currently in power on its own or as a senior coalition partner in 12 states, and as a junior partner in Jammu and Kashmir, and in the federal territory of Delhi. These states and Delhi have a total of 183 seats, or 90 short of the majority mark of 273 seats in the lower house. Compared to this, the BJP is currently in power on its own in five states (Gujarat, Madhya Pradesh, Chhattisgarh, Karnataka, and Goa), totaling 96 seats in parliament; and as junior partner in two more, Bihar and Punjab, totaling 53 seats.

Indian state party systems have been evolving toward bipolarity over the decades. Today nearly all the states—the notable exception being Uttar Pradesh, with its 80 seats—are bipolarized between two parties, or two coalitions, or a party and a co-alition. The way the Indian electoral system works, the main influence on a party's prospects for win-ning parliamentary seats in a particular state is whether it is one of the two leading parties in that state. If this is the case, it can benefit from a swing in its favor that will give it most of the seats in the state. This could be the case if it is in power in the state and runs a popular government perceived to be performing well. Alternatively, being in power could prove a liability if the government is per-ceived as performing poorly.

The Congress is one of the two leading parties in as many as 24 states and in all 7 federal territo-ries, including Delhi—totaling 342 seats in parlia-ment. However, it is not one of the two leading parties in four major states: Uttar Pradesh, Bihar, West Bengal, and Tamil Nadu, totaling as many as 201 seats. The prospect of the Congress winning a significant number of seats on its own from these states is quite limited (though not impossible), and the party has relied on coalition partners in the three most recent elections.

This means that, out of 543 elected seats in the lower house (2 members are nominated by the presi-dent), the Congress Party faces the almost impos-sible task of winning a majority of 273 from the 342 seats in states in which it is one of the two leading parties. Hence the imperative to find coalition part-ners, a strategy that goes against the grain for many older Congress leaders accustomed to being part of the sole ruling party for over 40 years until 1989.

Performing a similar calculation allows us to assess the position of the opposition BJP. The BJP is one of the two leading parties in 10 states and 5 federal territories, totaling 169 seats. With its cur-rent NDA allies, it is one of the two leading coali-tions in another three states with 101 seats. That makes a grand total of 270 seats, or just less than half of all lower house seats. Among these states and territories, the BJP faces the Congress as its principal opponent in 17 of them. Even with its allies, it is not one of the two leading parties in states and federal territories totaling 273 seats. Thus, to succeed in the upcoming national election, the BJP needs to expand its independent electoral appeal and forge more alliances, including possibly repairing broken alliances. Or it must be able to attract significant postelection coalition partners.

Confused Opposition

What might possibly help the Congress and its UPA allies are confusion and incoherence within the principal opposition party, the Hindu nationalist BJP, and within the BJP-led alliance, the National Democratic Alliance. The NDA has shrunk since its heyday when it was in power from 1998 to 2004 under Prime Minister Atal Bihari Vajpayee. Several key regional parties, which account for one of the two major parties in each of a number of big states, have left the NDA. These include the Telugu Desam Party of Andhra Pradesh, which was a vital prop of the NDA government; the Trinamool Congress, which later became, until 2012, the largest partner of the Congress in UPA II, and which is currently the ruling party of West Bengal; and the Biju Janata Dal, the ruling party of Orissa. Another electoral ally of 2004 that has broken with the BJP (though it was never part of the NDA) is the All India Anna DMK, currently the ruling party in Tamil Nadu.

What is worse for the BJP, its largest current ally, the Janata Dal (United)—with which it is in a co-alition ruling the large state of Bihar—has threat-ened to leave the NDA if the BJP chooses Modi, the divisive chief minister of Gujarat, as its prime min-isterial candidate. Modi stands accused of being responsible for the anti-Muslim riots of 2002 in Gujarat, in which about 2,000 people, mainly Mus-lims, were killed. Modi could rally the Hindu na-tionalist faithful. He could also appeal to a broad section of urban voters impressed by his steward-ship of the economic development of fast-growing Gujarat. Even so, he would certainly alienate not only India's minorities but also a significant number of moderate Hindus, and for these reasons would drive away existing or potential allies who depend to some extent on Muslim and Christian minority votes in their states. Thus a Modi candi-dacy could cut both ways. BJP strategists are, of course, aware of this.

However, they do not seem to have, or be able to decide on, a credible alternative to Modi. And Modi himself seems well aware of this. Since 2002 he has seen to it that his state has experienced no repeat of the anti-minority rioting, and he has assiduously tried to project himself as a leader who symbolizes growth and good governance. Gujarat's chief minister has wooed the Indian big business elite, which has largely reciprocated his overtures, and he has also tried to ride the anticorruption movement that has emerged over the past two years, rather than resort to minority-bashing rhetoric.

Nevertheless, it is safe to say the minorities remain deeply suspicious of Modi. Muslims and Christians total 15 percent of India's population. They represent an important swing vote in a substantial minority of parliamentary constituencies. They also make up a significant component of the voter base of several regional parties that the BJP might need as coalition partners before or after the next national election.

The great uncertainty is whether either the Congress or the BJP will garner a large enough number of seats to become the nucleus of a viable coalition, that is, one that can attract postelection partners from among regional parties (and leftist parties too, in the case of the Congress). It is quite possible that we will see a 1996-type situation, in which a minority coalition of regional (and possibly leftist) parties with external support from the Congress or the BJP forms the government.

It is also possible that no such viable coalition can be formed. In other words, the prospect of India without a stable governing coalition—whether established by the Congress Party, by the BJP, or by regional parties supported by either the Congress or the BJP—is not beyond the realm of possibility. Everything depends on the precise arithmetic of the legislature that is elected and the equations among the parties. If a sustainable coalition proves beyond reach, India might be in for another early election, as happened in the 1990s when three national elections were held in four years (1996, 1998, and 1999). This is the most worrisome scenario from the standpoint of stability and sound policy.

Leadership Doubts

Both major parties have leadership problems, which, though not crises, must be resolved to project a credible image before the next election. The Congress Party is most likely to retire Prime Minister Manmohan Singh in the event of forming a government in 2014 (he will be 81 by then), but it has not yet put forward the most talked about alternative, Rahul Gandhi, as its prime ministerial candidate. Gandhi has maintained long public silences on issues, occasionally broken by carefully crafted statements. This contrasts with Modi, the BJP's most likely candidate for prime minister, who is vocal on all manner of issues. Modi has increasingly dominated the media, including social media, since his third consecutive victory in Gujarat's assembly election in December 2012.

Gandhi has not, despite repeated invitations, taken up a cabinet position. He has preferred, since 2004, to work to rebuild the Congress as a broad-based and responsive political machine that can deliver electoral victories across the country. He has particularly focused on rebuilding the party in his home state of Uttar Pradesh, where it has been out of power since 1989 and was relegated to fourth place in the 2012 assembly election. His record in this effort has been mixed at best, which does not bode well for either him or the party.

However, he seems to see his role, like that of his mother Sonia Gandhi, the Congress's president, as a unifying symbol and rallying point for the party, remaining above factionalism and regionalism, rather than as the political executive of a government department. It is possible the Congress might go into the national election without naming a candidate for prime minister, as it did in 2004. But if faced with a strong, if controversial and divisive, BJP candidate in Modi, the strategy might not work.

The BJP also shows, despite the party's and Modi's aggressiveness, a streak of desperation. In recent state assembly elections it mostly retained what it already held, but it lost power in the small states of Uttarakhand and Himachal Pradesh, and wrested only tiny Goa from the Congress. It has lost four major allied parties, mentioned earlier, from its electoral coalition since 2004. A defeat in 2014 would be the BJP's third consecutive loss in a national election.

Electoral Wild Cards

The wild cards in the run-up to the national election, and in the process of government formation after it, will be key players in the various regional parties—that is, those occupying the non-Congress, non-BJP space in the Indian party system. Non-Congress, non-BJP parties collectively received 50 percent of the votes in the last national election. Actually the term "regional party" is a misnomer. Almost all of these are single-state parties. Even the Communist Party of India (Marxist), which has a base in three states, West Bengal, Kerala, and Tripura, is not a regional party, since its state strongholds are in three different regions. These parties in aggregate account for one of the two leading parties in as many as 11 major states totaling 315 seats.

Of the regional parties, three are long-standing allies of the BJP in the NDA: the Sikh party Akali Dal of Punjab, the Shiv Sena of Maharashtra, and the Janata Dal (United) of Bihar. Three more—the Telugu Desam Party of Andhra Pradesh, Biju Janata Dal of Orissa, and Asom Gana Parishad of Assam—will not ally with the Congress since it is their main rival in their states. They have allied with the BJP in the past and could do so again. A significant possibility, depending on the parliamentary election results, is a minority coalition of regional and leftist parties, supported from the outside by the Congress, as was the case with the short-lived United Front governments in 1996–98, or even a minority coalition (minus the left) supported by the BJP.

Part of the confusion in Indian politics stems from the fact that prospects for government formation and hence policy trajectories depend on the precise arithmetic of pre-electoral and post-electoral coalitions in a party system with a large number of regional parties that can go in various directions.

The Politics of Scandal

Since 2011, a large-scale anticorruption movement has emerged in civil society in response to graft scandals exposed by the media, and this has undermined the legitimacy of the Congress more than that of other parties. Several major scandals, involving amounts running possibly into billions of dollars, have erupted in recent years. Among the officials implicated are federal ministers and state chief ministers of the ruling UPA II coalition, including the Congress Party.

These scandals include the allegedly crooked sale of second-generation cell phone spectrum allocations in 2008, involving the former telecom minister A. Raja of the DMK, a coalition partner of the Congress; a 2010 Commonwealth Games scandal involving contracts awarded by Congress politician Suresh Kalmadi; a real estate scandal involving the former Maharashtra chief minister Ashok Chavan; a "coalgate" scandal over the allocation of coal mining permits to favored firms by the UPA II government; and most recently a payoff in an arms import deal. All of these cases have involved bribery charges in connection with the allocation of publicly owned or regulated resources to favored private firms, or with government contracts in the cases of the Commonwealth Games and arms imports allegations.

The scandals sparked a huge public agitation led by the charismatic, septuagenarian rural leader and anticorruption crusader Anna Hazare. Protesters demanded the passing of a law that would institute an ombudsman to investigate corruption charges against public officials, a process that could be activated by citizen complaints.

The Congress Party was put on the defensive, and the Anna Hazare movement appeared at first to be coordinating its positions and attacks on the government and ruling party with the BJP-led opposition. However, after huge demonstrations in Delhi and saturation media coverage, particularly in the summer of 2011 and much of 2012, the movement split and entered formal politics with the registration of a single-issue, anticorruption political party called the Common Mans Party. And this party has trained its attacks on both the Congress and the BJP.

The anticorruption movement is part of a wider arena of civil society groups and activist media that take up and magnify public discontent. This was again reflected in massive public agitation and media coverage concerning the issue of women's safety, following a horrific and deadly gang rape of a student in Delhi in December 2012. These largely urban, middle-class movements and the associated media coverage have unsettled politicians and the ruling parties at the national and stale levels. Many in the political class are not accustomed to such public outcry and activism, and for many a degree of corruption is routine.

The anticorruption movement initially was felt to have made the ruling Congress Party and its allies electorally vulnerable. However, the fallout also has affected the BJP, following corruption scandals associated with iron ore mining and sand quarrying in Karnataka and Uttarakhand, respectively, and corruption charge against Nitin Gadkari, the BJP president, who was forced step down from his post in January 2013.

Uncertainty Abroad

On the foreign policy front, there seem to be confusion and drift too. India's key security threats, Pakistan and China, are both nuclear powers with a long-standing covert cooperative relationship in the nuclear and missile areas. India has long and disputed borders and a history of conflict with both countries. Yet relations have not significantly improved with either Pakistan or China under the UPA II—in some respects they have deteriorated.

India-Pakistan relations took a nosedive after Pakistani terrorists attacked Mumbai in November 2008. However, despite an absence of meaningful action by Pakistan against the terror groups thought to be behind the attack, the UPA II sought to improve relations. Officials focused on improving trade ties in order eventually to boost political relations. Relations remain frosty and distrustful nevertheless. The number of shooting incidents along the de facto border in Kashmir has increased over the past year despite an official cease-fire.

China, likewise, has stepped up aggressive patrolling, and though there have been no shooting incidents, the number of intrusions along the undefined Line of Actual Control has increased over the past two years. Political relations with Beijing have not improved despite a rapid growth in trade, such that China has emerged as India's second largest trading partner. Beijing has indicated shifts on

Kashmir toward the Pakistani position, as well as reasserted its claims to the northeastern state of Arunachal Pradesh in its visa policy. China recently initiated work on three dams on the Brahmaputra River in Tibet without informing downstream India. And Pakistan reportedly has handed over management of its Gwadar port in the Arabian Sea, near the mouth of the Persian Gulf, to a Chinese company.

Relations with the United States, thought to be the key to the long-term support that India is perceived to need vis-à-vis an unstoppably rising China, have been adrift. This is so despite the land-mark Indo-US nuclear deal of 2008, negotiated by the UPA I government with the George W. Bush administration. That agreement opened up imports of civilian nuclear reactors, fuel, and components to India in exchange for some nonproliferation obligations, while India received de facto US acceptance of its existing weapons capabilities. The deal led to an expectation of realignment toward the United States, or at least a greater tilt in India's formally nonaligned posture. This has not quite happened under UPA II, leading to a degree of disappointment with India in the United States, and doubts about whether India can be a reliable partner.

The Indo-US nuclear deal, though subject to various interpretations, should have enabled a distinct Indian shift toward the United States, since it finessed the nonproliferation issue. This was the third and only remaining irritant in the relationship after the cold war-era Indian tilt toward Moscow and US tilt toward Pakistan, both of which had been corrected under Presidents Bill Clinton and Bush. However, India has placed no nuclear reactor import contract with US companies since then, preferring other suppliers. Nor did the United States win a deal to supply India with 126 multi-role combat aircraft, a deal that went last year to a French firm.

New Delhi has been hedging against China's rise by diversifying relationships with a range of powers, including the United States but not exclusively. The understanding of the world behind this strategy, a narrative that has been called "Nonalignment 2.0," is one in which the United States is relatively declining and a multipolarity of sorts is emerging, a trend that

India needs skillfully to navigate and exploit. Both India's strategic foreign policy orientation and Indo-US relations will depend to a major extent on whether the second Barack Obama administration, after its recently announced pivot of forces to Asia, will constrain or accommodate China. This issue will unfold over the next 12 months at a time when Indian politics is in a state of election-year uncertainty.

Indian governance continues to confront complex challenges that, in combination, present roadblocks to reforms. Contradictory pulls and pressures arising from a fragmented party system within a federal system lead to minority coalition governments at the federal level, while several states are ruled by opposition parties. A number of key economic reforms need action at the state level. In addition, a large part of the Indian population is still very poor and looks to government programs for sustenance. And graft, ultimately rooted in a corrupt campaign finance system, remains pervasive.

That Indian politics will be characterized by confusion and drift until the coming election seems certain today. What remains very uncertain is whether a strong and stable government—a government capable of liberalizing labor markets and privatizing public enterprises in order to lift the economy onto a track of sustained high growth, while enduring short-term political costs in doing so—will be formed and last its term.

DISCUSSION QUESTIONS

1) Vladimir Putin may seem like one of the most powerful and unrestrained presidents in the world, but in what ways is his power limited according to Frolov? What are the contradictions in his style of rule that may eventually result in him being able to wield less power? Given the prospects outlined by Frolov, why do leaders not restrain themselves more in their exercise of power?

2) How can you characterize where power lies in Iran's political system? What is the power of the president vis-à-vis the clerics? Does this piece tell us something only about a country like Iran that has a very unique political environment? Or does this suggest anything about the nature of executive power generally?

3) Can you lay out some of the calculations being made by participants in India's politics, drawing on the piece by Sridharan? Consider the voters first: What will shape their vote in upcoming elections, especially as it regards which parties will govern? Consider also the elites in political parties: What are they thinking about with regard to the elections and with regard to the prospect for forming coalitions? Does the image portrayed in this piece speak well to the robustness of India's democracy, or does it suggest that India's democracy is a mess?

Interest Groups, Political Parties, and Party Systems

The formal institutions that shape politics include the various branches of government, but many other political institutions are essential to understanding how government works. Especially important are those groups that contest elections and try to shape debates about policy, namely interest groups and political parties. In this section we consider how parties operate in different societies and how public opinion becomes aggregated into the political process. Different societies have party systems that manifest in different ways, such as a dominant single party, a two-party system, or a multi-party system. As you read the readings in this section, consider how interest groups (or indeed the citizenry at large) might integrate into the political process differently in these different party systems.

When considering how political parties operate, a common lament is that they end up being "too partisan." Loosely speaking, this argument goes that parties are concerned with winning elections and getting their own members into positions of political power, more than they are interested in the "common good" or overall "well-being of the country." This criticism takes different forms, and comparative perspectives can help us assess whether this is a universal truth or is a particular feature of certain types of party systems.

One perspective is adopted by Pietro Nivola in a piece for the Brookings Institution, a think tank (or policy analysis organization) based in Washington, D.C. Nivola offers the idea that partisanship itself can be welcomed. In a sense, Nivola argues, the United States is becoming more "parliamentary" or "majoritarian," with the two major parties voting much more like they are in lock-step. He argues this can enhance accountability and even promote civic engagement, as it becomes increasingly clear to voters what each party stands for. There are caveats for Nivola—mainly having to do with the fact that a small minority can block legislation, but this is more a problem of the legislature than one of partisanship itself.

Those debating the merits and drawbacks of the American two-party system often contrast it with the parliamentary systems of Europe. Looking at Germany, Clay Risen concludes that the parliamentary style of democracy has its own major problems. In particular, political parties tend to fragment, while the big "broad-based" parties in two-party systems are more coherent and push politics toward consensus. This debate about presidential and parliamentary democracies persists in many forms, with advocates around the world often suggesting that some of the ills of a particular political system could be resolved by shifting to another system.

Finally, we can consider how parties and interests play out in a country like China, where a single party dominates government and interest groups are tightly restricted. Tom Friedman's snapshot of "five brief news items" intimates that China is a society in transition: the old Communist party elite will increasingly recognize the need to be more responsive to the populace and its expressions of discontent. In an authoritarian (yet economically modernizing) system, these may not take the form of mass rallies or conventional interest group mobilization, but instead may percolate through the blogosphere and other venues. As Friedman notes, maintaining a stable society in the midst of inequality and potential discord will require a "two-way conversation" between the government and the governed. How this plays out will have significant implications for the ability of the Communist Party to remain China's dominant political force.

In Defense of Partisan Politics

PIETRO S. NIVOLA

"In Defense of Partisan Politics" by Pietro S. Nivola, The Brookings Institution, April 8, 2009. Reprinted by permission.

From the steps of the Capitol on January 20th, President Barack Obama appealed for an end to the politics of "petty grievances" and "worn-out dogmas." The year 2009 was supposed to mark the dawn of a post-partisan era. With any luck, Democrats and Republicans would stop quarreling, and would finally get down to work together. The time had come, exhorted the new president drawing from Scripture, to lay "childish" polemics aside.

But childish or not, America's partisan politics have remained as stubbornly intense and polarized as ever. To paraphrase more Scripture, the lambs remain unwilling to lie down with the lions. And there are few signs of partisan swords being turned into plowshares. Far from opening a new age of bipartisan comity in the House of Representatives, the president and the Democratic majority received not a single Republican vote in their first big legislative test, the roll call on the so-called American Recovery and Reinvestment Act (the "stimulus"). More recently, not one Republican in the Senate or the House voted for the concurrent resolution on the president's budget. More, not less, of such party-line voting probably lies ahead.

So here's a heretical thought: Maybe, among the many inflated expectations that we attach to the Obama presidency and should temper, those about the advent of "post-partisanship" ought to be lowered, drastically. In other words, get over it. The rough-and-tumble of our party politics is here to stay. What's more—and this is even greater heresy—not everything about that fact of political life is horrible.

Majoritarianism

The Democratic and Republican parties today are each more cemented in their ideologies and more distinct than they were a generation ago. In Congress, party lines used to be blurred by the existence of so-called liberal Republicans and truly conservative Democrats. Now those factions are dwindling species. Why they are dying out is a long story

that has been the object of an extensive study titled *Red and Blue Nation?* cosponsored by Brookings and the Hoover Institution at Stanford University. For present purposes, suffice it to recognize that the disputes between Republicans and Democrats are about more than "petty grievances" (though there are plenty of them, too); the party differences run deep and fundamentally reflect differing convictions held by large blocs of voters, not just their elected representatives. An example: Whereas a staggering 84 percent of Democrats seem to believe "it's the government's responsibility to make sure that everyone in the United States has adequate health care," only 34 percent of Republicans evidently concur, according to a reputable national poll taken last November.

Because both parties are more cohesive, they are also more disciplined. If you are a member of Congress and you basically agree with your party's position on most salient issues, why defect to the other side on key votes? Americans of the baby-boom generation are not accustomed to seeing this high degree of party unity. They remember the old days when the main way to do business on Capitol Hill was to cobble together ad-hoc coalitions. Want a civil rights bill? Get northern Democrats and Republican moderates on your side, and hope that you have enough votes to overpower the conservative phalanx of southern Democrats and states'-rights Republicans. Want more money for the Vietnam War in the 1960s? Combine solid support from that bipartisan conservative bloc with plenty of other hawkish stalwarts in both parties (think reliable GOP loyalists like Everett Dirksen but also Scoop Jackson Democrats), and you'd get the funds.

Increasingly, the contemporary party system bears scant resemblance to the one that prevailed a half-century ago. What it resembles instead is politics in most other periods of American history, for example the late nineteenth century when the two parties were also internally coherent and keenly at odds. During such periods, the American parties have behaved more like political parties in parliamentary regimes—where the in-party (the governing majority) rules, and the out-party (the minority) consistently forms a loyal opposition.

Notice this distinctive feature of the parliamentary model: Not only *can* the majority, voting in lockstep, prevail with no help from opposition members; all it needs on board in order to legislate is a *simple* majority of the legislators. Supermajorities—the requirement in the U.S. Senate to override a filibuster—are never the norm. A parliamentary system, in other words, operates much like our congressional budget reconciliation process where as little as a one-vote margin in the House and as little as 51 votes in the Senate suffice to adopt a bill.

There is much handwringing about the trend toward majoritarian—that is, parliamentary-style—politics in the United States. Democrats moaned when the GOP, led by George W. Bush, drove tax cuts through Congress on nearly a party-line vote with Vice President Cheney casting the tie-breaker. Now, Republicans will groan if the Obama administration and the Democratic congressional leadership opt to use the reconciliation procedure to ram health-care reform into law. But is all the lamentation justified?

Accountability

One of the advantages of parliamentary democracy is that the electorate knows what to expect. What you see (or vote for) is what you get. As America becomes parliamentary, if voters elect a Republican president and congressional majority, here's a good bet: Tax cuts will be on the way. If voters elect a Democratic president and congressional majority—running on a party platform that declares universal health care to be a "moral imperative"—guess what? Health-care legislation to extend coverage will happen. Now, granted one can debate the policy merits of either party's priorities. Robotic tax-cutting runs up deficits—and so almost certainly will health care that covers everybody. But if the voters have explicitly empowered their elected officials to do either of these things, who are "we" to stand in the way?

Further, the voters have plenty of opportunity to change their minds. If they decide that mistakes are being made—or that they prefer an alternative agenda to the one being proffered by the party in power—they can throw the rascals out. Indeed, in this country, unlike practically every other democracy, the public gets a chance to entertain that option with extraordinary frequency: every two years.

Nor, from the standpoint of democratic theory, is it easy to make an airtight case for why Congress and the president should be forced to muster supermajorities to enact their most important priorities. Ours, like any sound democracy, has to balance principles of majority rule with minority rights. But a political order in which technically just over 7 percent of a legislature—that is, a sub-group that possibly represents as little as 10 percent of the population—can have the last word, as our Senate arithmetic can imply, raises serious questions of democratic accountability and even legitimacy. Let's face it; making a regular practice of putting, in effect, veto-power in the hands of a minority is hard to square with a government of the people, by the people, for the people.

The Virtues of a Choice, Not an Echo

There is one other thing to say in defense of heightened partisanship: It has succeeded in making elections more interesting.

Voters have a tendency to become indifferent and apathetic when asked to choose between alternatives that display not "a dime's worth of difference," as the old saying went about our two-party system during the heyday of bipartisan comingling.

By contrast, as Marc J. Hetherington of Vanderbilt University demonstrates in a key chapter of *Red and Blue Nation?*, voter participation has surged as the partisan divide has grown sharper.

The electorate is not turned off by the chasm, and contestation, between the parties. On the contrary, Hetherington finds, the polarized political parties have animated voters of all stripes—liberals, conservatives, and moderates. Growing civic engagement and voter turnouts are hallmarks of a vibrant democracy, not of a "broken" one.

German Lessons

CLAY RISEN

This essay was originally published in *Democracy: A Journal of Ideas*.

Should progressives frustrated with our democracy pine for a parliamentary system? In a word—nein.

Germany's national elections took place on Sunday, September 27, a warm, clear fall day that brought people out to Berlin's sidewalk promenades, trying to soak up one last day of good weather before the long winter. My wife, two friends, and I, all of us political junkies, had plans to hit a few parks and museums, then settle on a bar to watch the returns once the polls closed at six. Later that night we'd work our way to one of the campaign parties around town.

At 6:05, just done with a leisurely bite at a garden café in Charlottenburg, we rang up another American friend with our evening agenda. "Not sure the parties will be swinging much longer," he said. "The election's just been called." With stunning accuracy, exit polls were already showing a decisive win for the coalition of Angela Merkel's Christian Democrats (CDU) and the pro-business Free Democrats (FDP). By 6:10, concession speeches were being prepared; within the hour, the election was over.

We scrambled to find a bar with a TV. There were crowded pubs everywhere—but the patrons were all watching soccer. After half an hour we found a bar with an unused flat screen. "Can we watch the election returns?" we asked the server. Judging by the look on her face, we might as well have asked about competitive knitting. But hey, we were paying customers, so she said yes. We watched for an hour, and not a single person joined us.

What a contrast to last November in Washington, when my wife and I bounced from crowded bar to bar watching the U.S. presidential election returns. To be fair, we were on the verge of electing the nation's first African-American president, while this year Germany was bringing to a merciful end what everyone, even some of the candidates, deemed the country's most boring campaign ever.

Then again, whether one considered the election "boring" speaks volumes about the difference between German and American political cultures. True, Merkel and her Social Democratic (SPD) opponent, Frank-Walter Steinmeier, made for excellent insomnia cures (a last-minute music video by the sexed-up "Steinmeier Girl" notwithstanding). This year, barely 70 percent of Germans voted, the lowest number in postwar history. But to an American observer, the election had all the elements of high political drama: The sudden, double-digit power of the far-left Linke party, the once-dominant center-left SPD fighting for relevance amid tanking poll numbers, the popularity of the pro-market center-right during a deep recession.

Germany is a vibrant parliamentary democracy, yet its body politic is asleep. Germans either trust their elected officials to take care of things, or they sink into a deep political apathy. The latter camp is growing: A recent poll showed only 49 percent of Germans had faith in their democratic institutions, dropping to 29 percent in the former East Germany. Yet aside from a small activist current, they rarely try to change things.

Next to European health care and European urban planning, the aspect of European life for which liberal Americans pine most often is the continent's parliamentary politics. Whenever I run down the litany of niche German political parties—alongside the Greens, the FDP, and the Linke, there's the Animal Protection Party, the new-age Violet Party, and the Retired People's Party, among others—for left-leaning American friends, they sigh and say, "I wish." Parties that actually represent people's interests? Coalitions built on cross-party compromise, rather than ideological stone walls? Wouldn't that be great, they say.

A progressive's dream. I agree. Or rather, I did, before I spent this previous August and September in Germany. After seeing German politics up close, I'll take my two-party system, thank you very much.

There is a lot to recommend the political structure in Germany. Just look at the results: Since the founding of the federal republic in 1949, it has held the country together through the era postwar re-building, the Cold War, the left-wing violence of the 1970s, the fall of the Berlin Wall, and reunification.

In the early postwar years, Germany, like the United States, had two massive "people's" parties, the center-right CDU and the center-left SPD, along with the much smaller, eccentric FDP, which over the last 60 years has aligned with both sides of the spectrum. For nearly 40 years, the SPD and CDU accounted for about 90 percent of the vote.

This worked, for a while. But already by the late 1960s, frustrations were growing. Because the parties are structured as membership organizations, with lifelong career ladders, it is almost impossible for grassroots movements, even inside the membership, to influence a party's course. The parties may represent "the people," but they are led by oligarchic central committees, which have little incentive to adapt in response to changes in voting patterns.

Little incentive—until it's too late. As in the United States, the left-wing radicalism of the 1960s and 1970s drew on deep generational and political contradictions in German society. But it lasted longer, and expressed itself much more violently, than in America because there was no party system to absorb it. By 1972, former radicals in the United States were campaigning for McGovern; in Germany, they were bombing U.S. Army bases.

Eventually, some of those radicals entered politics as the Green party; others shaved, put on suits, and joined the SPD. But the SPD bigwigs were unwilling to make room for them. Many of them were never entirely comfortable there, and out of frustration with SPD Chancellor Gerhard Schröder's welfare-law reforms of the early 2000s they left to form the Linke.

Clinton's welfare reforms of the 1990s also produced enormous disagreement on the left. But because there was nowhere for dissenting factions to go, they had to fight it out internally—and, over time, these centripetal forces created a new consensus, which formed the basis for Barack Obama's ride into the White House and the backbone of support for his progressive agenda. The German left, on the other hand, simply picked up its toys and went to play elsewhere, thanks to the centrifugal forces of the parliamentary system. The result is a rump center-left, an eco-centric postmaterialist left, and a self-righteous neo-Marxist far-left, none of which had anything constructive to say during the recent economic crisis, a time when, typically, left-wing, pro-government parties are needed most.

The constant proliferation of parties is an expression of the system's shortcomings, not its strengths; rather than adapt to sociopolitical changes, as America's does, it fragments. Having three left parties, each with its own agenda and suspicions, is no way to get progressive legislation through the Bundestag. The Democrats may not be perfect, but at least they stick together behind a set of principles about how the country should be run.

And just as the Linke is establishing its bona fides—it won an astounding 12 percent of the vote in September's election—along comes yet another fissure in German politics: the Pirate party, which won 2 percent of the vote in its first national campaign (and over 13 percent among first-time male voters). Here the split is generational; the Pirates, only semi-ironically named after Internet piracy, represent the young and online in German society, a class of voters who see the liberating potential of Internet politics but see absolutely no interest from the leading parties in exploiting it. As with the 1970s radicals, it's because the establishment doesn't think change is necessary—"the parties love control, and Internet politics means giving up some of that control," one web consultant to the Green party told me.

Of course, the Pirates aren't about to break the mold of German political parties. Like their elders, they represent a client base, not a universal vision. The notion of the "people's party" was always a sham built on an anachronistic, industrial-age politics that valued conformity over individuality. In the post-industrial era, those values are reversed, and as society fragments into "taste cultures" and sub-tribes, so too does European parliamentary politics. If you can't find a party that speaks for you, start your own.

Obviously, new, sustainable parties don't emerge every day. But Germany now has six factions (including the CDU's Bavarian sister party, the Christian Socialists) in the Bundestag, and each government is a cobbling together of divergent political interests, achieved only after lengthy negotiations—even the current, ideologically consistent CDU/FDP coalition took over a month to solidify. Such coalitions may have theoretical advantages, but in practice they encourage caution and incremental policymaking, lest one party should quit the team.

The problem is that the big decisions in contemporary politics—climate change, global terrorism, international financial reform—demand a policymaking coherence and stability that only broad-based, pragmatic parties like America's can provide. Not surprisingly, big changes, particularly on climate, are increasingly passed up the ladder to the EU, where less transparent, less democratic bodies can make the tough decisions that national parliaments can't.

Complaining about Washington infighting is practically a national pastime in the United States, but we'd do well to consider how much our two parties have achieved relative to Europe. Most of the things progressives like about Germany were established in the early postwar days or the unique moment of post-communist unification. Consider everything that, for better or worse, America's two parties have achieved over the last decade: The creation of a massive domestic security apparatus after 9/11, the invasion and occupation of two distant countries, a series of deep tax cuts, a Medicare drug benefit, an economic bailout, and the temporary takeover of large swaths of the banking and automotive sectors. At the time of this writing, the United States is on the verge of passing sweeping reforms of its health-insurance system, a mid-stream step that few countries could dream of achieving.

And while the two parties don't guarantee complete coherence, they play a vital role in corralling various levels of opinion and forcing Congress toward consensus. Just imagine if the United States had a parliamentary system like Germany's. We'd probably have a center-left and center-right party, greens, libertarians, and progressives, too; but we'd also have a Texas party, a farm-labor party, a right-wing-fundamentalist party, an America First party—in a large heterogeneous society, the possibilities are endless. We'd be Italy, or India. There's

no end to the shortcoming of the Republican-Democrat duopoly, but it's more effective than the alternative.

While televised soccer and the weather probably accounted for some of the diverted attention in Berlin on election day, everyday Germany has more or less given up on achieving substantial change through its party system. Well over half the respondents in pre-election polls said they didn't think it mattered who won; they felt secure in, or at least resigned to, the fact that the country would go along about the same as before, no matter who won.

Is this a function of German society, or its political structure? Both. But the clientelist, multi-party system has a lot to do with such apathy. Membership organizations have difficulty representing the views of non-members, even if they stand to win more votes; after all, those voters don't pay dues or elect the party leadership. At the same time, there aren't nearly enough parties to represent the wide spectrum of political stances present in even German society. The result is usually apathy, though at times—like the 1970s—it is apathy's opposite: rage.

And again, for all the complaining that Americans direct toward their parties, the Democrats and the GOP do a relatively good job of adapting and responding to voters' needs. Lacking a membership roster, but with a mandate to represent at least half the voting public, the two parties have to cast wide nets, and they have to recast them each election. Each time they do, they have to calibrate their message and adapt to voters' needs, hopes, and fears. Like a bickering couple celebrating their golden anniversary, Americans might not always like the parties we have, but we're committed to them. And when we want them to change, we grow active, not apathetic, because we know that it's relatively easy to do.

I take second place to no one in admiring the achievements of modern Germany: A social market, a sturdy welfare net, a robust educational system, a high savings rate, a thick pacifist streak, and an aggressive environmental consciousness. But after my time in Berlin, I'm convinced that these achievements have come despite its parliamentary structure, not because of it.

The Talk of China

THOMAS L. FRIEDMAN

Here is the story of today's China in five brief news items.

Story No. 1

For most of the last two weeks, Xi Jinping, the man tapped to become China's new Communist Party leader, was totally out of sight. That's right. The man designated to become China's next leader—in October or early November—had disappeared and only resurfaced on Saturday in two photos taken while he was visiting an agricultural college. They were posted online by the official Xinhua news agency. With the Chinese government refusing to comment on his whereabouts or explain his absence, rumors here were flying. Had he fallen ill? Was there infighting in the Communist Party? I have a theory: Xi started to realize how hard the job of running China will be in the next decade and was hiding under his bed. Who could blame him?

Chinese officials take great pride in how they have used the last 30 years to educate hundreds of millions of their people, men and women, and bring them out of poverty. Yet, among my Chinese interlocutors, I find a growing feeling that what's worked for China for the past 30 years—a huge Communist Party-led mobilization of cheap labor, capital and resources—will not work much longer. There is a lot of hope that Xi will bring long-delayed economic and political reforms needed to make China a real knowledge economy, but there is no consensus on what those reforms should be and there are a lot more voices in the conversation. Whatever top-down monopoly of the conversation the Communist Party had is evaporating. More and more, the Chinese people, from microbloggers to peasants to students, are demanding that their voices be heard—and officials clearly feel the need to respond. China is now a strange hybrid—an autocracy with 400 million bloggers, who are censored, feared and listened to all at the same time.

So Xi Jinping is certain to make history. He will be the first leader of modern China who will have to have a two-way conversation with the Chinese people *while* he tries to implement some huge political and economic reforms. The need is obvious.

Story No. 2

In March, Chinese authorities quickly deleted from the blogosphere photos of a fatal Beijing car crash, believed to involve the son of a close ally of President Hu Jintao. The car was a Ferrari. The driver was killed and two young women with him badly injured. "Photos of the horrific smash in Beijing were deleted within hours of appearing on microblogs and Web sites," The Guardian reported. "Even searches for the word 'Ferrari' were blocked on the popular Sina Weibo microblog. . . . Unnamed sources have identified the driver of the black sports car as the son of Ling Jihua, who was removed as head of the party's general office of the central committee this weekend." It was the latest in a string of incidents spotlighting the lavish lifestyles of the Communist Party elite.

Chinese authorities are so sensitive to these stories because they are the tip of an iceberg—an increasingly corrupt system of interlocking ties between the Communist Party and state-owned banks, industries and monopolies, which allow certain senior officials, their families and "princelings" to become hugely wealthy and to even funnel that wealth out of China. "Marx said the worst kind of capitalism is a monopolistic capitalism, and Lenin said the worst kind of monopolistic capitalism is state monopolistic capitalism—and we are practicing it to the hilt," a Chinese Internet executive remarked to me.

As a result, you hear more and more that "the risks of not reforming have become bigger than the risks of reforming." No one is talking revolution, but a gradual evolution to a more transparent, rule-of-law-based system, with the people having more formal input. But taking even this first gradual step is proving hard for the Communist Party. It may require a crisis (which is why a lot of middle-class professionals here are looking to get their money or themselves abroad). Meanwhile, the gaps between rich and poor widen.

Story No. 3

Last week, the official Xinhua news agency reported that authorities in the city of Macheng, in Hubei Province in central China, agreed to invest $1.4 million in new school equipment after photos of students and their parents carrying their own desks and chairs to school, along with their books, "sparked an outcry on the Internet. . . . The education gap in China has become a hot-button issue."

Story No. 4

President Hu Jintao suggested that it would be good if the people of Hong Kong learned more about the mainland, so Hong Kong authorities recently announced that they were imposing compulsory "moral and national education" lessons in primary and secondary schools. According to CNN, "the course material had been outlined in a government booklet called 'The China Model,' which was distributed to schools in July." It described China's Communist Party as "progressive, selfless and united" and "criticized multiparty systems as bringing disaster to countries such as the United States." High school students from Hong Kong, which enjoys more freedom than the mainland as part of the 1997 handover from Britain, organized a protest against Beijing's "brainwashing" that quickly spread to parent groups and universities. As a result, on Sept. 8, one day before local elections, Hong Kong's chief executive, Leung Chun-ying, Beijing's man there, announced the compulsory education plan was being dropped—to avoid pro-Beijing candidates getting crushed.

Story No. 5

A few weeks ago, Deng Yuwen, a senior editor of The Study Times, which is controlled by the Communist Party, published an analysis on the Web site of the business magazine Caijing. According to Agence France-Presse, Deng argued that President Hu Jintao and Prime Minister Wen Jiabao "had 'created more problems than achievements' during their 10 years in power. . . . The article highlighted 10 problems facing China that it said were caused by the lack of political reform and had the potential to cause public discontent, including stalled economic restructuring, income disparity and pollution. 'The essence of democracy is how to restrict government power; this is the most important reason why China so badly needs democracy,' Deng wrote. 'The overconcentration of government powers without checks and balances is the root cause of so many social problems.'" The article has triggered a debate on China's blogosphere.

This is just a sampler of the China that Xi Jinping will be inheriting. This is not your grandfather's Communist China. After three decades of impressive economic growth, but almost no political reforms, there is "a gathering sense of an approaching moment of transition that will require a different set of conditions for Chinese officials to maintain airspeed," observed Orville Schell, the Asia Society China expert. The rules are going to get rewritten here. Exactly how and when is impossible to say. The only thing that is certain is that it will be through a two-way conversation.

DISCUSSION QUESTIONS

1) Pietro Nivola seems to strike a counterintuitive note on partisanship. What is the basis for his argument that partisanship in Washington could be beneficial in certain ways? One of the assertions is about the United States becoming more "parliamentary" as a result, which begs the question: If Nivola thinks this is beneficial, should the United States not shift to a parliamentary system of government? Do you believe the United States should do so, and why or why not?

2) The pieces in this section illustrate different party systems. How do you think the structure of these party systems (such as single-party vs. multi-party systems) affects how interest groups participate in the political process differently? What about the citizenry at large? Do single-party and dominant-party systems (like China) imply that individuals and interest groups don't really matter in politics, since the same party always wins elections? Why or why not?

3) Consider the two-party system in the United States, in which the Democrats and Republicans routinely win nearly all national elections, even as Congress and the parties themselves are often unpopular and many people wish for a third party to emerge. What about the electoral system and the social realities in the United States raises obstacles to third parties? Or, why do you think the existing two-party system is so stable, seemingly making it impossible to move to a multi-party system?

Revolutions and Contention

One of the topics in comparative politics that students often find particularly fascinating is that of revolution and related forms of contention and conflict. Here the field tries to understand when and why people seek to bring about their preferred ends outside of formal political institutions (that is, not just through campaigning for and electing representatives, petitioning sitting politicians, and so forth). We also try to understand why some contentious efforts are successful and others are less so, and why different forms of contention—protests, social movements, revolutions, terrorism, civil war, and so forth—take place in different contexts. Needless to say, it is a large and interesting area of research.

Much of the public discussion about contention in recent years has focused on the Arab Spring revolts and the political developments to which they have given rise. You read about these revolts in Section 5. They will echo here, but it is important to recognize that contention takes many forms and occurs in many places, and so here we try to also highlight other places where contention is (and is not) taking place.

Our first reading, by the journalist James Fallows, looks at the relationship between contention in the Middle East and the seeming stability of China's authoritarian regime. Why, we might ask, has this revolt not spread to the world's largest authoritarian state? Fallows might say that it has, in the sense that some Chinese citizens have hoped to make a "Jasmine Revolution," but that the regime has successfully repressed their efforts. Of course, this may beg deeper questions about why the regime in China has been successful in suppressing revolt; these sorts of questions are for your further consideration and exploration.

There has been a great deal of protest activity in recent years (though it is hard to say whether there has been more or less than at other, comparable, times). Sometimes protest conforms to the expectations of old-fashioned theories, with workers demanding better conditions and more equitable distribution of wealth. On other occasions, though, protest surprises and even confounds analysts. An example is the wave of protests in Brazil in 2013. Our second piece, by Elizabeth Leeds of the Washington Office on Latin America, attempts to help analysts recover their footing, suggesting that these protests are understandable and not as radical a departure from the past as some have suggested.

Some have argued that the Internet and social media have dramatically changed protest activity. Often this is celebrated, with commentators noting that Facebook, Twitter, and other platforms expand the potential for mobilization. But the author of our third and final reading in this section, Bessma Momani, urges caution. Drawing briefly on discussions of recent protest actions in a variety of places, Momani suggests that social-media–based mobilization might undermine deliberative democracy and produce unintended consequences. Since many current students are active users of social media, you may ask yourself: What is the strongest argument you could make against Momani's perspective? And in return, what is the strongest reply that Momani and other skeptics might offer?

Arab Spring, Chinese Winter

JAMES FALLOWS

Just after the streets of Tunisia and Egypt erupted, China saw a series of "Jasmine" protests—until the government stopped them cold. Its methods were subtler than they had been at Tiananmen Square, and more insidious. Was the regime's defensive reaction just paranoia? Or is the Chinese public less satisfied— and more combustible—than it appears?

Something big is happening in China, and it started soon after the onset of the "Arab Spring" demonstrations and regime changes first in Tunisia and then in Egypt: the most serious and widespread wave of repression since the Tiananmen Square crackdowns 22 years ago. Of course, "worst since Tiananmen Square" does not mean "as bad as Tiananmen Square." As the government has taken pains to ensure, there have been no coordinated nationwide protests so far, and troops from the People's Liberation Army, in their instantly recognizable green uniforms, have not played the major role that they did then in containing dissent. Instead, enforcement around the country has been left mainly to regular police, typically in their dark-blue uniforms; the much-feared "urban management" patrols known as *chengguan*, also in dark blue; large reserve armies of plainclothesmen; and many other less visible parts of the state's internal-security apparatus, which now has a larger budget than China's regular military does.

Unlike in 1989, for most people in most of the country, life and business since the beginning of the Arab Spring have hummed along relatively normally. The main domestic concerns in China at the moment are rapid inflation, especially in food prices; a severe long-term nationwide drought (broken by occasional severe localized flooding), which has threatened farms in the country's normally wet southern provinces and brought Dust Bowl conditions to parts of the normally dry north; and widening scandals and public fear about tainted food supplies. In May, a report based on figures from the Chinese Ministry of Health showed that cancer had become the country's leading cause of death, which is an unusual and revealing distinction. In poorer countries, infectious diseases are usually the main killers; in richer ones, heart disease and other consequences of a sedentary, wealthy lifestyle. The rising prevalence of cancer, including in "cancer villages" near factories or mines in China's still-poor countryside, was taken even by Chinese commentators as another indication of the urgency of dealing with the environmental consequences of the country's nonstop growth. For modern China, though, all of these are familiar concerns.

A set of less familiar problems developed with amazing speed early in the year. In mid-January, Hu Jintao met Barack Obama in Washington, on what would be Hu's last official visit to the United States. In a little more than a year, Hu will finish his second five-year term as president and relinquish the job, presumably to anointee/Vice President Xi Jinping. The meetings in Washington were as constructive and positive-toned as such events can be. Obama gave Hu the gala White House state dinner (which my wife and I attended) that he had notably not received on his previous American visit: five years earlier, George W. Bush had offered Hu only a lunch at the White House, an omission the more startling given the standard Chinese practice of building even the most trivial business meeting around a celebratory banquet. Officials from both sides noted their areas of political and economic disagreement (arms sales to Taiwan, status of the Dalai Lama, etc.) but also signed numerous cooperative agreements, in fields ranging from clean-energy research to student exchanges and increased military interactions. President Ben Ali had been forced from power in Tunisia just days before Hu Jintao traveled to Washington. The Tahrir Square protests against Hosni Mubarak in Egypt began just after Hu returned to Beijing, and were soon followed by the uprisings in Jordan, Yemen, Syria, and Libya. The spread of protest from one Arab-Islamic country to its neighbors might have seemed predictable. Less so was the effect in China.

On Sunday afternoon, February 20, while Muammar Qaddafi's troops were shooting into unarmed crowds in Benghazi, a handful of Chinese staged the first of a projected series of weekly "Jasmine" protests designed to extend the spirit of the Arab Spring protests to several major Chinese cities. The demonstration in Beijing was held in front of a McDonald's restaurant at the Wangfujing intersection, not far from the Forbidden City and Tiananmen Square. That day, several dozen demonstrators were matched by about the same number of foreign reporters, plus large numbers of passersby and onlookers (Wangfujing on a weekend is one of Beijing's most jammed areas) and larger groups of uniformed and plainclothes police.

Among the onlookers was Jon Huntsman Jr. with his family. Huntsman, then in his last weeks as the U.S. ambassador to China before returning to run for the presidency, looked like a Chinese pop-culture caricature of a cool-cat American. He was wearing sunglasses—the day was cold but brilliantly clear—and a *Top Gun*–style brown-leather aviator jacket with a big American-flag patch on the left shoulder. He had become a well-known figure in Beijing, from his bike rides around town and his command of spoken Mandarin, and he was quickly picked out by Chinese in the crowd and captured on camera phones in photos and a video that soon spread across the Internet.

Even though Huntsman maintained that he'd been out on a family stroll and happened by the protest inadvertently, no one in China believed that, and the video of him with two strapping sons, misidentified as bodyguards, quickly circulated in China as proof that the United States was engineering the protests. I don't know whether Huntsman's presence was an accident. I do know that having America's senior representative on the scene was damaging, given the hypersensitivity of the Chinese government and many citizens to the merest hint of foreign meddling in domestic affairs. (On the most-circulated video, a Chinese man yells at Huntsman, "You want chaos for China, don't you?") It also illustrated the awkwardness of Huntsman's

staying on as ambassador to America's most important partner/rival country while publicly contemplating a run against the president who had appointed him.

Within two days, the street outside the Wangfujing McDonald's had been almost entirely blocked by out-of-nowhere "street repair" construction hoardings. The following Sunday, when the next Jasmine march was supposed to take place, almost no demonstrators appeared in Wangfujing. Instead there were large numbers of foreign reporters and tourists, and countless hundreds of security forces. Jasmine demonstrators in Shanghai mustered a larger showing that day, but that turned out to be a high-water mark. By late February, the Jasmine "movement" was on its way to being decisively shut down.

My wife and I were in China, mainly Beijing, through February and March, so we had a chance to see how this movement tentatively built itself and was then quelled, at least for a while. One of the realities hardest to convey about modern China (and *Atlantic* readers know that I certainly have tried over the years) is how life there can be simultaneously so wide-open and so tightly controlled. In most of the country and for most people's pursuits, this Chinese Winter that followed an Arab Spring left life looking normal. The economy kept growing; farmers worried about their crops and students about their tests; engineers designed new high-speed rail lines. I was in China mainly to report on the country's big high-tech ambitions, and there was absolutely nothing about my interviews or factory visits that was not business as usual.

Yet for those in China who defined their business as involving politics of any sort, the pressure was intense. First, in February, a large number of the country's human-rights and public-interest lawyers (yes, they exist) were arrested or detained, or were disappeared, in the style of Pinochet's Chile. Once they were gone, people they might have represented and defended—writers, professors, bloggers, activists of many sorts—were arrested or made to disappear too. The Nobel Committee expressed concern not just that the most recent recipient of the Peace Prize, the civil-rights activist Liu Xiaobo, was still imprisoned but that they had not heard anything from him for months. "Signs of tightening control have been visible for several years," Joshua Rosenzweig, a human-rights official in Hong Kong, wrote in March. "But the authorities are now employing a range of new, illegal methods to silence their critics . . . Most terrifying of all is the way in which enforced disappearance appears to have become almost routine."

Apart from Liu Xiaobo, the Chinese activist best known around the world is the artist Ai Weiwei. Inside China he had, among other causes, sought investigations into the lax building standards that led to thousands of schoolchildren's deaths in the Sichuan earthquake of 2008. On April 3 of this year, as he was about to board a plane in Beijing for Hong Kong, he was detained too. Eventually he was charged with tax evasion, and remained in legal jeopardy even after his release in June. "If the authorities can detain a figure of such stature arbitrarily and hold him incommunicado as long as they want with no access to family or legal counsel, then no one in China is safe from the whims and anxieties of those in power," Wei Jingsheng, who himself had served 15 years in prison for political crimes before being released to the United States in the 1990s, wrote in the *Christian Science Monitor* after the arrest.

I realize that a chronicle of such cases becomes tedious, especially with unfamiliar names. But every day, new names appeared—on foreign news sites, not in the Chinese press—along with other illustrations of a society politically closing up and cracking down. Conferences with international attendees were canceled at the last minute. So too, with one day's notice, was a prestigious annual debate tournament, among teams from 16 leading Chinese universities. The topic, a reconsideration of the ideals set out for China a century ago in the revolution that overthrew the last Qing emperor, in 1911, was deemed too sensitive. Foreign journalists were one by one called in "for tea," code for a cautionary talk with security officials. Usually the officials warned that the journalists would be expelled if they violated "rules"—some newly imposed, some long on the books but not enforced—requiring advance official permission before interviewing Chinese citizens.

Church meetings were disrupted. Members of "sensitive" ethnic groups—Tibetans, Muslim Uighurs, Inner Mongolians, all of whose home districts had been scenes of ongoing protest—came in for special scrutiny. One day in March, major boulevards in Beijing suddenly were lined with older women, bundled up in overcoats and with red armbands identifying them as public-safety patrols, who sat on stools at 20-yard intervals and kept watch for disruption. They had no practical effect except as reminders that the authorities were on guard and in control.

During the earliest stages of the Arab Spring, the mainstream Chinese media virtually ignored its existence. Then, as the drama in Egypt became unignorable, coverage in China emphasized the dangerous chaos and excesses. Then the theme became: whether or not such upheaval made sense for anyone else, it was the wrong way for China and would jeopardize the country's hard-won gains. *Global Times*, a nationalist paper, said of Western protests about Ai Weiwei's arrest: "The West's behavior aims at disrupting the attention of Chinese society and attempts to modify the value system of the Chinese people."

In a way, the most surprising and thoroughgoing change in Chinese daily life was in access to the Internet. As I wrote in these pages three years ago ("The Connection Has Been Reset," March 2008), the genius of China's Internet censorship has been its flexible repression. The filtering system known officially as Golden Shield and unofficially as the Great Firewall made finding unauthorized material just difficult enough that the great majority of Chinese citizens wouldn't bother. Meanwhile, enough loopholes and pressure valves remained open that people who really cared about escaping its confines always could. A very significant loophole took the form of the government's blind eye toward VPNs—"Virtual Private Networks," which gave anyone willing to spend a dollar or two a week safe passage through the Great Firewall. You signed up for a VPN service, you made your connection, and from that point on you prowled the Internet just as if you were logged on from London or New York.

People who could afford VPNs, including most foreigners and many in the Chinese elite, could view Internet censorship as a problem for the country but not personally for them. And most people assumed that this loophole would always stay open—how could universities or corporations do business otherwise? Even the man known in China as the father of the Great Firewall, a computer scientist (and university president!) named Fang Binxing, made waves in February by telling a leading Chinese newspaper that he kept six VPNs running on his computers at home.

That report was soon pulled from the paper's Web site—and at about that same time, serious disruption of VPN activity began. For a while I thought something was wrong with my computer. I'd try to get my e-mail, or to go to a foreign news site—and after a few minutes of waiting, I would realize that the connection was simply not ever going to get through. Part of the Great Firewall's power is that you don't see a message saying "access denied." Things just . . . don't work, and you can't be sure why. But officials from VPN companies said they were being targeted, in a way they'd never experienced before. "The Klingon Empire scored a couple of solid hits on the USS Enterprise," the CEO of one of the leading VPNs, Witopia, wrote to his customers in March (along with discreet tips on new ports and connections to try).

The VPN disruption seemed worst on weekends and was sometimes an absolute blackout for hours on end. My own theory, which no one I interviewed could disprove, was that this was a proof of concept for the security agencies—a demonstration that they could cut off channels to the outside world immediately, if the need arose. But even when the system was turned back on, the Internet in much of China was hobbled. If you have spent time in South Korea, Japan, or Singapore, you know that broadband systems there make the typical U.S. "high-speed" connection seem pokey. But China's Internet controls can seem like a return to the days of 1,200-baud dial-up access. After each Web click, it could take five, 10, 30 seconds for a page to appear. "Anyone bullish about China should come and try to use the internet here," an American graduate student named Matt Schiavenza wrote in a frustrated tweet this year. (Twitter, like Facebook and Blogger and many Google services, is unusable in China

without a VPN.) Or, as the head of a foreign tech company wrote to me in an e-mail early this year, "Ultimately, if they want to take the country's internet connections 'Third World,' none of us can prevent that."

After the Japanese earthquake in March, Bill Powell, a writer for *Time* who had gone to Fukushima from his base in Shanghai, told me about a site, AllThingsNuclear.org, whose information he considered most reliable and up-to-date. When Powell returned to China, he found that this site too was blocked by the Great Firewall. "What are they afraid of?" he wrote in a Web posting. "Or is the answer simply that these days, they are afraid of EVERYTHING?"

What the central Chinese leadership might be afraid of, and why, is the central political question about China now. The hair-trigger defensiveness of the government's response resembles that of a tottering Arab Spring regime, while overall the nation's prospects could not seem more different from, say, Egypt's. Economically, countries throughout the North Africa/Middle East crescent have been stagnant. China, as you might have heard, has been an economic success. Qaddafi, Mubarak, Ben Ali, and others have governed as if they had a lifetime hold on power. Hu Jintao and Wen Jiabao were not elected by the public, but they will give up power after two terms.

Egypt, Tunisia, Syria, and the like have discontented reserve armies of unemployed young men. Because of its one-child policy, China has, if anything, a shortage of young women and men, relative to the retirees they will have to support. This March, as the Chinese crackdown intensified, the Pew Global Attitudes Project released the results of surveys the previous year in China and Egypt, among other places. The contrast was stark. Twenty-eight percent of Egyptians were "satisfied" with their country's direction, down from 47 percent a few years earlier; 87 percent of Chinese were satisfied, up from 83 percent. Only 23 percent of Egyptians were optimistic about their own life prospects over the next five years, versus 74 percent of Chinese (and 52 percent of Americans). Surveys in China can be suspect, and Pew notes in the fine print that its Chinese survey sample was "disproportionately urban," under-weighting China's rural poor. Still, the general impression that most people in China buy into the prevailing system rings true.

Why, then, has the government reacted as if the country were on the brink of revolt? Do the Chinese authorities know something about their country's realities that groups like Pew have missed, and therefore understand that they are hanging by a thread? Or, out of reflex and paranoia, are they responding far more harshly than circumstances really require, in ways that could backfire in the long run?

While in China and afterward, I asked everyone I could: Is the government eerily perceptive, or destructively obtuse? There's no proof on either side, but here are the arguments for each view.

Those who think the government has good reason to be worried say that the accumulated tensions— political, economic, environmental, and social—of China's all-out growth have reached an unbearable extreme. By this interpretation, the seeming satisfaction of the Chinese public is a veneer that could easily crack. "If one were to read only the Party-controlled media, one might get the impression that China is prosperous, stable, and headed for an age of 'great peace and prosperity,'" Liu Xiaobo himself wrote, in an essay shortly before he was arrested. (The English version, translated by Perry Link of Princeton, will appear this fall in a collection of Liu's essays and poems, *No Enemies, No Hatred*.) He continued:

Not only from the Internet, but from foreign news sources as well as the internal documents of the regime itself—its 'crisis reports'—we know that more and more major conflicts, often involving violence and bloodshed, have been breaking out between citizens and officials all across China. The country rests at the brink of a volcano.

By June of this year, a wave of bombings, riots, and violent protests at widely dispersed sites across the country illustrated what Liu was warning about. The trigger of the uprisings varied city by city—ethnic tensions in some areas, beatings by police or *chengguan* in others—but they added to a mood of nationwide tension. "With rampant official corruption, inflation, economic disparity, and all sorts of social injustice and political tensions, the threat to the CCP rule is very much real," Cheng Li, who grew up in Shanghai and is now a specialist in Chinese politics at the Brookings Institution, told me this summer.

Five years ago, in his book *China's Trapped Transition*, Minxin Pei argued that China would be hitting a limit of its current economic growth scheme in about seven years' time, or about now. Pei, who is also originally from Shanghai and is now at Claremont McKenna College, in California, said that China's state-led development model would work wonderfully—up to a point. The same traits that made the country a miracle of the infrastructure-and-cheap-exports era would handicap it, he said, when it had to compete in higher-value industries and jobs, as it is now trying to do.

"If you were sitting in Hu Jintao's office, you would see the protests, the ethnic tensions," he told me recently, "and you might think, 'If we are not tough enough, things could quickly get out of control.'" From the central authorities' point of view, according to Pei, there is one clear lesson of Tiananmen Square: "They have learned from past experience in 1989 that you have to be very tough at the beginning, to nip things in the bud. It is much better to have overkill than underkill."

I heard similar sentiments from people now working in China, Chinese and foreign alike. For instance, a well-known economist in China, who asked not to be named, said that the government was worried precisely because it understood the difficulties of the economic adjustments ahead. "There is increasing awareness of how out-of-control the growth model has become, and it will require a sharp adjustment involving a growth slowdown," this person said. "The more aware the leaders are of the strains in the economy, the more worried they are about the difficulty of the adjustment"—mainly through layoffs, bankruptcies, and other economic shocks.

If, months or years from now, the volcano should explode and the veneer of control should crack, it will be easy to find evidence that this was inevitable all along. When I asked an academic at one of China's leading universities how he would explain the government's harshness, he wrote in an e-mail that the level of public discontent was extreme:

It is hard to get anyone in Beijing under the age of 30 to indicate anything but contempt for the government, and I suspect this is true in a lot of other cities. There really is a sense among young people and college students that everyone is grabbing everything they can, and it is noteworthy that princelings [children of senior party leaders] no longer want to be investment bankers but rather want to be private equity investors. In other words, getting paid millions for your connections isn't interesting anymore. Owning the whole lot is better.

Premier Wen Jiabao is seen as the big-hearted "grandpa" of China, always the first to visit disaster scenes. His son, Winston Wen, has an M.B.A. from Northwestern and has worked in private equity.

The other view is that the situation in China is indeed tense—but that it has always been tense, and that so many people have so much to lose from any radical change, that the country's own buffering forces would contain a disruption even if the government weren't cracking down so hard.

The main reason is that for all the complaints and dissatisfactions with today's Communist rule, there is no visible alternative—in part, of course, because the government has worked so hard to keep such alternatives from emerging. This is a less satisfying side of the argument to advance. You look worse if you turn out to be wrong, and it seems unimaginative to say that an uneasy status quo might go on indefinitely. Still, it is what I would guess if forced to choose.

I asked Chas Freeman what he made of China's current turmoil. He is a former diplomat who served as Richard Nixon's interpreter during his visit to China in 1972. Because Freeman was working during the discussions between Nixon and Zhou Enlai, he knows that one of the most famous stories about Zhou is not true. Half the commencement speakers in America have quoted Zhou's alleged response when asked whether the French Revolution had been a success: "Too soon to tell." Ah, those far-seeing Chinese! In fact, Freeman points out, Zhou was not talking about the French Revolution of 1789. He was talking about the upheavals that began in France in 1968 and had not fully simmered down by the time he and Nixon talked.

When it came to contemporary China, Freeman said that he takes seriously the complaints about economic inequality, ethnic tension, and other potential sources of instability. But, he said, they remind him of conversations he had when living in Taiwan in the 1970s, before Chiang Kai-Shek's Kuomintang party had moved from quasi-military rule to open elections. "People would say they are corrupt, they have no vision, they have a ridiculous ideology we have to kowtow to, but that no one believes in practice," he told me. "And I would say, 'If they're so bad, why don't you get rid of them?' That would be greeted with absolute incredulity." Taiwanese of that era would tell him that, corrupt or not, the party was steadily bringing prosperity. Or that there was no point in complaining, since the party would eliminate anyone who challenged its rule. The parallel with mainland China was obvious. A generation later, Taiwan had become democratized.

Conceivably, that is what another generation might mean for the mainland—especially if the next wave of rulers are less hair-trigger about security, and more concerned about the lobotomizing effects on their society of, for instance, making it so hard to use the Internet. Which in turn is part of a climate that keeps their universities from becoming magnets for the world's talent, which in turn puts a drag on China's attempts to foster the Apples, Googles, GEs of the future. We don't know, but we can guess that whatever China's situation is, a generation from now, we will be able to look back and find signs that it was fated all along. "People predicted the fall of the Chinese Communist Party in 1989, and it didn't happen," Perry Link told me. "People did not predict the fall of the Soviet Union in 1991, and it did happen. I'm sure that whatever happens in China, or doesn't, we will be able to look back and say why." If only it were possible to do that now.

Protests in Brazil: Digging Beneath the Surface

ELIZABETH LEEDS

"Protests in Brazil: Digging Beneath the Surface," by Elizabeth Leeds, Washington Office on Latin America, August 1, 2013. Reprinted with permission.

Brazil's recent country-wide demonstrations protesting a broad range of political and social conditions are interesting for reasons that go well beyond the specific issues raised by the protesters.

First, the content of the protests themselves and the tepid response of the government of President Dilma Rousseff show how out of touch the Worker's Party (*Partido dos Trabalhadores*, PT) has become with the enthusiastic and large portion of the population that first elected Lula in 2002. This same influential base re-elected him in 2006 and then elected Dilma as his successor in 2010, albeit with less excitement. Despite running on a platform that condemned corruption, Lula and Dilma's PT has been plagued by continuous corruption scandals throughout its 11-year rule, sending the message that politics have remained business as usual. Indeed, polls show that most protesters and those in the population they symbolize find government institutions and political parties in general unable and unwilling to represent their demands.

The economic policies started by Fernando Henrique Cardoso in the 1990s and continued by both Lula and Dilma stabilized the economy and raised Brazil to a world economic power status. Domestically, poverty alleviation policies, the expansion of opportunities for higher education, and increased availability of credit for those previously excluded from the consumer economy have created a new segment of the middle class. But while Brazil has been lauded for its middle-class growth, this new group finds itself heavily indebted and reliant on woefully inadequate public services—especially regarding health, primary and secondary education, and transportation.

While the catalyst for the demonstrations was the Free Transportation Movement (*Movimento Passe Livre*, MPL), the protests quickly escalated. Aided by social media, the protests became an outlet for the pent-up demands and frustrations of the broad segment of the middle and working classes that do not profit from Brazil's economic growth. In addition, the emergence of Brazil's version of the Millenium generation (students and recently graduated twenty-somethings struggling with under- and unemployment) augmented the participation and enthusiasm of the demonstrations. These segments were outraged by the vast sums (approximately US$14 billion) being spent by the government on preparations for the World Cup in 2014 and Olympics in 2016 while neglecting basic public services. Corruption and lack of transparency in awarding construction contracts has strengthened the disillusionment.

The violent reaction of the police in most cities shows how unprepared they were to deal with large demonstrations. Middle class protestors—who experienced what poorer segments of the population live through routinely—added curbing police violence to their demands.

Certain media outlets have focused on the presumably amorphous and largely leaderless nature of the protests, but that view neglects the social context of Brazil's vibrant civil society and history of highly effective social movements. While the MPL started the process, in each of the 100 cities nationwide where local protests erupted, local social movements and civil society organizations already involved a wide variety of issues were ready to intensify the struggle. In Rio, for example, corruption, misplaced spending, unnecessary low-income neighborhood removals linked to the mega-events, and police violence have been addressed by such organizations as Meu Rio , Comité Popular Rio Copa e Olimpíadas, Rio on Watch (a project of Catalytic Communities), and Redes da Maré, to name a few. And while the media concentrated on protests in Rio's city center, the state government headquarters, and the governor's apartment in Rio's affluent south zone, little attention was paid to demonstrations at a number of

Rio's squatter communities (*favelas*), whose populations are affected even more severely by the lack of effective public spending and police misconduct.

Soon after the first protests erupted, Dilma took the initiative to meet with the MPL leaders, mayors, governors, and the judiciary to address the popular demands. Her response was to create the National Pact (*Pacto Nacional*)—a series of hasty measures seen largely as band-aid solutions to problems with health, education, corruption, and the electoral system—all with an eye on next year's presidential elections. For example, her proposal to address public health inadequacies was to create a National Pact for Health, which includes importing foreign doctors from Portugal, Spain, and Cuba to work in rural and out-lying urban areas. The doctors, in addition to being unfamiliar with local contexts, would not even have to pass licensing exams in Brazil. The proposal ignores the fact that Brazil does not lack doctors. Rather, there is a poor distribution of doctors throughout the country, as well as abysmal conditions in public clinics and hospitals in these areas, which often lack basic equipment, medicine, and salaries for public health personnel. Brazil's per capita health spending is from one-third to one-half less than its neighbors Argentina, Uruguay, and Paraguay.

Finally, of all the issues raised by the protestors, the one totally ignored by Dilma was public safety. The reaction of the police to the demonstrations shows a total lack of preparedness in dealing with large scale protests—the size of which Brazil had not seen since the early 1990s when President Fernando Collor was impeached. While the vast majority of demonstrators acted peacefully, there was a small minority of vandals (*vândalos*), who threw molotov cocktails, smashed bank and store windows, and looted. This minority created a climate in which police indiscriminately arrested civilians and made use of non-lethal weapons (pepper spray, tear gas, and rubber bullets) against all demonstrators. This criminalization of democratic expression set back the limited advances the police have made in the last decade to improve relations with society. While the jurisdiction of the police is largely at the state level in Brazil, the federal government has the opportunity and resources—and indeed the duty—to set national guidelines for the use of force. Leaving public safety and the police out of the National Pact marginalizes the police forces and maintains the status quo, allowing the police to become the scapegoat for the very ills of society that are being protested.

App-Powered Protests Put Democracy in Peril
Elections Are the Only True Measure of Faith in a Government and Its Policy Ideas

BESSMA MOMANI

Should we have democracy on demand?

Spain, Turkey, Brazil, Egypt have experienced forms of it. What other country might be next to feel the wrath of people power?

In the past few years, TV news cameras have gone from capital to capital to film the anger of people demanding change from their governments.

Europeans have taken to the streets to oppose economic austerity policies—demanded by the IMF and eurozone powerhouses in exchange for sorely needed money to shore up public finances.

In Turkey, an urban planning issue turned a small green space into a national crisis for a third-term president who was viewed as a populist leader.

In Brazil, people poured into the streets to tell its democratically elected president that policy priorities should be transportation, solving inequities and better education—not flashy international games.

And most recently, Egyptians went into the streets to sanction and endorse a military coup, launched to restore order over a failing economy and undignified presidency.

Getting millions into the streets to call for change can be as easy as having a tweet go viral. Meet in the square in 140 characters or less: just one day of unrest, if the conditions are right, is all that it takes to get your democratically elected government to listen to your demands.

Is this a crisis for democratic rule or a new liberating way to achieve accountability from governments during elected tenures? I'm afraid it's the former.

Before there was a Facebook page for everything, democracy was built on the bargaining of ideas at political party conventions. The exchange of ideas involved lengthy philosophical debates in town halls; political representatives needed to knock on doors to explain their ideological views and answer tough and complex policy questions. Political leaders had to sweat out national debates to prove they were the right person for the top job. Social movements needed to agree on ideological platforms to create political parties.

There are no perfect democracies, and yes there can be elitism, classism, racism, ageism and sexism that give an advantage to some over others. But there is a reason democracy was built in a way that allowed for a slow and healthy exchange of ideas. Political bargaining was not horse-trading favours as pictured on popular TV dramas. It was about finding compromise on tough issues like "how much control should government have in cultural products and services?" "Should government be a primary investor in public infrastructure?" "Should foreign investment be encouraged?"

A vibrant and healthy democracy was one that created broad-based policies supported by some political consensus, which took hard work and compromise to achieve.

Some might argue that people power in the streets of Rio de Janeiro or Cairo is simply a form of populist veto power on a government's mandate. Why should a nation wait for the completion of an elected leader's term to demand change? Aren't these protests just a quasi-referendum on a government's performance?

Here's the inherent challenge: how do you measure street protests as an indication of majoritarian will? How do we know that the millions in the streets of Madrid, protesting their government's spending cuts, represent the view of Spain's mainstream? The same can be asked of the millions gathered in Cairo's Tahrir Square. More importantly, are those gathered in protest in agreement on the same alternative policy to that proposed by their government?

The truth is we don't know. This is why there's a process of political bargaining and a ballot box. Elections are the only true measure of faith in a government and its policy ideas.

Why are these mass protests new? It is because we—the people—live in a hyper-connected reality with information and communication on demand. It is not merely impatience with government, but a quest for immediate accountability that drives these mass demonstrations.

These are inherently good intentions to improve democracy—and they urgently point to the need for a conversation on how to make this system of governance more accountable and responsive to the needs of the people. But this critical discussion can't and won't take place in the streets and squares of a capital near you. It is time to realize that there is simply no app for democracy.

DISCUSSION QUESTIONS

1) In the first reading in this section, James Fallows points to the notable contrast between the events of the Arab Spring and the persistence of authoritarian rule in China. What accounts for the difference? Why do you suppose so many Middle Eastern states witnessed contentious activity at the same time?

2) Some scholars think that revolutions and social movements tend to happen as soon as opportunities for mobilization emerge. Others think that the main determinants are changing patterns of grievances. What do the readings in this section suggest about these debates? Can you develop a theory of protest that brings together both opportunities and grievances?

3) In recent years, many have stressed the role that social media has played in social protest. In this section's third reading, Bessa Momani expresses concerns about possible negative consequences of activists' reliance on technological mediation. On balance, which view do you think is best? How might we weigh the pros and cons of such technologies? What could Twitter activists learn from Momani's critique?

Nationalism and Ethno-National Conflict

Virtually everyone in the modern world has a national identity, either through their own choosing or through others ascribing it to them. These identities are very consequential: this is true for many reasons, but one of the most important among them is the fact that most modern states claim to govern on the behalf of a nation. As such, one's national identity matters for how one will be treated.

Some view nationalism as a good thing; others see it as bad and dangerous. Both views are too simple. Nationalism and national identity are closely linked, for example, to democracy, since nationalism places such emphasis on popular sovereignty. And people get a sense of pride from identification with the nation. Our first reading, by the international relations scholar Stephen Walt, focuses on how nationalism impacts people's enjoyment of athletic contests like the Olympics. Walt emphasizes that our shared nationality makes us root for people with whom we have no actual connection and that reflecting on this experience tells us something about what it is to have a national identity.

But what is a nation, and how do we know one when we see one? Many groups consider themselves to be nations, even if they do not possess a full-fledged nation-state. Mobilizing around such national identities produces both good and bad outcomes. The largely peaceful desire for greater autonomy in Scotland (in the United Kingdom), Quebec (Canada), or Catalonia (Spain) might be considered examples. On the one hand, (at least some) people clearly derive value from their sense of belonging to Scottish, Quebecois, or Catalan groups. Sometimes this is mainly about the right to speak one's preferred language and to live one's preferred traditions in a certain region of a country. On the other hand, such groups' desire for greater autonomy and, possibly, independence might produce conflict and both political and economic difficulties. Political scientists and policy makers debate how to respond to such issues, with some arguing for federal or consociational institutions and others arguing for efforts at assimilation. Our second reading considers the Catalan case, and it shows how language is a particular factor that matters in the formation and articulation of nationhood.

Nationalism and national identity also impact policy making in other ways, perhaps especially foreign policy. On the one hand, "economic nationalism" can cause policy makers to favor domestic producers (or consumers), sometimes through protectionism and subsidies. On the other hand, *sometimes* nationalism may encourage expansionist or even hostile foreign policies. At the same time, if often does not: consider the fact that virtually every modern polity attempts to legitimate itself through nationalism and national identity, and you will likely see that nationalism cannot always lead to these bad outcomes. It may be that a good deal of popular analysis focuses on memorable cases and misses the more boring, but perhaps more common, cases in which nationalism is relatively benign. A recent example is the debate about the nationalism of Japan's Prime Minister Shinzo Abe. In the past, Japanese nationalism was sometimes linked to militarism, most notably in the years leading up to and including World War II. Abe is regarded by some as encouraging a kind of nationalism reminiscent of this tradition, or at least roughly friendly to it. In our third piece, the noted scholar of Japanese nationalism, Kevin Doak, argues that this is a misreading, and that Abe is actually a proponent of what political scientists call "civic nationalism."

Sometimes, though, group differences (whether the groups are understood to be different nations, ethnicities, or something else) do indeed lead to more serious problems, such as intergroup violence and, in the most nightmarish cases, genocide. Scholars of comparative politics debate what causes such conflict: Is it really about nationalism and ethnic attachment, or perhaps about weak states and predatory elites, or perhaps some other factors like poverty? In our fourth reading, Stefan Wolff considers a variety of theories of ethnic conflict, emphasizing efforts to explain both the spread and the escalation of conflict and looking at conflicts in and around the Sudan (now two countries, the Sudan and South Sudan) and the former Yugoslavia in recent decades.

What the Olympics Can Teach Us about Nationalism

STEPHEN M. WALT

Like most of you, I'm spending some time these days watching the Olympics. It's especially fun to see more obscure sports like fencing, table tennis, and beach volleyball get their moments in the sun, and there are always a few upsets and feel-good stories to keep us riveted. And for the record, I thought that utterly wacky opening ceremony was flat-out brilliant.

But given my day job, I can't help but see the Olympics as a sublimely teachable moment about nationalism. Every Olympic year I ask my students who they rooted for, and whether they got a subtle thrill when one of their countrymen won. Are they disappointed when one of their fellow nationals loses out? Of course, the vast majority of students admit that they tend to do just that, and I'll confess to similar instincts myself.

But the next question I ask them is "Why? Why do you care? Is it because you know the actual people involved?" Of course not. I don't root for Ryan Lochte of the United States over Yannick Agnel of France because I know them both personally, and I happen to like Lochte more, or because my personal knowledge of the two tells me that Lochte is more deserving in some larger sense (i.e., he works harder, has overcome more obstacles, etc.). I have no idea, yet for some silly reason I get a certain pleasure when some American I've never even met does well. This tendency is even more true about team events: I really have no way of knowing if the American team is nicer, smarter, more ethical, etc., than any of their foreign rivals. Yet I find myself cheering for a bunch of strangers who for all I know might be mostly jerks.

But even though I know all this, most of the time I can't quite stop myself from being inwardly pleased when the Stars and Stripes is up on the podium, and I can't help feeling a bit disappointed when some American individual or team flames out. Some of this tendency may be due to the fact that coverage here in the United States tends to focus on the American athletes (and in a pretty flattering way), but that is itself both a reflection of nationalism (NBC knows that American viewers want to watch their countrymen) and one of the things that reinforces those beliefs.

Which is of course why my students say much the same thing, no matter where they are from. This feature of nationalism is what Benedict Anderson famously meant by the phrase "imagined community." A nation is a group of people that imagines itself to be part of a common family, even though most of the members do not know each other personally (and might not like each other if they did). Yet they have the sense of being tied together, to the extent that when one member of the groups succeeds (or fails) it actually affects how other members who don't even know them feel.

This tendency isn't absolute, of course (i.e., there may be some U.S. athletes I don't care much for, just as there are some members of the Boston Red Sox I've never warmed to very much). And in those cases, I won't be sorry if they don't emerge triumphant. But the general rule applies, because nationalism remains an incredibly powerful political force. Try it on yourself the next time you turn on the Games.

Language and Nationalism: Catalonian Confusion

THE ECONOMIST

© The Economist Newspaper Limited, London (November 27, 2012).

The weekend's election seems to have cleared up little about the prospects for Catalonian independence. The governing party, which campaigned for Catalonia's right to self-determination but not (yet) outright immediate independence, lost seats. An outright secessionist party gained seats, but so did a party vociferously opposed to independence. Overall, parties affiliated with the self-determination movement will now have a majority.

What are the linguistic factors at play? Catalan is an ancient language, recorded at least since the 11th century in a form clearly distinct from vulgar Latin. This age puts it roughly on par with the much bigger neighbouring French and Castillian Spanish. Unlike neighbouring Occitan/Provençal (also found in writing a thousand years ago), Catalan is the vibrant majority language of its territory still today. A 2001 census of Catalonia found that 4.6m of the 6.2m in the Catalan autonomous region spoke Catalan (and 3.1m could write it). Unfortunately, this doesn't distinguish levels of competency, though we can probably assume that people comfortable writing Catalan speak it well. Just 340,000 (5%) say they do not understand Catalan. Compare that to the *Basque autonomous region*, where 52% say they speak Basque "not at all". Basque separatism may be better known, but Catalan is healthier in Catalonia than Basque is in the Basque region.[1]

Though the newspapers this week are talking mainly about Catalonia's frustration over its subsidy to the Spanish budget, linguistic factors have been part of Catalan nationalism for a long time. Franco tried to ban nearly all written use of Catalan for decades, before relaxing policies to allow for limited cultural use. Public speaking of anything but Spanish was discouraged under the slogan *una bandera, una patria, una lengua*. Most attempts to crush a language simply make speaking it a point of defiant pride, and this was no exception. But the gap between speaking and writing skills in Catalonia show that to a certain extent, Franco succeeded, at least, in making Catalan

more a language of private and informal life than of public and official use.

Catalan faces another threat: those 2001 census numbers above are not entirely safe from change, Catalans feel. Until the Spanish economy tanked, many migrants came from Latin America to Spain, and especially to wealthy Catalonia, looking for work. They brought Spanish, and in the bigger cities, felt little need to learn Catalan. (It is perfectly possible to live in Barcelona without speaking Catalan; it would be difficult without speaking Spanish.) Add to that the problem of what Catalan nationalists call "internal migration" from the rest of Spain, and Catalans do not feel that their language's future is assured. Having fought for tolerance of Catalan, the nationalist movement is accused of intolerance towards Spanish. In schools for example, Catalan is the primary language by law. As one member of the Institut d'Etudis Catalans once told me, though, Catalan nationalists don't consider this to be "intolerance". He simply wanted Catalan in Catalonia to be like Italian in Italy, German in Germany or French in France.

And that is the rub of nationalism: Catalonia isn't like Germany or Italy yet. A nation-state has the sovereign right to insist on the primacy of one language. Catalans constitute Europe's biggest language group without a state[2]: some 11.5m people speak the language, according to Wikipedia (meaning almost half of them are outside the Catalonian autonomous region in Spain). This puts Catalan on rough par with Greek, Bulgarian or Swedish.

---

1   These numbers are incomplete. Basque spills into other provinces, especially Navarre, and into France. Catalan extends into France, too, as well as down the coast into Valencia, and to the Balearic Islands. But the rough numbers show clearly enough that of the two, Catalan is on the stronger footing.

2   This excludes the Kurds. Though Turkey is an EU candidate and part of Turkey is clearly in Europe, the Kurds are more accurately considered to be in the Middle East.

In short: the weekend's election may not have re-solved the picture, but Catalan nationalism is noth-ing to scoff at. With political, cultural and economic factors all pushing the same way, the idea that sepa-ratism will blow over may be wishful thinking. Our pre-election leader encouraged Spain to consider more formal and elaborate federalism instead, and recognise that Catalonia, the Basque country and perhaps Galicia are "cultural nations within Spain". Would that be enough for the nationalists? Maybe, maybe not, but the elections showed that a majority is certainly not happy with where things stand today.

Shinzo Abe's Civic Nationalism

KEVIN DOAK

"Japan Chair Platform: Shinzo Abe's Civic Nationalism" by Kevin Doak, Center for Strategic & International Studies, May 15, 2013. Reprinted by permission of the Center for Strategic & International Studies.

There's an old saw among nationalism scholars, and it goes like this: "I'm a patriot, you're a nationalist, but (you and I can agree that) he's a racist." There's a lot to learn from these few words about the politics of nation-alism, and especially the politics of misunderstanding and misrepresenting the nationalism of others. We tend to see our own nationalism as a good thing, that of our closest allies as acceptable but risky, and that of third parties as dangerous in the extreme.

I was reminded of this tendency during Shinzo Abe's first term as prime minister. The U.S. media in particular was filled with charges, claims and innuendos that Abe was something between a risky nationalist and a dangerous racist—all with little to no evidence, of course. It was just another instance of poorly informed rhetoric in the service of a pol-itical agenda. In general, Americans tend to see na-tionalism in Japan only through the exceptional lens of Imperial Japan's military actions, particu-larly during and after the attack on Pearl Harbor. That is, when we hear of Japanese "nationalism," what often is implied is the peculiar form of "stat-ism" (*kokkashugi*) that dominated politics and cul-ture during wartime Japan even though—as Maruyama Masao emphasized—*kokkashugi* is not really a form of nationalism at all.[1] All concern about accurately grasping what nationalism really is pushed aside, the only question of interest often seems to be only whether Japan is "returning" to the "nationalism" [statism] of the wartime.

Because of these misunderstandings and biases, many today are probably mystified—or worse, horrified—by the tremendous public support for Abe and his LDP in the last election. Does this mean that the Japanese people are becoming "nationalis-tic" (ie., militaristic or statists)? How could they reelect such a horrible nationalist? Well, since the peace-loving postwar Japanese couldn't possibly really like a nationalist, this must have been a pro-test vote, which will be corrected in the next elec-tion of the House of Councilors (HC) this summer. The Japanese people must have voted for Abe in spite of, not because of, his nationalism. Such are the machinations many go through to square the 2012 election results with their misconception of Abe and his relationship to nationalism.

Perhaps the LDP will not win the upcoming HC election later this year. Or maybe they will. I do not intend to prophesy about future elections but to argue that if we do not understand the funda-mentals of Japanese nationalism, and particularly the important role Abe is playing in democratiz-ing Japanese nationalism, we will continue to mis-apprehend the basic political dynamics that are unfolding in Japan today.

1   Maruyama, Chapter 1 "Introduction: The Nation and Nationalism," *Studies in The Intellectual History of Tokugawa Japan*, trans. Mikiso Hane, (Princeton University Press, 1974), p. 324.

The first and most important thing to understand about Japanese nationalism is that there are two words for nationalism in the Japanese lexicon (and *kokkashugi* [statism] is not one of them): *minzokushugi* and *kokuminshugi*. When a person speaking or thinking in Japanese makes reference to "nationalism," he must choose which of these two terms to employ. And that choice makes a difference. Each form of nationalism, *minzokushugi* or *kokuminshugi*, has its own political and cultural history in modern Japan, as I have documented elsewhere.[2] Simply put, the former is best understood as "ethnic nationalism" and the latter as "civic nationalism." And it is a mistake to assume that only the political right is nationalistic. Separate studies by Gayle and Takekawa have demonstrated that the left (eg., Marxists, *Asahi* newspaper) remains quite strongly attached to nationalism, but of the ethnic variety, whereas more conservative intellectuals and media outlets (eg. *Yomiuri* newspaper) are more inclined toward civic nationalism.[3]

Ethnic nationalism has appealed to the left in postwar Japan for many reasons, most importantly that it provides a socio-cultural identity that need not find expression in laws and political institutions (here we can intuit the reason some ethnic nationalists were dismayed by the Diet passing the Act on the National Flag and Anthem in 1999). But ethnic nationalism has also been positioned as "Asian nationalism" at least since the 1955 Bandung Conference; in contrast, civic nationalism has from its very beginning in modern Japan and throughout East Asia been seen as the favorite of pro-Western governments, Christian minorities and intellectuals thought to be tainted by Western ways of thinking. Recently, historians in Japan and the West have recognized that ethnic nationalism was given a boost by the effects of Japan's loss of its multiethnic empire after World War II. The first decades after 1945 were a heyday of ethnic nationalism in Japan, and only in the last few decades have we seen the tables turned and civic nationalism rise to the fore.

Shinzo Abe is one of the leaders in this current renaissance of civic nationalism in Japan. But few in the West appear to know this, perhaps because few of them actually have read his 2006 book in Japanese, *Toward a Beautiful Country* (republished

largely intact as *Toward a New Country* this year). At the heart of the book is "Chapter 3: What is Nationalism?" Sports provide the key metaphor for Abe in explaining nationalism that is democratic and nationalism that is not. He speaks of his fascination as a young boy watching the parades for the Tokyo Olympics, but this pride clearly comes from how athletes would represent Japan—not from their blood but from what they would do as competitors in the games. He writes with pride also about how naturalized Japanese like Alessandro "Alex" Santos fought for Japan in World Cup soccer games. "Alex" and his fellow Brazilian-Japanese "Ramos" are embraced for what they are: fellow Japanese compatriots, men made Japanese by law, not by blood or ethnicity. And finally, Abe directly rejects ethnic nationalism by pointing to the example of Australian Gold Medalist, Cathy Freeman, whose Australian national identity coexists with her aboriginal identity. "Nationalism," Abe concludes, "can be translated in various ways, but if we dare to render it as ethnic nationalism (*minzokushugi*), then Cathy Freeman would not be able to carry both banners (Australian and Aboriginal) without being ripped apart within by this nationalism."[4] Throughout the book, Abe consistently renders the Japanese nation as *kokumin* (civic nation) not as *minzoku* (ethnic nation), a distinction made not only conceptually but also through his description of how democratic nationalism functions in practice.

Those who wish to know what concrete difference Abe's civic nationalism might make in particular policy issues are well-advised to read Abe's book. But to appreciate how this renaissance of

2 Kevin M Doak, *A History of Nationalism in Modern Japan: Placing the People* (Brill, 2007); Japanese translation, *Ōgoe de utae, 'Kimigayo' o* (PHP, 2009).
3 Curtis Anderson Gayle, *Marxist History and Postwar Japanese Nationalism* (RoutledgeCurzon, 2003); Shun'ichi Takekawa, "Forging Nationalism from Pacifism and Internationalism: A Study of *Asahi* and *Yomiuri*'s New Year's Day Editorials, 1953-2005." *Social Science Japan Journal* vol. 10, no. 1 (April 2007).
4 Abe Shinzō, *Atarashii kuni e* (Bungei Shunju, 2013), p. 102.

civic nationalism is deeply linked to the policies Abe seeks to establish, one merely needs to read the concluding lines from *Toward a New Country*:

> Thus, when we line up all the issues that Japan faces, not just the North Korean kidnapping issue, but even the territorial questions, the U.S.-Japan relationship or even economic issues like the TPP, I believe they all come from the same root. Is this not the price we have had to pay for enjoying economic prosperity while kicking these problems down the road, without a clear consciousness that the life and treasure of the Japanese civic nation (*Nihon kokumin*) and the territory of Japan are to be protected by the Japanese government's own hands? Truly, "escape from the postwar regime" is still the most important theme for Japan, just as it was five years earlier when I was the prime minister.
>
> During the last general election, the LDP raised the slogan, "Take Back Japan." This did not mean only to take back Japan from the Democratic Party government. I'll go so far as to say that we are in a battle to take back the country of Japan from post-war history by the hands of the Japanese people (*Nihon kokumin*).[5]

---

5   Abe, *Atarashii kuni e*, p. 254.

Conflicts without Borders

STEFAN WOLFF

"Conflicts without Borders" by Stefan Wolff, May/June 2008. Reprinted by permission of *The National Interest*.

Many governments around the world identify stopping and stemming "ethnic and religious hatreds" as a major foreign-policy priority. Quite simply, in the words of the 2006 U.S. National Security Strategy, such "conflicts do not stay isolated for long and often spread or devolve into humanitarian tragedy or anarchy." Yet, ethnic conflicts do not simply appear out of thin air. They can be traced primarily to the decisions of political leaders. The spread of ethnic conflict is not automatic either. For existing ethnic conflicts to move beyond their original borders, the relevant actors—ethnic communities, states and other private interest groups—need to make a choice. If they choose to expand the conflict, they need three things: the motive, the means and the opportunity.

Ethnic conflict spreads in two principal patterns: diffusion and escalation. Diffusion means that the existence of one ethnic conflict leads to the occurrence of others, either elsewhere in the same state or in other, often neighboring, states. Escalation, on the other hand, describes a situation in which more actors become involved in the same conflict as belligerent parties.

The traditional patterns of the spread of ethnic conflict exhibit close links between escalation and diffusion and typically occur when ethnic groups mobilized on the basis of some combination of greed, grievance or security concerns confront each other, the states in which they live or both. Ethnic groups, states or a combination of both can drive these conflicts. They are predominantly played out on a regional level (e.g., in the western Balkans, in the Greater Middle East) and involve not only the immediate neighbors of an ongoing conflict, but they also draw in regional and great powers.

The literature on ethnic conflict is full of different theories about its ultimate causes. There are three common explanations. One focuses on cost-benefit calculations or "greed": conflicts happen when profit is to be made. A second sees social, political, economic and other grievances as powerful explanations as well. Here, the argument is that conflict happens when people are dissatisfied with their status compared to other groups in society or feel that their status is threatened. So conflict can become a strategy either to change or defend the status quo. Finally, the third considers the so-called security dilemma as central among the causes of ethnic conflict. When people perceive their survival as individuals and members of a group is at risk, they seek to avert this threat by using violence preemptively against those who they consider to be the main source of the threat.

In most ethnic conflicts, participants are motivated by a mix of profit, status and security considerations. This is important for the diffusion of ethnic conflict because one conflict can only spread within or beyond a given country if people elsewhere are receptive to it. They must be motivated to pursue their interests by means of conflict, and they need the means and opportunity to do so.

The conflict in Sudan is primarily driven by ethnic groups. In the Darfur crisis, the government, through the Arab Janjaweed militias, is targeting local Darfurian communities. The government claims their attacks originally came in response to the western rebel groups—the Sudanese Liberation Army and the Justice and Equality Movement—challenging President Omar al-Bashir, but many label the conflict genocide.

When the thirty-year civil war between north and south was approaching a negotiated settlement in the first years of the twenty-first century, the rebel groups elsewhere in the country wanted a greater share in the emerging new political and economic bargain as well. Their motive was improved political and economic status. Neighboring Chad, in particular, was motivated to play a role in the conflict by its keen interest in weakening the regime in Khartoum; the Chadian government alleged that Sudan was the main sponsor of antigovernment rebels in Chad.

The Sudanese government had the means to carry out repression in Darfur in the form of the Janjaweed militia. The western rebel groups, in the meantime, benefited from easy access to bases in Chad and received arms and equipment from there (as well as from Eritrea).

Opportunities presented by ongoing negotiations and international involvement in Sudan combined with motivation and means to make conflict possible. Having learned the "lesson" that violence pays by seeing it bring the government to the negotiating table, ready to make concessions, the movements in

Darfur launched attacks against government forces. They even had a Plan B (for some of them it may even have been Plan A): if the government did not respond with concessions but with increased repression, then surely a humanitarian emergency would result. The international community would take sides with the local movements, shifting the balance of power away from the government.

As this case shows, the causes of the spread of ethnic conflict come not just from the local or state levels. This becomes more clear when one considers why neither Plan A nor Plan B of the Darfur movements worked. The Sudanese government was in a very favorable position that allowed it to pursue a policy of ruthless repression in Darfur. Equally as important as the existence of the means and motive was the international-opportunity structure. Initially, the African Union and UN mediators in the north-south conflict hesitated to become involved for fear of jeopardizing a settlement. This allowed Khartoum to negotiate a separate deal with the south and exclude Darfur from the so-called Comprehensive Peace Agreement of 2005. It was the close economic partnership between Sudan and China that protected the former from any hard-hitting action by the UN Security Council, despite the gravity of the human-rights violations in Darfur.

As the situation in Darfur worsened with mass killings and refugee flows, there was a second wave of diffusion, this time spreading directly into Chad and leading to an almost-successful coup against the government there. Military operations conducted by regular Chadian forces in Sudan in response in early 2008 also illustrate that escalation and diffusion are often closely linked.

Kosovo is another illustrative example of the complexity of the spread of ethnic conflict. At the extreme end, not just a case of diffusion or escalation, but simply the precedent set by Kosovo's independence is seen as a potential cause of conflict proliferation. Here, the initial conflict was also driven by ethnic antagonisms: Serbs and Albanians equally sought full control of Kosovo.

Control of means played an important part in halting the spread of the conflict. For ten years, successive preventive deployment missions—by the UN and later NATO and the EU—made sure that

Macedonia was not dragged into the violence that engulfed the western Balkans throughout the 1990s. On the other hand, not having curbed the proliferation of small arms from Albania to Kosovo was one of the major facilitating factors that made the rise of the Albanian Kosovo Liberation Army (KLA) possible from the mid-1990s onward. The rise of the KLA—which called for the independence of Kosovo and was considered a terrorist group with links to organized crime, including by many in the West—was also aided significantly by a "tax" collected among diaspora Albanians in Western Europe and the United States.

The NATO-led intervention in 1999, motivated primarily by concerns over the grave violation of human rights in Kosovo, was an early example of escalation. At that time, Russia, too, resisted Western policy but eventually accepted Kosovo's UN-led administration under Security Council Resolution 1244. Almost ten years on, Russian resistance to Kosovo's unilateral declaration of independence and its recognition is far more uncompromising. While Russia has neither the means nor the opportunity to engage the West militarily, it may well contribute to the diffusion of the Kosovo conflict, albeit in a different way.

Kosovo is presented by Russia, and others, as an opportunity, a dangerous precedent for the creation of new states by unilateral acts of those seeking to realize their claim to self-determination through secession. That Kosovo has been able to pursue this path and find relatively widespread international recognition, it is argued, will inspire secessionist movements elsewhere to follow the Kosovo example. That it is unlikely this line of reasoning will have any practical merit— after all, even Russia has so far refused to recognize separatist regions across the former Soviet Union—is less important.

The very fact that self-determination movements elsewhere can now cite the case of Kosovo is likely to make the settlement of some of these conflicts more difficult because movements elsewhere will refer to Kosovo as a precedent based not only on the view of Russia, but also strengthened by similar pronouncements from China, Spain, Romania, Slovakia and Greece to name but a few. This has already affected, and will continue to

affect, places as diverse as Sri Lanka, Indonesia, the Philippines, Thailand, India, China, Somaliland, south Sudan, Ethiopia and Tanzania.

Yet, diffusion is also likely much closer to Kosovo: Macedonia, with its roughly 25 percent ethnic Albanian population right across the border from Kosovo, and Bosnia and Herzegovina, with its highly discontent Serbian community, are perhaps the most likely early "victims" of diffusion. On the other hand, escalation in the sense of external belligerents entering the frame is unlikely. A strong NATO and EU military presence on the ground across the Balkan region will prevent or at least swiftly contain local violence. The still-feasible promise of closer relations with, and eventual membership in, the European Union is also likely to calm any desire for major trouble.

The "diffusion qua precedent" in the case of Kosovo when it comes to opportunities is instructive. Regardless of how one feels about the legitimacy and legality of Kosovo's unilateral declaration of independence, there is little if any need to turn it into an almighty precedent. Russia may be right in insisting that short of a new UN Security Council resolution, only a consensual separation of Kosovo from Serbia would have been legal under current international law. But waving the big stick of Kosovo as a precedent is counterproductive, not least in relation to any of the conflicts in Russia's own neighborhood. By the same token, the refusal, so far, to recognize Kosovo by several European governments such as Spain, Greece, Cyprus, Slovakia and Romania establishes a precedent where there is none—and a wrong one at that.

Kosovo is unique and requires a unique response—rejecting its independence with reference to other cases undermines this position and strengthens the very separatist forces that are meant to be deterred. By delaying or denying international recognition to Kosovo out of concern for the implications that such a move might have on suspected separatist movements in their own countries, these states are sending exactly the wrong message. For one, they equate their own problems with those of Kosovo. Yet, neither of these countries has Serbia's track record of past persistent and grave human-rights violations. Nor do people living in areas like Spain's

Basque Country give the same strong support to independence as do some 90 percent of current inhabitants of Kosovo. Moreover, Northern Cyprus, another often-cited area that could "abuse" Kosovo as a precedent, in fact seeks reunification with the south. In 2004, they approved of a unsponsored plan to that effect, which was rejected by the south. So neither of these two cases, nor the situations in Slovakia and Romania involving ethnic Hungarians, are comparable to the situation in Kosovo.

When the spread of conflict is not driven by ethnic groups, it is driven by states. This is apparent in Iraq, an equally complex case of diffusion and escalation. Turkey's recent invasion of the Kurdistan region of northern Iraq was motivated by its own security concerns in relation to the terrorist Kurdistan Workers' Party (PKK), which has waged an insurgency against successive Turkish governments for over two decades. The threat from the PKK and Kurdish demands vis-à-vis Turkey in general, however, is perceived to have increased as a result of developments in Iraq. This also increases Turkey's motivation to be involved. The 2005 constitution formally established Kurdistan as a region in Iraq with far-reaching powers of self-government, including its own military forces. On the one hand, this allegedly gives Kurds in Turkey more incentives to ask for an equally advantageous status. More importantly, perhaps, it also means that Kurdish popular sentiment in Iraq might provide a power base and safe haven for the PKK, from which the terrorist organization may reinvigorate its campaign in Turkey.

Yet, the threat of diffusion and escalation does not end there. Other states could be equally motivated to play a part in the conflict. There are also sizable Kurdish communities in Iran and Syria. Further complicating matters, Iran and Saudi Arabia back different sides of another conflict driven by radicalized religious groups: the sectarian civil war between Sunni and Shia within Iraq. This could easily escalate further into a proxy war for regional hegemony. In addition, Iran, more than Saudi Arabia, also has an interest in making life as difficult as possible for the multinational coalition in Iraq, and has escalated the various interlinked conflicts in the Middle East, if only by using proxy forces like Hezbollah and Islamic Jihad.

Policy responses should take these actors' concerns into account and focus on eliminating potential spoilers of any settlement. So irredeemable PKK terrorists must be sidelined and deprived of their political and power bases. But this can only succeed if it happens in combination with acknowledging and addressing the legitimate grievances of Kurds by the Turkish government (a policy that has already begun), and a Kurdish acceptance, on both sides of the border, that violence is an unsuitable means to pursue otherwise legitimate ends. Above all, the current borders in the region must be recognized explicitly. This involves respect for the territorial integrity of both Iraq and Turkey, as well as for the right of Kurds in Iraq to their autonomous region.

The Turkish-Kurdish example indicates just how difficult it will be to remove motivations from the equation of diffusion and escalation of ethnic conflict. In many other cases, immediate success in this respect is likely to be equally difficult to achieve.

More recent, "nontraditional" patterns of diffusion and escalation reveal varied means and follow a different and more dangerous logic. Over the past several years, evidence has grown that there are increasing and solid links between ethnic conflicts on the one side and international terrorism and organized crime on the other. This has also created a new dynamic for the spread of ethnic conflict, and one that is much more difficult to tackle with the traditional set of responses aimed at containing and eventually settling such conflicts.

The links between conflict, crime and terrorism are, for example, particularly obvious in Southeast Asia, involving the Philippines, Indonesia, Malaysia and Thailand. At the center of a regional fundamentalist Islamic terror network is a group called Jemaah Islamiyah. It maintains links with similar groups, including the Abu Sayyaf Group and the Moro Islamic Liberation Front in the southern Philippines, the Malaysian Kampulan Mujahedin, insurgent groups in southern Thailand, such as the Pattani United Liberation Organization, and the Free Aceh Movement in Indonesia. These links are primarily based on shared experiences of senior commanders in the anti-Soviet Afghan war in the 1980s and 1990s. They manifest themselves today in joint training, recruitment, financing and operational cooperation, and often involve direct and indirect links to terrorist groups in the Middle East, including al-Qaeda.

The various groups have exploited local grievances and grafted themselves onto preexisting ethnic conflicts, forming a dangerous, symbiotic partnership with local insurgents. They offer local fighters access to funds and know-how and receive in return a base from which they can wage their very own brand of jihad. This jihadist connection, however, should not make us overlook the fact that the environment of ethnic conflict in Asia also proves fertile ground for organized crime and draws on it as a major source of funds for armed struggles. The Abu Sayyaf group, for one, finances its activities primarily with the proceeds of kidnapping. Other groups in Burma, Bangladesh and northeast India are involved in the production and smuggling of drugs.

While similar types of escalation are underway in Africa and have already had a certain measure of success in the east (specifically Kenya, Tanzania and Uganda), the Horn (Eritrea, Ethiopia, Somalia) and Nigeria, the strategy of implanting Islamic jihad in any of Europe's ethnic conflicts has so far been relatively ineffective. Here, the major new dimension of spread is organized crime. In Kosovo, various groups have long been involved with drug smuggling, gunrunning and human trafficking. Kosovar Albanian mafia groups today control much of western Europe's prostitution. And Transnistria in Moldova, an unrecognized separatist entity, is a major source and transport route for drugs, cigarettes and women destined for the sex industry in Europe.

The general point here is not to criminalize what are often legitimate grievances of suppressed population groups, but to highlight that ethnic conflict spreads in very different ways. Even in an age when international terrorism is seen as the greatest scourge, ethnic conflicts—no matter how far away they happen—pose serious security challenges and need to be tackled.

For the most part, ethnic conflicts are political conflicts. They can be resolved in a bargaining process in which all parties can agree on institutions, rules and regulations that allow them to resolve their disagreements by political rather than violent means. Sensible policy responses need to take account of the causes and consequences of traditional and nontraditional patterns of diffusion and escalation if they want to succeed.

Removing the motive for people to spread ethnic conflict would be the most likely strategy of sustainable success. This would mean addressing greed, grievance and security concerns of ethnic communities, states and private interest groups. Obviously, this is easier said than done, not least because it is often rather difficult, if not outright impossible, to disentangle the various actors' claims, especially if they have become interwoven over long periods of time. Removing motivations is more likely to be possible in cases where criminal and international terrorist involvement is minimal. Here, policy responses must start by taking the concerns of all actors involved seriously and striving for comprehensive bargains using pressures and incentives alike to make solutions sustainable. It also means using the traditional mechanisms to prevent spread: eliminating potential spoilers, stopping flows of arms, money and "expertise" to susceptible areas, and diaspora support.

Not creating the kind of opportunity in which developments in one ethnic conflict can, beyond all proportions, have global ramifications is primarily a responsibility of political leaders. Rather than letting themselves be driven by short-term domestic concerns (presidential elections in Cyprus, parliamentary elections in Spain, a weak presidency in Romania, etc.), political leaders need to show skill, vision and responsibility when dealing with matters of ethnic conflict and its diffusion and escalation.

Settling ethnic conflicts before they can spread and preventing them before they happen would of course be the most sensible strategy of all. Yet, we have to be realistic about the extent to which this is possible now and in the future. Effective policies prioritize political solutions but are willing to draw on a wide range of other options, including military and judicial ones, to deal with the unholy trinity of ethnic conflict, organized crime and international terrorism. This is the best way to remove the motivations, seize the means and eliminate the opportunities to allow ethnic conflict to spread. Taking this approach will not resolve all ethnic conflicts or prevent the emergence of new ones, but it will put an effective stop to the spread of existing ones.

DISCUSSION QUESTIONS

1) The readings in this section discuss instances in which nationalism is, on balance, a benign development, but also some in which nationalism seems linked to destructive processes. How might one generate a theory to account for when nationalism takes more benign forms and when it becomes more problematic? What might be risk factors for the latter outcome? How could your theory be empirically tested?

2) In at least one of the cases discussed in this section (proponents of a separate Catalan nation-state, or at least greater regional autonomy for Catalonia), language is a major issue of concern to nationalists. Do you think this is likely to be generalizable across cases? Does linguistic difference always lead to identity difference? And is identity difference possible in the context of shared language? As you think about these issues, consider cases like Switzerland, Canada, and the many polities of Spanish America.

3) Is national identity always based on "ethnic" criteria? What does this mean? Do both "civic" and "ethnic" versions of nationalism exist? If so, what are the implications of this distinction? Could it help us to predict the behavior of nation-states?

Gender, Race, and Ethnicity

Most comparative political scientists probably hope for a world free of inequalities based on gender, race, ethnicity, and sexual orientation. We do not, however, live in such a world at present. Indeed, in many countries, ethnic or racial differences link to forms of economic, civil, and politic inequalities, and in virtually all countries women are less likely than men to hold political office. The field of comparative politics asks many questions about this state of affairs. First, it tries to document and understand differences in this respect. Not only do levels of inequality vary, but the very ideas of gender, race, and ethnicity differ across cultural contexts. Second, it tries to understand the sources of inequalities. For example, is explicit discrimination to blame? Structural inequities? Historical legacies? Finally, much work in political science looks at potential policy responses to race-, gender-, and ethnicity-based inequality, trying to figure out what can reduce it most effectively. Considerable attention is focused on institutional policies like quotas and reserved seats, probably because institutional rules of this sort are the easiest to engineer (this is not to say that engineering them is easy, but just that it is easier than, say, directly redressing the unequal distribution of assets or income in society).

This section has three readings, which reflect these themes. The first is an article from *The Economist* on race in Brazil. Many scholars have pointed out that race does not have exactly the same meaning in Brazil and other parts of Latin America as it does in places like the United States. Boundaries between groups have historically been more fluid in Brazil, for example. Indeed, many Brazilians have denied that racism is even an issue in their country. Yet there is considerable evidence that inequality and race are related in Brazil. As the reading points out, figuring out what is going on with this relationship and how to resolve it is a complicated task.

The second reading looks at global opinions about homosexuality. Produced by an important social science research organization, this piece compares survey data from a number of countries concerning attitudes toward gays and lesbians. The study finds striking differences: in general, European countries are highly tolerant/affirming, and countries in several other regions are less so. As you know, scholars in comparative politics try to explain variation of this sort, wondering why something like attitudes towards homosexuality would vary so much across cultures. The authors of the piece have hypotheses that are consistent with their data. For one, economic development seems to encourage tolerance. For another, religion's influence seems to reduce it. However, it is not clear that these relationships are causal: they *may* be, but the report's data cannot examine this beyond noting correlations. Moreover, as the report's authors point out, there are exceptions to these general relationships. For example, China exhibits fairly low religiosity (in relative terms) but also exhibits relatively high intolerance of homosexuality. Can you think of other factors that might account for country-level variation about these matters?

The final reading in this section is by the political scientist Sarah Bush and considers the ways in which attention to gender is increasingly prevalent in democracy promotion. Her main emphasis is on the use of gender quotas, which are institutional design tools through which some groups and organizations seek to expand women's political representation. As you will see, she considers both the potential benefits and limitations of quotas when applied to different circumstances. What do you think about the likely utility of gender quotas? Can you think of alternative or supplementary methods to reduce inequalities of this sort?

Race in Brazil: Affirming a Divide

THE ECONOMIST

©The Economist Newspaper Limited, London (January 28, 2012).

In April 2010, as part of a scheme to beautify the run-down port near the centre of Rio de Janeiro for the 2016 Olympic games, workers were replacing the drainage system in a shabby square when they found some old cans. The city called in archaeologists, whose excavations unearthed the ruins of Valongo, once Brazil's main landing stage for African slaves.

From 1811 to 1843 around 500,000 slaves arrived there, according to Tânia Andrade Lima, the head archaeologist. Valongo was a complex, including warehouses where slaves were sold and a cemetery. Hundreds of plastic bags, stored in shipping containers parked on a corner of the site, hold personal objects lost or hidden by the slaves, or taken from them. They include delicate bracelets and rings woven from vegetable fibre; lumps of amethyst and stones used in African worship; and cowrie shells, a common currency in Africa.

It is a poignant reminder of the scale and duration of the slave trade to Brazil. Of the 10.7m African slaves shipped across the Atlantic between the 16th and 19th centuries, 4.9m landed there. Fewer than 400,000 went to the United States. Brazil was the last country in the Americas to abolish slavery, in 1888.

Brazil has long seemed to want to forget this history. In 1843 Valongo was paved over by a grander dock to welcome a Bourbon princess who came to marry Pedro II, the country's 19th-century emperor. The stone column rising from the square commemorates the empress, not the slaves. Now the city plans to make Valongo an open-air museum of slavery and the African diaspora. "Our work is to give greater visibility to the black community and its ancestors," says Ms Andrade Lima.

This project is a small example of a much broader re-evaluation of race in Brazil. The pervasiveness of slavery, the lateness of its abolition, and the fact that nothing was done to turn former slaves into citizens all combined to have a profound impact on Brazilian society. They are reasons for the extreme socioeconomic inequality that still scars the country today.

Neither Separate nor Equal

In the 2010 census some 51% of Brazilians defined themselves as black or brown. On average, the income of whites is slightly more than double that of black or brown Brazilians, according to IPEA, a government-linked think-tank. It finds that blacks are relatively disadvantaged in their level of education and in their access to health and other services. For example, more than half the people in Rio de Janeiro's *favelas* (slums) are black. The comparable figure in the city's richer districts is just 7%.

Brazilians have long argued that blacks are poor only because they are at the bottom of the social pyramid—in other words, that society is stratified by class, not race. But a growing number disagree. These "clamorous" differences can only be explained by racism, according to Mário Theodoro of the federal government's secretariat for racial equality. In a passionate and sometimes angry debate, black Brazilian activists insist that slavery's legacy of injustice and inequality can only be reversed by affirmative-action policies, of the kind found in the United States.

Their opponents argue that the history of race relations in Brazil is very different, and that such policies risk creating new racial problems. Unlike in the United States, slavery in Brazil never meant segregation. Mixing was the norm, and Brazil had many more free blacks. The result is a spectrum of skin colour rather than a dichotomy.

Few these days still call Brazil a "racial democracy". As Antonio Riserio, a sociologist from Bahia, put it in a recent book: "It's clear that racism exists in the US. It's clear that racism exists in Brazil. But they are different kinds of racism." In Brazil, he argues, racism is veiled and shamefaced, not open or institutional. Brazil has never had anything like the Ku Klux Klan, or the ban on interracial marriage imposed in 17 American states until 1967.

Importing American-style affirmative action risks forcing Brazilians to place themselves in strict racial categories rather than somewhere along a spectrum, says Peter Fry, a British-born, naturalised-Brazilian anthropologist. Having worked in southern Africa, he says that Brazil's avoidance of "the crystallising of race as a marker of identity" is a big advantage in creating a democratic society.

But for the proponents of affirmative action, the veiled quality of Brazilian racism explains why racial stratification has been ignored for so long. "In Brazil you have an invisible enemy. Nobody's racist. But when your daughter goes out with a black, things change," says Ivanir dos Santos, a black activist in Rio de Janeiro. If black and white youths with equal qualifications apply to be a shop assistant in a Rio mall, the white will get the job, he adds.

The debate over affirmative action splits both left and right. The governments of Dilma Rousseff, the president, and of her two predecessors, Luiz Inácio Lula da Silva and Fernando Henrique Cardoso, have all supported such policies. But they have moved cautiously. So far the main battleground has been in universities. Since 2001 more than 70 public universities have introduced racial admissions quotas. In Rio de Janeiro's state universities, 20% of places are set aside for black students who pass the entrance exam. Another 25% are reserved for a "social quota" of pupils from state schools whose parents' income is less than twice the minimum wage—who are often black. A big federal programme awards grants to black and brown students at private universities.

These measures are starting to make a difference. Although only 6.3% of black 18- to 24-year-olds were in higher education in 2006, that was double the proportion in 2001, according to IPEA. (The figures for whites were 19.2% in 2006, compared with 14.1% in 2001). "We're very happy, because in the past five years we've placed more blacks in universities than in the previous 500 years," says Frei David Raimundo dos Santos, a Franciscan friar who runs Educafro, a charity that holds university-entrance classes in poor areas. "Today there's a revolution in Brazil."

One of its beneficiaries is Carolina Bras da Silva, a young black woman whose mother was a cleaner. As a teenager she lived for a while on the streets of São Paulo. But she is now in her first year of social sciences at Rio's Catholic University, on a full grant. "Some of the other students said 'What are you doing here?' But it's getting better," she says. She wants to study law and become a public prosecutor.

Academics from some of Brazil's best universities have led a campaign against quotas. They argue firstly that affirmative action starts with an act of racism: the division of a rainbow nation into arbitrary colour categories. Assigning races in Brazil is not always as easy as the activists claim. In 2007 one of two identical twins who both applied to enter the University of Brasília was classified as black, the other as white. All this risks creating racial resentment. Secondly, opponents say affirmative action undermines equality of opportunity and meritocracy—fragile concepts in Brazil, where privilege, nepotism and contacts have long been routes to advancement.

Proponents of affirmative action say these arguments sanctify an unjust status quo. And formally meritocratic university entrance exams have not guaranteed equality of opportunity. A study by Carlos Antonio Costa Ribeiro, a sociologist at the State University of Rio de Janeiro, found that the factors most closely correlated to attending university are having rich parents and studying in private school.

In practice, many of the fears surrounding university quotas have not been borne out. Though still preliminary, studies tend to show that *cotistas*, as they are known, have performed academically as well as or better than their peers. That may be because they have replaced weaker "white" students who got in merely because they had the money to prepare for the exam.

Nelson do Valle Silva, a sociologist at the Federal University of Rio de Janeiro, says that the backlash against quotas would have been even stronger if access to universities were not growing so fast. For now, almost everyone who passes the exam gets in somewhere. It also helps, he says, that many universities have adopted less controversial "social quotas". Mr Fry agrees that affirmative action has "become a fait accompli". He attributes the declining resistance to guilt, indifference and the fear of being accused of racism.

The Battle for Jobs

For black activists, the next target is the labour market. "As a black man, when I go for a job I start from a disadvantage," says Mr Theodoro. He notes that the United States, which is only 12% black, has a black president and numerous black politicians and millionaires. In Brazil, in contrast, "we have nobody". That is not quite true: apart from footballers and singers, Brazil has a black supreme-court justice (appointed by Lula) and senior military and police officers. But they are exceptional. Only one of the 38 members of Ms Rousseff's cabinet is black (though ten are women). Stand outside the adjacent headquarters of Petrobras, the state oil company, and the National Development Bank in Rio at lunchtime, and "all the managers are white and the cleaners are black," says Frei David.

Some private-sector bodies are starting to espouse racial diversity in recruitment. The state and city of Rio de Janeiro have both passed laws reserving 20% of posts in civil-service exams for blacks, though they are yet to be implemented. If unemployment rises from today's record low, job quotas are likely to create even more controversy than university entrance has.

What stands out from a decade of debate about affirmative action is that it is being implemented in a very Brazilian way. Each university has taken its own decisions. The federal government has tried to promote the policy, but not impose it. The supreme court is sitting on three cases addressing racial quotas. Some lawyers suspect it is deliberately dragging its heels in the hope that society can sort the issue out.

Society itself is indeed changing fast. Many of the 30m Brazilians who have left poverty over the past decade are black. Businesses are taking note: many more cosmetics are aimed at blacks, for example. The mix of passengers on internal flights now bears some resemblance to Brazil, rather than Scandinavia. Until recently, the only black actors in television soap operas played maids; now one Globo soap has a black male lead. Much of this might have happened without affirmative action.

The question facing Brazil is whether the best way to repair the legacy of slavery is to give extra rights to darker-skinned Brazilians. Yes, say the government and the black movement. Given the persistence of racial disadvantage that is understandable.

But the approach carries clear risks. Until the invasion of American academic ideas, most Brazilians thought that their country's racial rainbow was among its main assets. They were not wholly wrong. Mr do Valle Silva, a specialist in social mobility, finds that race affects life chances in Brazil but does not determine them. And if positive discrimination becomes permanent, a publicly funded industry of entitlement may grow up to entrench it and to promote divisive racial politics.

There may be better ways to establish genuine equality of opportunity and rights. Brazil has had anti-discrimination legislation since the 1950s. The 1988 constitution made both racial abuse and racism crimes. But there have been relatively few prosecutions. That is partly because of racism in the judiciary. But it is also because judges and prosecutors think the penalties are too harsh: anyone accused of racism must be held in jail both before and after conviction. And in Rio de Janeiro the black movement's preference for affirmative action led the state government to lose interest in measures aimed at attacking racial prejudice, according to a study by Fabiano Dias Monteiro, who ran the state's anti-racist helpline before it was scrapped in 2007.

The hardest task is to change attitudes. Many Brazilians simply assume blacks belong at the bottom of the pile. Supporters of affirmative action are right to say that the country turned its back on the problem. But American-style policies might not be the way to combat Brazil's specific forms of racism. A combination of stronger legal action against discrimination and quotas for social class in higher education to compensate for weak public schools may work better.

The Global Divide on Homosexuality: Greater Acceptance in More Secular and Affluent Countries

PEW RESEARCH GLOBAL ATTITUDES PROJECT

"The Global Divide on Homosexuality." Pew Research Center, Washington, D.C. (June 4, 2013). http://www.pewglobal
.org/2013/06/04/the-global-divide-on-homosexuality/. Reprinted by permission of the Pew Research Center's Global
Attitudes Project.

Overview

As the United States and other countries grapple with the issue of same-sex marriage, a new Pew Research Center survey finds huge variance by region on the broader question of whether homosexuality should be accepted or rejected by society.

The survey of publics in 39 countries finds broad acceptance of homosexuality in North America, the European Union, and much of Latin America, but equally widespread rejection in predominantly Muslim nations and in Africa, as well as in parts of Asia and in Russia. Opinion about the acceptability of homosexuality is divided in Israel, Poland and Bolivia.

Attitudes about homosexuality have been fairly stable in recent years, except in South Korea, the United States and Canada, where the percentage saying homosexuality should be accepted by society has grown by at least ten percentage points since 2007. These are among the key findings of a new survey by the Pew Research Center conducted in 39 countries among 37,653 respondents from March 2 to May 1, 2013.[1]

The survey also finds that acceptance of homosexuality is particularly widespread in countries where religion is less central in people's lives. These are also among the richest countries in the world. In contrast, in poorer countries with high levels of religiosity, few believe homosexuality should be accepted by society.

Age is also a factor in several countries, with younger respondents offering far more tolerant views than older ones. And while gender differences are not prevalent, in those countries where they are, women are consistently more accepting of homosexuality than men.

Where Homosexuality is Most Accepted

The view that homosexuality should be accepted by society is prevalent in most of the European Union. The view that homosexuality should be accepted by society is prevalent in most of the European Union countries surveyed. About three-quarters or more in Spain (88%), Germany (87%), the Czech Republic (80%), France (77%), Britain (76%), and Italy (74%) share this view, as do more than half in Greece (53%). Poland is the only EU country surveyed where views are mixed; 42% say homosexuality should be accepted by society and 46% believe it should be rejected.

Canadians, who already expressed tolerant views in 2007, are now even more likely to say homosexuality should be accepted by society; 80% say this, compared with 70% six years ago. Views are not as positive in the U.S., where a smaller majority (60%) believes homosexuality should be accepted. But Americans are far more tolerant today than they were in 2007, when 49% said homosexuality should be accepted by society and 41% said it should be rejected.

Opinions about homosexuality are also positive in parts of Latin America. In Argentina, the first country in the region to legalize gay marriage in 2010, about three-quarters (74%) say homosexuality should be accepted, as do clear majorities in Chile (68%), Mexico (61%) and Brazil (60%); about half of Venezuelans (51%) also express acceptance. In contrast, 62% of Salvadorans say homosexuality should be rejected by society, as do nearly half in Bolivia (49%).

In the Asia/Pacific region, where views of homosexuality are mostly negative, more than seven-in-ten in Australia (79%) and the Philippines (73%) say homosexuality should be accepted by society; 54% in Japan agree.

Where Homosexuality is Rejected

Publics in Africa and in predominantly Muslim countries remain among the least accepting of homosexuality. In sub-Saharan Africa, at least nine-in-ten in Nigeria (98%), Senegal (96%), Ghana (96%), Uganda (96%) and Kenya (90%) believe

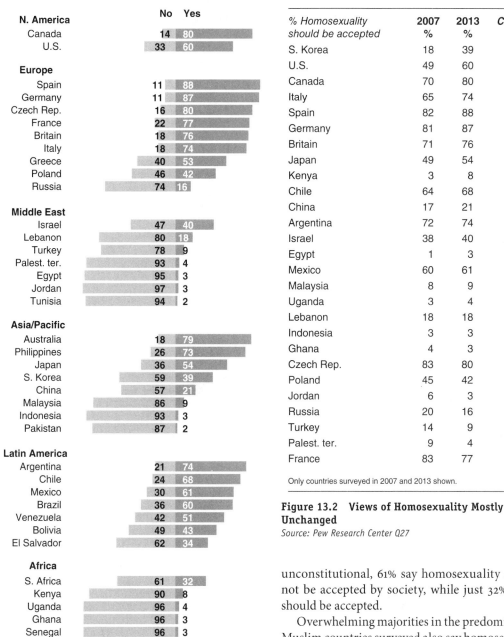

N. America

	No	Yes
Canada	14	80
U.S.	33	60

Europe

	No	Yes
Spain	11	88
Germany	11	87
Czech Rep.	16	80
France	22	77
Britain	18	76
Italy	18	74
Greece	40	53
Poland	46	42
Russia	74	16

Middle East

	No	Yes
Israel	47	40
Lebanon	80	18
Turkey	78	9
Palest. ter.	93	4
Egypt	95	3
Jordan	97	3
Tunisia	94	2

Asia/Pacific

	No	Yes
Australia	18	79
Philippines	26	73
Japan	36	54
S. Korea	59	39
China	57	21
Malaysia	86	9
Indonesia	93	3
Pakistan	87	2

Latin America

	No	Yes
Argentina	21	74
Chile	24	68
Mexico	30	61
Brazil	36	60
Venezuela	42	51
Bolivia	49	43
El Salvador	62	34

Africa

	No	Yes
S. Africa	61	32
Kenya	90	8
Uganda	96	4
Ghana	96	3
Senegal	96	3
Nigeria	98	1

Figure 13.1   Should Society Accept Homosexuality?
Source: Pew Research Center Q27

% Homosexuality should be accepted	2007 %	2013 %	Change
S. Korea	18	39	+21
U.S.	49	60	+11
Canada	70	80	+10
Italy	65	74	+9
Spain	82	88	+6
Germany	81	87	+6
Britain	71	76	+5
Japan	49	54	+5
Kenya	3	8	+5
Chile	64	68	+4
China	17	21	+4
Argentina	72	74	+2
Israel	38	40	+2
Egypt	1	3	+2
Mexico	60	61	+1
Malaysia	8	9	+1
Uganda	3	4	+1
Lebanon	18	18	0
Indonesia	3	3	0
Ghana	4	3	−1
Czech Rep.	83	80	−3
Poland	45	42	−3
Jordan	6	3	−3
Russia	20	16	−4
Turkey	14	9	−5
Palest. ter.	9	4	−5
France	83	77	−6

Only countries surveyed in 2007 and 2013 shown.

Figure 13.2   Views of Homosexuality Mostly Unchanged
Source: Pew Research Center Q27

unconstitutional, 61% say homosexuality should not be accepted by society, while just 32% say it should be accepted.

Overwhelming majorities in the predominantly Muslim countries surveyed also say homosexuality should be rejected, including 97% in Jordan, 95% in Egypt, 94% in Tunisia, 93% in the Palestinian territories, 93% in Indonesia, 87% in Pakistan, 86% in Malaysia, 80% in Lebanon and 78% in Turkey.

Elsewhere, majorities in South Korea (59%) and China (57%) also say homosexuality should not be accepted by society; 39% and 21%, respectively, say it should be accepted. South Korean views, while

homosexuality should not be accepted by society. Even in South Africa where, unlike in many other African countries, homosexual acts are legal and discrimination based on sexual orientation is

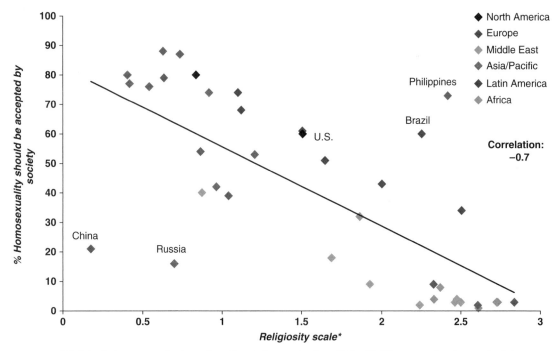

* Religiosity is measured using a three-item index ranging from 0–3, with "3" representing the most religious position. Respondents were coded as "1" if they believe faith in God is necessary for morality; "1" if they say religion is very important in their lives; and "1" if they pray at least once a day. The mean score for each country is used in this analysis. Religiosity scores for the U.S., Britain, France, Germany, Spain and Japan are from the Spring 2011 Global Attitudes Survey.

Figure 13.3   Less Tolerance for Homosexuality in More Religious Countries
Source: Pew Research Center Q27

still negative, have shifted considerably since 2007, when 77% said homosexuality should be rejected and 18% said it should be accepted by society.

Religiosity and Views of Homosexuality

There is a strong relationship between a country's religiosity and opinions about homosexuality.[2] There is far less acceptance of homosexuality in countries where religion is central to people's lives—measured by whether they consider religion to be very important, whether they believe it is necessary to believe in God in order to be moral, and whether they pray at least once a day.

There are some notable exceptions, however. For example, Russia and China receive low scores on the religiosity scale, which would suggest higher levels of tolerance for homosexuality. Yet, just 16%

of Russians and 21% of Chinese say homosexuality should be accepted by society. Conversely, Brazilians and Filipinos are considerably more tolerant of homosexuality than their countries' relatively high levels of religiosity would suggest.

In Israel, where views of homosexuality are mixed, secular Jews are more than twice as likely as those who describe themselves as traditional, religious or ultra-Orthodox to say homosexuality should be accepted (61% vs. 26%); just 2% of Israeli Muslims share this view.

Gender and Age and Views of Homosexuality

In most of the countries surveyed, views of homosexuality do not differ significantly between men and women. But in the countries where there is a

% Homosexuality should be accepted	Men %	Women %	Diff
Israel	31	48	+17
Venezuela	44	59	+15
Britain	69	83	+14
Japan	47	61	+14
Chile	62	74	+12
Greece	47	59	+12
France	72	82	+10
U.S.	55	65	+10

Only countries with a double-digit gender gap shown.

Figure 13.4 Gender Gap on Views of Homosexuality
Source: Pew Research Center Q27

% Homosexuality should be accepted	18–29 %	30–49 %	50+ %
U.S.	70	64	52
Canada	87	82	75
Britain	79	82	71
France	81	79	74
Germany	87	90	84
Italy	86	80	67
Spain	90	91	85
Greece	66	62	40
Poland	47	43	38
Czech Rep.	84	87	72
Russia	21	17	12
Turkey	9	7	10
Egypt	3	2	3
Jordan	5	1	1
Lebanon	27	17	10
Palest. ter.	5	3	--
Tunisia	3	2	1
Israel	40	44	35
Australia	--	83	77
China	32	19	15
Indonesia	4	2	3
Japan	83	71	39
Malaysia	7	10	11
Pakistan	2	2	2
Philippines	78	71	68
S. Korea	71	48	16
Argentina	81	78	62
Bolivia	53	43	27
Brazil	74	60	46
Chile	78	70	57
El Salvador	43	33	24
Mexico	70	60	52
Venezuela	57	51	45
Ghana	3	3	2
Kenya	7	9	--
Nigeria	0	1	3
Senegal	5	2	2
S. Africa	35	32	28
Uganda	3	2	7

Some figures for the Palestinian territories, Australia and Kenya not shown due to small sample sizes.

Figure 13.5 Age and Views of Homosexuality
Source: Pew Research Center Q27

gender gap, women are considerably more likely than men to say homosexuality should be accepted by society.

In Japan, Venezuela and Greece, where about six-in-ten women say homosexuality should be accepted (61% in Japan and 59% in Venezuela and Greece), fewer than half of men share this view (47%, 44% and 47%, respectively). About half of women in Israel (48%) express positive views of homosexuality, compared with just 31% of men. And, while majorities of women and men in Britain, Chile, France and the U.S. say homosexuality should be accepted by society, women are more likely than men to offer this view by at least ten percentage points.

In many countries, views of homosexuality also vary across age groups, with younger respondents consistently more likely than older ones to say homosexuality should be accepted by society. Age differences are particularly evident in South Korea, Japan, and Brazil, where those younger than 30 are more accepting than those ages 30–49 who, in turn, are more accepting than those ages 50 and older.

For example, in Japan, 83% of those younger than 30 say homosexuality should be accepted, compared with 71% of 30–49 year-olds and just 39% of those 50 and older. Similarly, 71% of South Koreans in the younger age group offer positive views of homosexuality, but just about half of 30–49 year-olds (48%) and 16% of those 50 or older do. In Brazil, about three-quarters of those younger than 30 (74%) say homosexuality should be accepted, compared with 60% of those in the middle category and 46% of those 50 or older.

In the EU, solid majorities across age groups in Britain, France, Germany, Spain, Italy and the Czech Republic express positive views of homosexuality, although Italians and Czechs ages 50 and older are considerably less likely than younger people in these countries to say homosexuality should be accepted. At least eight-in-ten Italians younger than 30 (86%) and ages 30–49 (80%) share this view, compared with 67% of those ages 50 and older. In the Czech Republic, 84% of those ages 18–29 and 87% of those 30–49 say homosexuality should be accepted, while 72% of those ages 50 and older agree.

In Greece, where acceptance of homosexuality is not as prevalent as in most of the EU countries surveyed, majorities of 18–29 year-olds (66%) and 30–49 year-olds (62%) say homosexuality should be accepted by society; far fewer Greeks ages 50 and older (40%) share this view.

People ages 50 and older in the U.S., Canada, Argentina, Bolivia and Chile are also less likely than those in the two younger age groups to say homosexuality should be accepted by society, although at least half of those 50 and older in all but Bolivia are accepting, including 75% in Canada. In the U.S., 70% of those ages 18–29 and 64% of those ages 30–49 are accepting of homosexuality, compared with about half of Americans ages 50 and older (52%). In Bolivia, however, 53% of 18–29 year-olds and 43% of 30–49 year-olds say homosexuality should be accepted, but just 27% of those in the older group share this view.

Mexicans and Chinese ages 18–29 are more likely than those in each of the other two age groups to offer positive views of homosexuality, but there is no significant difference between the views of 30–49 year-olds and those 50 or older. And in Russia, El Salvador and Venezuela, those younger than 30 are more tolerant of homosexuality than are those ages 50 and older, while the views of those ages 30–49 do not vary considerably from those in the youngest and oldest groups.

Across the predominantly Muslim countries surveyed, as well as in the six sub-Saharan countries, solid majorities across age groups share the view that homosexuality should be rejected by society. In Lebanon, however, there is somewhat more acceptance among younger respondents; 27% of Lebanese younger than 30 say homosexuality should be accepted, compared with 17% of 30–49 year-olds and 10% of those 50 or older.

NOTES

1. Results for India are not reported due to concerns about the survey's administration in the field.

2. Religiosity is measured using a three-item index ranging from 0–3, with "3" representing the most religious position. Respondents were coded as "1" if they believe faith in God is necessary for morality; "1" if they say religion is very important in their lives; and "1" if they pray at least once a day. The mean score for each country is used in this analysis.

Promoting Women's Political Representation Overseas

SARAH BUSH

"Promoting Women's Political Representation Overseas" by Sarah Bush. This article originated as a brief for the Scholars Strategy Network, January 2013 (http://www.scholarsstrategynetwork.org/).

Women make up over half of the world's population—but they hold only about one-fifth of the seats in national legislatures across the globe. American foreign policies are pushing to increase this important form of women's representation, using tactics ranging from training programs for female politicians to constitutional assistance and subtle diplomatic pressures. Efforts have stepped up sharply over the past three decades. Back in the 1980s, my research suggests, U.S.-funded efforts to promote democracy around the world paid almost no attention to women's political engagement. In contrast, today, about ten percent of all such projects deal with women's rights and political representation.

Why are U.S. officials spending millions of dollars each year to increase the female presence in the world's legislatures? We can't say that it is because the United States leads the world by example. According to the Inter-Parliamentary Union, the United States is tied with Morocco as just the eighty-second "best" country in the world in terms of women's representation. Regardless of the work still to be done at home, U.S. leaders are pushing women's cause abroad because they think it is both the right thing to do and the smart thing to do. The degree of gender equity in a country has been linked to economic development and democratization. In addition, aid supporting women in politics is something even foreign dictators are willing to tolerate. This strategy is therefore appealing not only for U.S. diplomats, but also for non-governmental organizations with U.S. funding that are trying to gain a foothold in closed societies.

Progress toward equal participation and greater political leverage for women can, however, be tricky. Increasing women's numbers in national legislatures around the world is a goal that has been pursued especially through legally-enforced gender quotas. But scholarly research shows that such quotas can be a mixed bag. There are upsides and downsides, and American foreign policymakers would be well advised to look for additional tools in certain circumstances.

What Gender Quotas Are Supposed to Do

"Gender quota" laws designed to increase women's political representation come in various forms. Gender quota laws can reserve a special set of seats in the legislature for women, so that only women can run for election to those seats. Quotas can also require a certain number of women to be on the lists of candidates that go to voters, leaving voters to make the final choices.

As with any kind of affirmative action, critics of gender quotas have raised various concerns about their fairness and efficacy. But despite ongoing controversies and questions, quotas are increasing in number—and have now spread to every region of the world. In fact, quotas influence national parliamentary elections in more than half of the world's countries, according to data compiled by the Quota Project, an initiative of the International Institute for Democracy and Electoral Assistance, which promotes democratic practices around the world.

The Good News about Quotas

The good news: research shows that quotas can improve women's political representation.

Research shows that quotas can improve women's representation in politics—both by reliably increasing the number of females elected to office and by changing the substance of policy-making.

- Looking across a wide swathe of countries and years, researchers have shown that adopting a quota is a key determinant of the number of women in a country's legislature—topping other important factors such as a country's religious heritage, democratic traditions, level of economic development, and even the proportion of girls enrolled in secondary schools."
- In India, local council seats are reserved for women through random selection. That kind of quota permits very rigorous studies of the impact of quotas. Well-designed studies have found that, even after quotas are withdrawn, their prior existence boosts the likelihood of women being elected. Quotas can also reduce negative stereotypes about women. Indeed, the presence of female officeholders can really matter. Research shows that councils with quotas adopt different types of policies than councils without them.

Where Quotas Fall Short

Yet gender quotas are hardly a panacea. In the developing world, the adoption of quotas in various countries does not correlate with the overall level of democracy. Nor are quotas related to other important indicators of higher socio-political standing for women. Countries with gender quotas now include Afghanistan, Azerbaijan, and Jordan, none of which is a paragon of freedom or gender equality.

But, quotas do not always equal democracy.

How do gender quotas get adopted in such countries? My research finds that international pressures and encouragement are key. In fact, nations that lack other democratic credentials often seek to signal their commitment to democracy to the international community by adopting gender quotas. They hope that having more women in office will help them attract generous foreign aid or enhance their country's overall reputation and international legitimacy. If many countries use quotas for symbolic purposes, simply to mimic democracy rather than practice it, we should wonder whether quotas in and of themselves can reliably enhance women's participation in non-democratic settings.

Looking to the Future

Gender quotas for legislatures produce a tangible female presence, and they may meaningfully boost women's involvement in politics. But in countries that are fundamentally not democratic in other ways, the sheer number of female legislators may not tell us as much as we imagine about the country's progress.

American policymakers determined to promote democracy abroad, especially in closed societies, may do better by redoubling other kinds of efforts. Promoting the development of political parties and free and fair elections may be even more important than getting a few token female insiders seated in legislatures. Overall democratization through freedom to organize and speak and compete for office may be the best way to ensure that the voices of regular women are really being heard in their countries' governments.

DISCUSSION QUESTIONS

1) One of the readings in this section discusses the use of quotas to increase the political power of underrepresented groups. What do you suppose are the main objections opponents of such techniques use to critique them? How do their proponents respond to these objections?

2) The reading in this section on race makes clear that boundaries between groups based on "race" and "ethnicity" are very different in places like Brazil and the United States. But where do you think these differences come from? Why would race and ethnicity be constructed in different ways in different countries? Which factors might be most important in this connection?

3) The reading on changing attitudes towards homosexuality across the globe points to some notable differences across countries (indeed, across groups of countries). What does the observable pattern of attitudes towards gays and lesbians suggest about the possible causes of intolerance?

Religion, Ideology, and Politics

Over the years, comparative social science has changed its mind several times concerning the importance of religion and ideology. Great classical theorists like Emile Durkheim and Max Weber considered them fundamentally important. By the mid-to-late twentieth century, however, and especially after the end of the Cold War, many social scientists believed that major ideological questions had been settled and that ideological polarization and rivalry was largely a thing of the past, consensus having emerged that capitalism and liberal democracy were best for everyone. As for religion, even the classical authors tended to believe that modernization implied "secularization," or the weakening of religion, and by the mid-to-late twentieth century the conventional wisdom in comparative politics and related fields was that religion's influence would continue to shrink until it was no longer an important factor in politics.

These views—or, at least, naïve formulations of them—are no longer tenable. While the impact of modernization on religion is a subject of some debate, religion clearly has not disappeared from modern politics. As such, many scholars have turned to discussing how different religious traditions, and ways for organizing religion's relationship to public life, affect democracy and democratic institutions.

A subject of particular interest in contemporary global politics has been the relationship between Islam and democracy. Some have asserted that Islam is somehow intrinsically hostile to democracy, a view rejected by most political scientists. Others have asked about whether different religious traditions, including Islam, have different implications for how religion and public life might be structured in a democratic polity. The first reading in this section is part of a recent lecture by the distinguished political scientists Alfred Stepan and the late Juan Linz on this subject.

Debating the continuing relevance of ideology may be even more complicated. There are clear examples of states where nonliberal ideologies remain important and are given official endorsement (e.g., Bolivia, Cuba, Ecuador, Iran, North Korea, Venezuela). Perhaps the most interesting case is China, which has seen dramatic reforms that reversed many of the prescriptions of Maoism. This has led some to believe that China is simply joining the liberal consensus. Yet its authoritarian political system persists. Our second reading, a short piece by Aaron Friedberg, suggests that there are still important ideological differences between China and the United States, and he tries to succinctly summarize how each country looks to the other through their own ideological lenses.

The third reading in this section is an excerpt from a recent essay by Francis Fukuyama, one of the scholars most famous for previously arguing that the liberal consensus made ideological conflict and debate largely obsolete. In this piece, Fukuyama tries to understand why expanding income inequality has not engendered *more* ideological debate and speculates about what an emergent ideology could look like.

Democratization Theory and the "Arab Spring"

ALFRED STEPAN AND JUAN J. LINZ

Stepan, Alfred, and Juan J. Linz. "Democratization Theory and the 'Arab Spring.'" *Journal of Democracy* 24:2 (2013), 15, 17–20. © 2013 National Endowment for Democracy and The Johns Hopkins University Press. Reprinted with permission of Johns Hopkins University Press.

[. . .]

Conflicts concerning religion, or between religions, did not figure prominently in either the success or failure of third-wave attempts at democratic transition. The Roman Catholic Church of course played an important and positive role in the democratic transitions in Poland, Chile, and Brazil. But conflicts over religion, which were so crucial in Europe in earlier historical periods, were not prominent. For this and other reasons, religion was undertheorized in scholarly writing about the third wave. Yet the hegemony, perceived or actual, of religious forces over much of civil society in the Arab world, especially in the countryside, had no parallel in the third wave. Thus the central role that Islam has played in the Arab Spring presents students of democratization with a novel phenomenon, and prompts them accordingly to come up with new concepts and fresh data to shed light upon it.

Samuel P. Huntington argued controversially that religion, especially Islam, would set major limits to further democratization. That suggested to one of us (Alfred Stepan) the idea of exploring what democracy and religion need, and do not need, from each other in order that each may flourish.[1] Stepan argued that neither *laïcité* of the French sort (generally recognized not merely as secularist but as positively antireligious), nor a type of secularism that decrees a complete separation between religion and the state, was empirically necessary for democracy to emerge.

What was needed for both democracy and religion to flourish? The answer was a significant degree of institutional differentiation between religion and the state. This situation of differentiation Stepan summed up as the "twin tolerations." In a country that lives by these two tolerations, religious authorities do not control democratic officials who are acting constitutionally, while democratic officials do not control religion so long as religious actors respect other citizens' rights. Many different patterns of relations among the state, religion, and society are compatible with the twin tolerations. There are, in other words, "multiple secularisms."

This term fits even the EU democracies. France retains a highly separatist, somewhat religion-unfriendly pattern of secularism with roots in the French Revolution. Germany, like Austria, Belgium, the Netherlands, and Switzerland, displays a very different pattern of state-religion relations that in German law is called "positive accommodation." In the German case, this includes a state role in collecting taxes for the Roman Catholic and Lutheran churches. The twin-tolerations model, of course, can incorporate countries with established churches—overall, a third of the EU's 27 member states have established churches, with the Lutheran Church filling this role in Denmark, Finland, and Sweden, as well as the non-EU states of Iceland and Norway. All the varieties of secularism in Europe are consistent with religious toleration and democracy.[2]

The crucial point is that multiple forms of secularism can be friendly to democracy and the twin tolerations. It should be better known than it is—particularly in most Arab countries—that close to 300 million Muslims have been living under democracy for each of the past ten years in the Muslim-majority countries of Albania, Indonesia, Senegal, and Turkey. If one adds the roughly 178 million Muslims who are natives of Hindu-majority India, the total number of Muslims living in democracies outside the West begins to approach half a billion. The Indian experience may be of particular interest, for it means that India had to be historically imagined—not to mention governed for the last six decades—as a democracy that incorporates a huge number of Muslim citizens.

India provides strong evidence against the presumption that there is something "exceptionalist" about Muslim attitudes toward democracy. In a recent survey with 27,000 respondents, India's Hindus and Muslims alike reported themselves as supporters of democracy at an equally high 71 percent.[3] Nearby in overwhelmingly Muslim Pakistan, the cognate figure was a mere 34 percent. That Indian Muslims should back democracy at more than twice the rate of their coreligionists who live just across the border—in a country with a far more checkered democratic history—underlines the great political contextuality of religion. With that in mind, we should look at the Muslim world's newly emergent democracies (Indonesia and Senegal, for example) and ask first if there have been any new conceptual emphases in Islamic political theology that have aided democratization in these places. Next, we should ask whether any new public policies regarding religion have been friendly to the twin tolerations while assisting democracy's rise.

On the conceptual and theological front, we note a growing emphasis on the importance of the Koranic verse (2:256) that categorically asserts, "There shall be no compulsion in religion." And as the Indonesian civil society leader, politician, and political scientist Amien Rais points out: "The Koran does not say anything about the formation of an Islamic state, or about the necessity and obligations on the part of Muslims to establish a Sharia or Islamic State."[4] Indonesian Muslim leaders say things like this often in order to argue against the imposition of *shari'a* in their country. To date, none of the Muslim-majority democracies has established *shari'a* as its legal code, and none has made Islam its established religion.[5]

We can draw similar examples from Tunisia, which in 2012 became the first Arab country in more than three decades to receive a ranking of 3 or better for political rights on the 7-point Freedom House scale (in which 1 is most free and 7 is least free). Many pan-Arabists or pan-Islamists, not to mention backers of a global Islamic caliphate, often voice doubts about the legitimacy of individual states and the value of democracy in them. Yet in Tunisia as in Indonesia, some influential Islamic advocates of democracy have used the key Koranic concepts of consensus, consultation, and justice to argue that democracy will be most effective and

most legitimate if it relates to the *specificities* of its citizens' histories in a particular state. For example, Rachid Ghannouchi of Ennahda, Tunisia's governing Islamist party since 2011, frequently says that his party should embrace the historic specificity that Tunisia for more than sixty years has had the Arab world's most progressive and women-friendly family code.[6]

Another concept that is becoming important in Tunisia is not "secularism" as such (in Arabic the word for secularism, *almaniyah*, carries antireligious overtones), but rather the concept of a civil state (*dawla madaniyah*) instead of a religious state. In a civil state, religion (in keeping with the twin tolerations) respects democratic prerogatives—the people are sovereign, and they make the laws. Yet a civil state also respects some prerogatives of religion and its legitimate role in the public sphere. In a May 2011 interview, both Ghannouchi and Tunisia's future prime minister, Hamadi Jebali of Ennahda, spoke extensively of the political imperative of a "civil state."[7]

What are some of the public policies and practices that have encouraged mutual respect between religion and democracy in Indonesia, Senegal, and also India?

First, all three actively contribute to the celebration of more religions than does Western Europe. For example, Denmark, France, Germany, the Netherlands, Sweden, and Switzerland decree a combined total of 76 religious holidays on which workers, by law, enjoy a paid day off. Every such holiday comes from the Christian calendar; none are for minority religions. Indonesia, by contrast, has six such official Islamic holidays, and seven additional holidays to cover days sacred to such minority religions as Buddhism, Christianity, Confucianism, and Hinduism. Senegal has seven public Islamic holidays, and six for the less than one-tenth of the population that is Roman Catholic. Senegal also subsidizes pilgrimages to Rome for Catholic citizens. India has five official Hindu holidays, and ten to accommodate its many minority religions. All three countries also offer state funding to different religions, especially for religious schools and hospitals.

India, Indonesia, and Senegal also embrace greater degrees of policy cooperation between the state and religion than would be found under

French-style *laïcité* or even U.S. doctrines of church-state accommodation. In all three countries, discussions between religious authorities and representatives of the democratic state have often led to policy consensus. In both Indonesia and Senegal, education-ministry specialists have worked with Islamic authorities to agree on mutually acceptable curricula, accreditation standards, and texts on the history of religion and Islam. One happy result has been that more parents than ever are choosing to send their daughters to school. Among Indonesians aged 11 to 14 today, 96 percent of boys and 95 percent of girls are literate.

In Senegal, the state asked the secretary-general of the National Association of Imams to inquire whether there is a Koranic basis for female genital mutilation (FGM). After study, the secretary-general sent all the Sufi orders a 43-page report saying that nothing in the Koran or early Islamic sources commands this custom or even indicates that it was ever practiced in the families of Muhammad and his companions. The imam concluded by asserting that a proper understanding of Islam required all imams to cooperate with state officials in a joint campaign—its effectiveness later certified by the UN—to combat FGM.[8]

Such examples put in question the political wisdom of John Rawls's injunction to take religion "off the political agenda" lest it interfere with the "overlapping moral consensus" that democracy requires. If democracy-inhibiting religious arguments are already on the political agenda, should Muslim leaders and activists who favor democracy not vigorously enter the public arena to show, from *within* their own tradition, that Islam and democracy are in fact compatible? Moreover, would it not be a good thing if more people in Arab countries—where "secularism" is too often seen as intrinsically hostile to religion—knew of the progress that Indonesia and Senegal have made toward relating religion, state, and society in ways that are friendly to both Islam and democracy?

[. . .]

NOTES

1. Alfred Stepan, "Religion, Democracy, and the 'Twin Tolerations,'" *Journal of Democracy* 11 (October 2000): 37–57. For a longer version, see Alfred Stepan, "The World's Religious Systems and Democracy: Crafting the 'Twin Tolerations,'" *Arguing Comparative Politics* (Oxford: Oxford University Press, 2001), pp. 213–254.

2. Alfred Stepan, "The Multiple Secularisms of Modern Democratic and Non-Democratic Regimes," in Craig Calhoun, Mark Juergensmeyer, and Jonathan VanAntwerpen, eds., *Rethinking Secularism* (New York: Oxford University Press, 2011), pp. 114–144.

3. See Alfred Stepan, Juan J. Linz, and Yogendra Yadav, *Crafting State Nations: India and Other Multinational Democracies* (Baltimore: Johns Hopkins University Press, 2011), pp. 70–71.

4. Mirjam Künkler and Alfred Stepan, "An Interview with Amien Rais," *Journal of International Affairs* 61 (Fall–Winter 2007): 205–218.

5. Stepan, "The Multiple Secularisms of Modern Democratic and Non-Democratic Regimes," p. 117.

6. Alfred Stepan, "Tunisia's Transition and the Twin Tolerations," *Journal of Democracy* 23 (April 2012): 94–97.

7. Stepan, "Tunisia's Transition."

8. For more detail on these and other examples of policy cooperation between religious and state officials in Indonesia and Senegal, see Alfred Stepan, "Rituals of Respect: Sufis and Secularists in Senegal in Comparative Perspective," *Comparative Politics* 44 (July 2012): 379–401.

In U.S.–China Relations, Ideology Matters

AARON FRIEDBERG

Is there an ideological basis for the emerging rivalry between the United States and the People's Republic of China? This question is at the heart of an article that I recently published in *The National Interest* and which I address at greater length in my forthcoming book.

It is sometimes said that because China is no longer a "Communist country" ideology is no longer a factor in U.S.-China relations. Like most truisms about China ("economic growth will lead inevitably to democracy;" "treat China like an enemy and it will become one") this one is, at best, only partly true. China's present leaders may not longer be Marxists, but they are most certainly Leninists; they believe that the one party authoritarian regime they lead should continue in power and they are determined to crush any opposition or dissent. Preserving CCP rule is the ultimate aim of all elements of Chinese policy, foreign as well as domestic.

As seen from Beijing, the United States appears as a crusading liberal democratic hegemon, intent on undermining the authority of regimes of which it disapproves and ultimately of remaking the entire world in its own image. This fear colors the Chinese government's perception of every aspect of U.S. policy and shapes its assessment of America's activities across Asia, which it believes are aimed at encircling it with pro-U.S. democracies.

The American people, meanwhile, are inclined to view with skepticism and distaste a regime that they regard as oppressive, illiberal, and potentially aggressive. While it is usually dressed in diplomatic language, the long-term aim of U.S. policy towards China is, in fact, to encourage "regime change," albeit gradually and by peaceful means.

Differences in ideology thus tend to heighten the mistrust and competitive impulses that are rooted in the dynamics of geopolitics. Since Athens and Sparta, dealings between dominant powers and fast-rising potential challengers have always been fraught with tension and have often resulted in conflict. Relations between the United States and China were never going to be smooth but, for as long as it persists, the ideological gap that now separates them is going to make it much harder to achieve a stable *modus vivendi*.

Now for the good news: if China *does* liberalize there is good reason to hope that relations between the two Pacific powers will improve, perhaps markedly. Hardcore "realists" doubt this, arguing that China's interests and policies will remain essentially the same, regardless of the character of its domestic regime. But this is a dubious assertion. A strong, democratic China would certainly seek a leading role in its region. But it would also be less fearful of internal instability, less threatened by the presence of democratic neighbors, more confident of its own legitimacy, and less prone to seek validation at home through the domination and subordination of others. For its part, while it will resist the efforts of an authoritarian regime to displace it from the region, the United States would probably be willing eventually to relinquish its position in Asia to a democratic China.

The Future of History: Can Liberal Democracy Survive the Decline of the Middle Class?

FRANCIS FUKUYAMA

Reprinted by permission of FOREIGN AFFAIRS, Volume 91, Number 1, January/February 2012. Copyright © 2012 by the Council on Foreign Relations, Inc. www.ForeignAffairs.com.

[. . .]

There is today a broad global consensus about the legitimacy, at least in principle, of liberal democracy. In the words of the economist Amartya Sen, "While democracy is not yet universally practiced, nor indeed uniformly accepted, in the general climate of world opinion, democratic governance has now achieved the status of being taken to be generally right." It is most broadly accepted in countries that have reached a level of material prosperity sufficient to allow a majority of their citizens to think of themselves as middle class, which is why there tends to be a correlation between high levels of development and stable democracy.

Some societies, such as Iran and Saudi Arabia, reject liberal democracy in favor of a form of Islamic theocracy. Yet these regimes are developmental dead ends, kept alive only because they sit atop vast pools of oil. There was at one time a large Arab exception to the third wave, but the Arab Spring has shown that Arab publics can be mobilized against dictatorship just as readily as those in Eastern Europe and Latin America were. This does not of course mean that the path to a well-functioning democracy will be easy or straightforward in Tunisia, Egypt, or Libya, but it does suggest that the desire for political freedom and participation is not a cultural peculiarity of Europeans and Americans.

The single most serious challenge to liberal democracy in the world today comes from China, which has combined authoritarian government with a partially marketized economy. China is heir to a long and proud tradition of high-quality bureaucratic government, one that stretches back over two millennia. Its leaders have managed a hugely complex transition from a centralized, Soviet-style planned economy to a dynamic open one and have done so with remarkable competence—more competence, frankly, than U.S. leaders have shown in the management of their own macroeconomic policy recently. Many people currently admire the Chinese system not just for its economic record but also because it can make large, complex decisions quickly, compared with the agonizing policy paralysis that has struck both the United States and Europe in the past few years. Especially since the recent financial crisis, the Chinese themselves have begun touting the "China model" as an alternative to liberal democracy.

This model is unlikely to ever become a serious alternative to liberal democracy in regions outside East Asia, however. In the first place, the model is culturally specific: the Chinese government is built around a long tradition of meritocratic recruitment, civil service examinations, a high emphasis on education, and deference to technocratic authority. Few developing countries can hope to emulate this model; those that have, such as Singapore and South Korea (at least in an earlier period), were already within the Chinese cultural zone. The Chinese themselves are skeptical about whether their model can be exported; the so-called Beijing consensus is a Western invention, not a Chinese one.

It is also unclear whether the model can be sustained. Neither export-driven growth nor the top-down approach to decision-making will continue to yield good results forever. The fact that the Chinese government would not permit open discussion of the disastrous high-speed rail accident last summer and could not bring the Railway Ministry responsible for it to heel suggests that there are other time bombs hidden behind the façade of efficient decision-making.

Finally, China faces a great moral vulnerability down the road. The Chinese government does not force its officials to respect the basic dignity of its citizens. Every week, there are new protests about land seizures, environmental violations, or gross corruption on the part of some official. While the country is growing rapidly, these abuses can be swept under the carpet. But rapid growth will not continue forever, and the government will have to pay a price in pent-up anger. The regime no longer has any guiding ideal around which it is organized; it is run by a Communist Party supposedly committed to equality that presides over a society marked by dramatic and growing inequality.

So the stability of the Chinese system can in no way be taken for granted. The Chinese government argues that its citizens are culturally different and will always prefer benevolent, growth-promoting dictatorship to a messy democracy that threatens social stability. But it is unlikely that a spreading middle class will behave all that differently in China from the way it has behaved in other parts of the world. Other authoritarian regimes may be trying to emulate China's success, but there is little chance that much of the world will look like today's China 50 years down the road.

Democracy's Future

There is a broad correlation among economic growth, social change, and the hegemony of liberal democratic ideology in the world today. And at the moment, no plausible rival ideology looms. But some very troubling economic and social trends, if they continue, will both threaten the stability of contemporary liberal democracies and dethrone democratic ideology as it is now understood.

The sociologist Barrington Moore once flatly asserted, "No bourgeois, no democracy." The Marxists didn't get their communist utopia because mature capitalism generated middle-class societies, not working-class ones. But what if the further development of technology and globalization undermines the middle class and makes it impossible for more than a minority of citizens in an advanced society to achieve middle-class status?

There are already abundant signs that such a phase of development has begun. Median incomes in the United States have been stagnating in real terms since the 1970s. The economic impact of this stagnation has been softened to some extent by the fact that most U.S. households have shifted to two income earners in the past generation. Moreover,

as the economist Raghuram Rajan has persuasively argued, since Americans are reluctant to engage in straightforward redistribution, the United States has instead attempted a highly dangerous and inefficient form of redistribution over the past generation by subsidizing mortgages for low-income households. This trend, facilitated by a flood of liquidity pouring in from China and other countries, gave many ordinary Americans the illusion that their standards of living were rising steadily during the past decade. In this respect, the bursting of the housing bubble in 2008–9 was nothing more than a cruel reversion to the mean. Americans may today benefit from cheap cell phones, inexpensive clothing, and Facebook, but they increasingly cannot afford their own homes, or health insurance, or comfortable pensions when they retire.

A more troubling phenomenon, identified by the venture capitalist Peter Thiel and the economist Tyler Cowen, is that the benefits of the most recent waves of technological innovation have accrued disproportionately to the most talented and well-educated members of society. This phenomenon helped cause the massive growth of inequality in the United States over the past generation. In 1974, the top one percent of families took home nine percent of GDP; by 2007, that share had increased to 23.5 percent.

Trade and tax policies may have accelerated this trend, but the real villain here is technology. In earlier phases of industrialization—the ages of textiles, coal, steel, and the internal combustion engine—the benefits of technological changes almost always flowed down in significant ways to the rest of society in terms of employment. But this is not a law of nature. We are today living in what the scholar Shoshana Zuboff has labeled "the age of the smart machine," in which technology is increasingly able to substitute for more and higher human functions. Every great advance for Silicon Valley likely means a loss of low-skill jobs elsewhere in the economy, a trend that is unlikely to end anytime soon.

Inequality has always existed, as a result of natural differences in talent and character. But today's technological world vastly magnifies those differences. In a nineteenth-century agrarian society, people with strong math skills did not have that many opportunities to capitalize on their talent. Today, they can become financial wizards or software engineers and take home ever-larger proportions of the national wealth.

The other factor undermining middle-class incomes in developed countries is globalization. With the lowering of transportation and communications costs and the entry into the global work force of hundreds of millions of new workers in developing countries, the kind of work done by the old middle class in the developed world can now be performed much more cheaply elsewhere. Under an economic model that prioritizes the maximization of aggregate income, it is inevitable that jobs will be outsourced.

Smarter ideas and policies could have contained the damage. Germany has succeeded in protecting a significant part of its manufacturing base and industrial labor force even as its companies have remained globally competitive. The United States and the United Kingdom, on the other hand, happily embraced the transition to the postindustrial service economy. Free trade became less a theory than an ideology: when members of the U.S. Congress tried to retaliate with trade sanctions against China for keeping its currency undervalued, they were indignantly charged with protectionism, as if the playing field were already level. There was a lot of happy talk about the wonders of the knowledge economy, and how dirty, dangerous manufacturing jobs would inevitably be replaced by highly educated workers doing creative and interesting things. This was a gauzy veil placed over the hard facts of deindustrialization. It overlooked the fact that the benefits of the new order accrued disproportionately to a very small number of people in finance and high technology, interests that dominated the media and the general political conversation.

The Absent Left

One of the most puzzling features of the world in the aftermath of the financial crisis is that so far, populism has taken primarily a right-wing form, not a left-wing one.

In the United States, for example, although the Tea Party is anti-elitist in its rhetoric, its members vote for conservative politicians who serve the interests of precisely those financiers and corporate elites they claim to despise. There are many explanations for this phenomenon. They include a deeply embedded belief in equality of opportunity rather than equality of outcome and the fact that cultural issues, such as abortion and gun rights, crosscut economic ones.

But the deeper reason a broad-based populist left has failed to materialize is an intellectual one. It has been several decades since anyone on the left has been able to articulate, first, a coherent analysis of what happens to the structure of advanced societies as they undergo economic change and, second, a realistic agenda that has any hope of protecting a middle-class society.

The main trends in left-wing thought in the last two generations have been, frankly, disastrous as either conceptual frameworks or tools for mobilization. Marxism died many years ago, and the few old believers still around are ready for nursing homes. The academic left replaced it with postmodernism, multiculturalism, feminism, critical theory, and a host of other fragmented intellectual trends that are more cultural than economic in focus. Postmodernism begins with a denial of the possibility of any master narrative of history or society, undercutting its own authority as a voice for the majority of citizens who feel betrayed by their elites. Multiculturalism validates the victimhood of virtually every out-group. It is impossible to generate a mass progressive movement on the basis of such a motley coalition: most of the working- and lower-middle-class citizens victimized by the system are culturally conservative and would be embarrassed to be seen in the presence of allies like this.

Whatever the theoretical justifications underlying the left's agenda, its biggest problem is a lack of credibility. Over the past two generations, the mainstream left has followed a social democratic program that centers on the state provision of a variety of services, such as pensions, health care, and education. That model is now exhausted: welfare states have become big, bureaucratic, and inflexible; they are often captured by the very organizations that administer them, through public-sector unions; and, most important, they are fiscally unsustainable given the aging of populations virtually everywhere in the developed world. Thus, when existing social democratic parties come to power, they no longer aspire to be more than custodians of a welfare state that was created decades ago; none has a new, exciting agenda around which to rally the masses.

An Ideology of the Future

Imagine, for a moment, an obscure scribbler today in a garret somewhere trying to outline an ideology of the future that could provide a realistic path toward a world with healthy middle-class societies and robust democracies. What would that ideology look like?

It would have to have at least two components, political and economic. Politically, the new ideology would need to reassert the supremacy of democratic politics over economics and legitimate anew government as an expression of the public interest. But the agenda it put forward to protect middle-class life could not simply rely on the existing mechanisms of the welfare state. The ideology would need to somehow redesign the public sector, freeing it from its dependence on existing stakeholders and using new, technology-empowered approaches to delivering services. It would have to argue forthrightly for more redistribution and present a realistic route to ending interest groups' domination of politics.

Economically, the ideology could not begin with a denunciation of capitalism as such, as if old-fashioned socialism were still a viable alternative. It is more the variety of capitalism that is at stake and the degree to which governments should help societies adjust to change. Globalization need be seen not as an inexorable fact of life but rather as a challenge and an opportunity that must be carefully controlled politically. The new ideology would not see markets as an end in themselves; instead, it would value global trade and investment to the extent that they contributed to a flourishing middle class, not just to greater aggregate national wealth.

It is not possible to get to that point, however, without providing a serious and sustained critique of much of the edifice of modern neoclassical economics, beginning with fundamental assumptions such as the sovereignty of individual preferences and that aggregate income is an accurate measure of national well-being. This critique would have to note that people's incomes do not necessarily represent their true contributions to society. It would have to go further, however, and recognize that even if labor markets were efficient, the natural distribution of talents is not necessarily fair and that individuals are not sovereign entities but beings heavily shaped by their surrounding societies.

Most of these ideas have been around in bits and pieces for some time; the scribbler would have to put them into a coherent package. He or she would also have to avoid the "wrong address" problem. The critique of globalization, that is, would have to be tied to nationalism as a strategy for mobilization in a way that defined national interest in a more sophisticated way than, for example, the "Buy American" campaigns of unions in the United States. The product would be a synthesis of ideas from both the left and the right, detached from the agenda of the marginalized groups that constitute the existing progressive movement. The ideology would be populist; the message would begin with a critique of the elites that allowed the benefit of the many to be sacrificed to that of the few and a critique of the money politics, especially in Washington, that overwhelmingly benefits the wealthy.

The dangers inherent in such a movement are obvious: a pullback by the United States, in particular, from its advocacy of a more open global system could set off protectionist responses elsewhere. In many respects, the Reagan-Thatcher revolution succeeded just as its proponents hoped, bringing about an increasingly competitive, globalized, friction-free world. Along the way, it generated tremendous wealth and created rising middle classes all over the developing world, and the spread of democracy in their wake. It is possible that the developed world is on the cusp of a series of technological breakthroughs that will not only increase productivity but also provide meaningful employment to large numbers of middle-class people.

But that is more a matter of faith than a reflection of the empirical reality of the last 30 years, which points in the opposite direction. Indeed, there are a lot of reasons to think that inequality will continue to worsen. The current concentration of wealth in the United States has already become self-reinforcing: as the economist Simon Johnson has argued, the financial sector has used its lobbying clout to avoid more onerous forms of regulation. Schools for the well-off are better than ever; those for everyone else continue to deteriorate. Elites in all societies use their superior access to the political system to protect their interests, absent a countervailing democratic mobilization to rectify the situation. American elites are no exception to the rule.

That mobilization will not happen, however, as long as the middle classes of the developed world remain enthralled by the narrative of the past generation: that their interests will be best served by ever-freer markets and smaller states. The alternative narrative is out there, waiting to be born.

DISCUSSION QUESTIONS

1) Consider critically Fukuyama's claims about the form that any future ideology is likely to take. Do you agree with his prognosis? Why or why not? Can you make an alternative prediction?

2) Assume for the sake of argument that both extreme claims about the relationship between religion and democracy are false (that is, that the religious background of a country determines its democratic character or that religious culture has absolutely no impact or implications for democracy). Chart out the elements of a middle ground position on the relationship between religion and democracy. Use examples drawn from the real world to illustrate your position.

3) Aaron Friedberg suggests that there are enduring ideological differences between the United States and China and that we can see this if we try to consider how the actions and positions of each of these countries appear from within the perspective of the other. Does this imply that all comparative political analysis is perspectival? If so, are there any limitations to this, or does it consign us to relativism?

Section 15

Comparative Politics and International Relations

Comparative politics and international relations are often treated as distinct subfields of political science. There is a reason for this: comparative politics *tends* to be about country- or regional-level processes and to make use of the comparative method, whereas international relations tends to be about the interaction of state and nonstate actors on the global stage. It should go without saying, though, that this analytical distinction does not mean that, in reality, comparative politics and international relations can be seamlessly distinguished from each other. What happens inside states influences how those states act on the international stage, and international events, forces, and processes influence domestic developments.

One of the major claims that has been made in recent years is that we are witnessing widespread globalization. Understood in a certain way, this is obviously true. Capital, labor, and information move more freely across the world now than they did in earlier times. Stronger claims about globalization, though, are more contentious. Note that they might actually undercut the distinction we drew above between international relations and comparative politics. In other words, if the breakdown of state and national borders gets to a certain point, and if geography is essentially irrelevant, this implies that domestic political institutions and other features of the cultures of individual polities have weakened considerably.

The first two readings in this section debate strong and weak versions of the globalization thesis. In the first of them, *New York Times* columnist Thomas Friedman makes his famous argument that "the world is flat," which means, in essence, that old geographical differences in economic opportunity no longer matter very much: we are all on an increasingly level playing field. The strong version of this argument is disputed in our second reading by Pankaj Ghamawat, who suggests that there is a great deal of exaggeration in such claims. This is followed by our third reading, a more descriptive piece from the *Economist*, which deals with the growth of diaspora trade networks. [Please note: no promises, but your instructor may offer you extra credit if you can correctly identify, without help from an online source, the Led Zeppelin albums from which each of the subtitles in this piece is drawn.] As global migration has increased, we see numerous examples of groups who trade with members of their own group across national borders. In some respects, this piece walks a line between the two that precede it, showing ways in which international processes and domestically rooted attachments interact.

The final selection here, by Bruce Russett, moves beyond the discussion of trade and globalization, even though it continues to address those themes in part. Russett is documenting the prospects for ever-greater peace in the twenty-first century. One major potential cause for greater peace is the increase in democracy around the world, with the attendant notion (building on the argument of philosopher Immanuel Kant) that democracies are unlikely to fight wars against one another. Other major factors are the increase in economic interdependence (to which the Friedman piece speaks) and the roles of international organizations in mitigating conflict. Consider in this selection how factors like democracy *within* countries (i.e., the realm of comparative politics) affect the relations *between* countries.

It's a Flat World, After All

THOMAS L. FRIEDMAN

In 1492 Christopher Columbus set sail for India, going west. He had the Nina, the Pinta and the Santa Maria. He never did find India, but he called the people he met "Indians" and came home and reported to his king and queen: "The world is round." I set off for India 512 years later. I knew just which direction I was going. I went east. I had Lufthansa business class, and I came home and reported only to my wife and only in a whisper: "The world is flat."

And therein lies a tale of technology and geoeconomics that is fundamentally reshaping our lives—much, much more quickly than many people realize. It all happened while we were sleeping, or rather while we were focused on 9/11, the dot-com bust and Enron—which even prompted some to wonder whether globalization was over. Actually, just the opposite was true, which is why it's time to wake up and prepare ourselves for this flat world, because others already are, and there is no time to waste.

I wish I could say I saw it all coming. Alas, I encountered the flattening of the world quite by accident. It was in late February of last year, and I was visiting the Indian high-tech capital, Bangalore, working on a documentary for the Discovery Times channel about outsourcing. In short order, I interviewed Indian entrepreneurs who wanted to prepare my taxes from Bangalore, read my X-rays from Bangalore, trace my lost luggage from Bangalore and write my new software from Bangalore. The longer I was there, the more upset I became—upset at the realization that while I had been off covering the 9/11 wars, globalization had entered a whole new phase, and I had missed it. I guess the eureka moment came on a visit to the campus of Infosys Technologies, one of the crown jewels of the Indian outsourcing and software industry. Nandan Nilekani, the Infosys C.E.O., was showing me his global video-conference room, pointing with pride to a wall-size flat-screen TV, which he said was the biggest in Asia. Infosys, he explained, could hold a virtual meeting of the key players from its entire global supply chain for any project at any time on that supersize screen. So its American designers could be on the screen speaking with their Indian software writers and their Asian manufacturers all at once. That's what globalization is all about today, Nilekani said. Above the screen there were eight clocks that pretty well summed up the Infosys workday: 24/7/365. The clocks were labeled U.S. West, U.S. East, G.M.T., India, Singapore, Hong Kong, Japan, Australia.

"Outsourcing is just one dimension of a much more fundamental thing happening today in the world," Nilekani explained. "What happened over the last years is that there was a massive investment in technology, especially in the bubble era, when hundreds of millions of dollars were invested in putting broadband connectivity around the world, undersea cables, all those things." At the same time, he added, computers became cheaper and dispersed all over the world, and there was an explosion of e-mail software, search engines like Google and proprietary software that can chop up any piece of work and send one part to Boston, one part to Bangalore and one part to Beijing, making it easy for anyone to do remote development. When all of these things suddenly came together around 2000, Nilekani said, they "created a platform where intellectual work, intellectual capital, could be delivered from anywhere. It could be disaggregated, delivered, distributed, produced and put back together again—and this gave a whole new degree of freedom to the way we do work, especially work of an intellectual nature. And what you are seeing in Bangalore today is really the culmination of all these things coming together."

At one point, summing up the implications of all this, Nilekani uttered a phrase that rang in my ear. He said to me, "Tom, the playing field is being leveled." He meant that countries like India were now able to compete equally for global knowledge work as never before—and that America had better get ready for this. As I left the Infosys campus that evening and bounced along the potholed road back to Bangalore, I kept chewing on that phrase: "The playing field is being leveled."

"What Nandan is saying," I thought, "is that the playing field is being flattened. Flattened? Flattened? My God, he's telling me the world is flat!"

Here I was in Bangalore—more than 500 years after Columbus sailed over the horizon, looking for a shorter route to India using the rudimentary navigational technologies of his day, and returned safely to prove definitively that the world was round—and one of India's smartest engineers, trained at his country's top technical institute and backed by the most modern technologies of his day, was telling me that the world was flat, as flat as that screen on which he can host a meeting of his whole global supply chain. Even more interesting, he was citing this development as a new milestone in human progress and a great opportunity for India and the world—the fact that we had made our world flat!

This has been building for a long time. Globalization 1.0 (1492 to 1800) shrank the world from a size large to a size medium, and the dynamic force in that era was countries globalizing for resources and imperial conquest. Globalization 2.0 (1800 to 2000) shrank the world from a size medium to a size small, and it was spearheaded by companies globalizing for markets and labor. Globalization 3.0 (which started around 2000) is shrinking the world from a size small to a size tiny and flattening the playing field at the same time. And while the dynamic force in Globalization 1.0 was countries globalizing and the dynamic force in Globalization 2.0 was companies globalizing, the dynamic force in Globalization 3.0—the thing that gives it its unique character—is individuals and small groups globalizing. Individuals must, and can, now ask: where do I fit into the global competition and opportunities of the day, and how can I, on my own, collaborate with others globally? But Globalization 3.0 not only differs from the previous eras in how it is shrinking and flattening the world and in how it is empowering individuals. It is also different in that Globalization 1.0 and 2.0 were driven primarily by European and American companies and countries. But going forward, this will be less and less true. Globalization 3.0 is not only going to be driven more by individuals but also by a much more diverse—non-Western, nonwhite—group of individuals. In Globalization 3.0, you are going to see every color of the human rainbow take part.

"Today, the most profound thing to me is the fact that a 14-year-old in Romania or Bangalore or the Soviet Union or Vietnam has all the information, all the tools, all the software easily available to apply knowledge however they want," said Marc Andreessen, a co-founder of Netscape and creator of the first commercial Internet browser. "That is why I am sure the next Napster is going to come out of left field. As bioscience becomes more computational and less about wet labs and as all the genomic data becomes easily available on the Internet, at some point you will be able to design vaccines on your laptop."

Andreessen is touching on the most exciting part of Globalization 3.0 and the flattening of the world: the fact that we are now in the process of connecting all the knowledge pools in the world together. We've tasted some of the downsides of that in the way that Osama bin Laden has connected terrorist knowledge pools together through his Qaeda network, not to mention the work of teenage hackers spinning off more and more lethal computer viruses that affect us all. But the upside is that by connecting all these knowledge pools we are on the cusp of an incredible new era of innovation, an era that will be driven from left field and right field, from West and East and from North and South. Only 30 years ago, if you had a choice of being born a B student in Boston or a genius in Bangalore or Beijing, you probably would have chosen Boston, because a genius in Beijing or Bangalore could not really take advantage of his or her talent. They could not plug and play globally. Not anymore. Not when the world is flat, and anyone with smarts, access to Google and a cheap wireless laptop can join the innovation fray.

When the world is flat, you can innovate without having to emigrate. This is going to get interesting. We are about to see creative destruction on steroids.

How did the world get flattened, and how did it happen so fast?

It was a result of 10 events and forces that all came together during the 1990's and converged right around the year 2000. Let me go through them briefly. The first event was 11/9. That's right—not 9/11, but 11/9. Nov. 9, 1989, is the day the Berlin Wall came down, which was critically important because it allowed us to think of the world as a single space. "The Berlin Wall was not only a symbol of keeping people inside Germany; it was a way of preventing a kind of global view of our future," the Nobel Prize-winning economist Amartya Sen said. And the wall went down just as the windows went up—the breakthrough Microsoft Windows 3.0 operating system, which helped to flatten the playing field even more by creating a global computer interface, shipped six months after the wall fell.

The second key date was 8/9. Aug. 9, 1995, is the day Netscape went public, which did two important things. First, it brought the Internet alive by giving us the browser to display images and data stored on Web sites. Second, the Netscape stock offering triggered the dot-com boom, which triggered the dot-com bubble, which triggered the massive overinvestment of billions of dollars in fiber-optic telecommunications cable. That overinvestment, by companies like Global Crossing, resulted in the willy-nilly creation of a global undersea-underground fiber network, which in turn drove down the cost of transmitting voices, data and images to practically zero, which in turn accidentally made Boston, Bangalore and Beijing next-door neighbors overnight. In sum, what the Netscape revolution did was bring people-to-people connectivity to a whole new level. Suddenly more people could connect with more other people from more different places in more different ways than ever before.

No country accidentally benefited more from the Netscape moment than India. "India had no resources and no infrastructure," said Dinakar Singh, one of the most respected hedge-fund managers on Wall Street, whose parents earned doctoral degrees in biochemistry from the University of Delhi before emigrating to America. "It produced people with quality and by quantity. But many of them rotted on the docks of India like vegetables. Only a relative few could get on ships and get out. Not anymore, because we built this ocean crosser, called fiber-optic cable. For decades you had to leave India to be a professional. Now you can plug into the world from India. You don't have to go to Yale and go to work for Goldman Sachs." India could never have

afforded to pay for the bandwidth to connect brainy India with high-tech America, so American shareholders paid for it. Yes, crazy overinvestment can be good. The overinvestment in railroads turned out to be a great boon for the American economy. "But the railroad overinvestment was confined to your own country and so, too, were the benefits," Singh said. In the case of the digital railroads, "it was the foreigners who benefited." India got a free ride.

The first time this became apparent was when thousands of Indian engineers were enlisted to fix the Y2K—the year 2000—computer bugs for companies from all over the world. (Y2K should be a national holiday in India. Call it "Indian Interdependence Day," says Michael Mandelbaum, a foreign-policy analyst at Johns Hopkins.) The fact that the Y2K work could be outsourced to Indians was made possible by the first two flatteners, along with a third, which I call "workflow." Workflow is shorthand for all the software applications, standards and electronic transmission pipes, like middleware, that connected all those computers and fiber-optic cable. To put it another way, if the Netscape moment connected people to people like never before, what the workflow revolution did was connect applications to applications so that people all over the world could work together in manipulating and shaping words, data and images on computers like never before.

Indeed, this breakthrough in people-to-people and application-to-application connectivity produced, in short order, six more flatteners—six new ways in which individuals and companies could collaborate on work and share knowledge. One was "outsourcing." When my software applications could connect seamlessly with all of your applications, it meant that all kinds of work—from accounting to software-writing—could be digitized, disaggregated and shifted to any place in the world where it could be done better and cheaper. The second was "offshoring." I send my whole factory from Canton, Ohio, to Canton, China. The third was "open-sourcing." I write the next operating system, Linux, using engineers collaborating together online and working for free. The fourth was "insourcing." I let a company like UPS come inside my company and take over my whole logistics operation—everything from filling my orders online to delivering my goods to repairing them for customers when they break. (People have no idea what UPS really does today. You'd be amazed!). The fifth was "supply-chaining." This is Wal-Mart's specialty. I create a global supply chain down to the last atom of efficiency so that if I sell an item in Arkansas, another is immediately made in China. (If Wal-Mart were a country, it would be China's eighth-largest trading partner.) The last new form of collaboration I call "informing"—this is Google, Yahoo and MSN Search, which now allow anyone to collaborate with, and mine, unlimited data all by themselves.

So the first three flatteners created the new platform for collaboration, and the next six are the new forms of collaboration that flattened the world even more. The 10th flattener I call "the steroids," and these are wireless access and voice over Internet protocol (VoIP). What the steroids do is turbocharge all these new forms of collaboration, so you can now do any one of them, from anywhere, with any device.

The world got flat when all 10 of these flatteners converged around the year 2000. This created a global, Web-enabled playing field that allows for multiple forms of collaboration on research and work in real time, without regard to geography, distance or, in the near future, even language. "It is the creation of this platform, with these unique attributes, that is the truly important sustainable breakthrough that made what you call the flattening of the world possible," said Craig Mundie, the chief technical officer of Microsoft.

No, not everyone has access yet to this platform, but it is open now to more people in more places on more days in more ways than anything like it in history. Wherever you look today—whether it is the world of journalism, with bloggers bringing down Dan Rather; the world of software, with the Linux code writers working in online forums for free to challenge Microsoft; or the world of business, where Indian and Chinese innovators are competing against and working with some of the most advanced Western multinationals—hierarchies are being flattened and value is being created less and less within vertical silos and more and more through horizontal collaboration within companies, between companies and among individuals.

Do you recall "the IT revolution" that the business press has been pushing for the last 20 years?

Sorry to tell you this, but that was just the prologue. The last 20 years were about forging, sharpening and distributing all the new tools to collaborate and connect. Now the real information revolution is about to begin as all the complementarities among these collaborative tools start to converge. One of those who first called this moment by its real name was Carly Fiorina, the former Hewlett-Packard C.E.O., who in 2004 began to declare in her public speeches that the dot-com boom and bust were just "the end of the beginning." The last 25 years in technology, Fiorina said, have just been "the warm-up act." Now we are going into the main event, she said, "and by the main event, I mean an era in which technology will truly transform every aspect of business, of government, of society, of life."

As if this flattening wasn't enough, another convergence coincidentally occurred during the 1990's that was equally important. Some three billion people who were out of the game walked, and often ran, onto the playing field. I am talking about the people of China, India, Russia, Eastern Europe, Latin America and Central Asia. Their economies and political systems all opened up during the course of the 1990's so that their people were increasingly free to join the free market. And when did these three billion people converge with the new playing field and the new business processes? Right when it was being flattened, right when millions of them could compete and collaborate more equally, more horizontally and with cheaper and more readily available tools. Indeed, thanks to the flattening of the world, many of these new entrants didn't even have to leave home to participate. Thanks to the 10 flatteners, the playing field came to them!

It is this convergence—of new players, on a new playing field, developing new processes for horizontal collaboration—that I believe is the most important force shaping global economics and politics in the early 21st century. Sure, not all three billion can collaborate and compete. In fact, for most people the world is not yet flat at all. But even if we're talking about only 10 percent, that's 300 million people—about twice the size of the American work force. And be advised: the Indians and Chinese are not racing us to the bottom. They are racing us to the top. What China's leaders really want is that the next generation of underwear and airplane wings not just be "made in China" but also be "designed in China." And that is where things are heading. So in 30 years we will have gone from "sold in China" to "made in China" to "designed in China" to "dreamed up in China"—or from China as collaborator with the worldwide manufacturers on nothing to China as a low-cost, high-quality, hyperefficient collaborator with worldwide manufacturers on everything. Ditto India. Said Craig Barrett, the C.E.O. of Intel, "You don't bring three billion people into the world economy overnight without huge consequences, especially from three societies"—like India, China and Russia—"with rich educational heritages."

That is why there is nothing that guarantees that Americans or Western Europeans will continue leading the way. These new players are stepping onto the playing field legacy free, meaning that many of them were so far behind that they can leap right into the new technologies without having to worry about all the sunken costs of old systems. It means that they can move very fast to adopt new, state-of-the-art technologies, which is why there are already more cellphones in use in China today than there are people in America.

If you want to appreciate the sort of challenge we are facing, let me share with you two conversations. One was with some of the Microsoft officials who were involved in setting up Microsoft's research center in Beijing, Microsoft Research Asia, which opened in 1998—after Microsoft sent teams to Chinese universities to administer I.Q. tests in order to recruit the best brains from China's 1.3 billion people. Out of the 2,000 top Chinese engineering and science students tested, Microsoft hired 20. They have a saying at Microsoft about their Asia center, which captures the intensity of competition it takes to win a job there and explains why it is already the most productive research team at Microsoft: "Remember, in China, when you are one in a million, there are 1,300 other people just like you."

The other is a conversation I had with Rajesh Rao, a young Indian entrepreneur who started an electronic-game company from Bangalore, which today owns the rights to Charlie Chaplin's image for mobile computer games. "We can't relax," Rao said. "I think in the case of the United States that is

what happened a bit. Please look at me: I am from India. We have been at a very different level before in terms of technology and business. But once we saw we had an infrastructure that made the world a small place, we promptly tried to make the best use of it. We saw there were so many things we could do. We went ahead, and today what we are seeing is a result of that. There is no time to rest. That is gone. There are dozens of people who are doing the same thing you are doing, and they are trying to do it better. It is like water in a tray: you shake it, and it will find the path of least resistance. That is what is going to happen to so many jobs—they will go to that corner of the world where there is the least resistance and the most opportunity. If there is a skilled person in Timbuktu, he will get work if he knows how to access the rest of the world, which is quite easy today. You can make a Web site and have an e-mail address and you are up and running. And if you are able to demonstrate your work, using the same infrastructure, and if people are comfortable giving work to you and if you are diligent and clean in your transactions, then you are in business."

Instead of complaining about outsourcing, Rao said, Americans and Western Europeans would "be better off thinking about how you can raise your bar and raise yourselves into doing something better. Americans have consistently led in innovation over the last century. Americans whining—we have never seen that before."

Rao is right. And it is time we got focused. As a person who grew up during the cold war, I'll always remember driving down the highway and listening to the radio, when suddenly the music would stop and a grim-voiced announcer would come on the air and say: "This is a test. This station is conducting a test of the Emergency Broadcast System." And then there would be a 20-second high-pitched siren sound. Fortunately, we never had to live through a moment in the cold war when the announcer came on and said, "This is a not a test."

That, however, is exactly what I want to say here: "This is not a test."

The long-term opportunities and challenges that the flattening of the world puts before the United States are profound. Therefore, our ability to get by doing things the way we've been doing them—which is to say not always enriching our secret sauce—will not suffice any more. "For a country as wealthy we are, it is amazing how little we are doing to enhance our natural competitiveness," says Dinakar Singh, the Indian-American hedge-fund manager. "We are in a world that has a system that now allows convergence among many billions of people, and we had better step back and figure out what it means. It would be a nice coincidence if all the things that were true before were still true now, but there are quite a few things you actually need to do differently. You need to have a much more thoughtful national discussion."

If this moment has any parallel in recent American history, it is the height of the cold war, around 1957, when the Soviet Union leapt ahead of America in the space race by putting up the Sputnik satellite. The main challenge then came from those who wanted to put up walls; the main challenge to America today comes from the fact that all the walls are being taken down and many other people can now compete and collaborate with us much more directly. The main challenge in that world was from those practicing extreme Communism, namely Russia, China and North Korea. The main challenge to America today is from those practicing extreme capitalism, namely China, India and South Korea. The main objective in that era was building a strong state, and the main objective in this era is building strong individuals.

Meeting the challenges of flatism requires as comprehensive, energetic and focused a response as did meeting the challenge of Communism. It requires a president who can summon the nation to work harder, get smarter, attract more young women and men to science and engineering and build the broadband infrastructure, portable pensions and health care that will help every American become more employable in an age in which no one can guarantee you lifetime employment.

We have been slow to rise to the challenge of flatism, in contrast to Communism, maybe because flatism doesn't involve ICBM missiles aimed at our cities. Indeed, the hot line, which used to connect the Kremlin with the White House, has been replaced by the help line, which connects everyone in America to call centers in Bangalore. While the other end of the hot line might have had Leonid Brezhnev threatening nuclear war, the other end of the help line just has a soft voice eager to help you sort out your AOL bill or collaborate with you on a new piece of software. No, that voice has none of the menace of Nikita Khrushchev pounding a shoe on the table at the United Nations, and it has none of the sinister snarl of the bad guys in "From Russia With Love." No, that voice on the help line just has a friendly Indian lilt that masks any sense of threat or challenge. It simply says: "Hello, my name is Rajiv. Can I help you?"

No, Rajiv, actually you can't. When it comes to responding to the challenges of the flat world, there is no help line we can call. We have to dig into ourselves. We in America have all the basic economic and educational tools to do that. But we have not been improving those tools as much as we should. That is why we are in what Shirley Ann Jackson, the 2004 president of the American Association for the Advancement of Science and president of Rensselaer Polytechnic Institute, calls a "quiet crisis"—one that is slowly eating away at America's scientific and engineering base.

"If left unchecked," said Jackson, the first African-American woman to earn a Ph.D. in physics from M.I.T., "this could challenge our pre-eminence and capacity to innovate." And it is our ability to constantly innovate new products, services and companies that has been the source of America's horn of plenty and steadily widening middle class for the last two centuries. This quiet crisis is a product of three gaps now plaguing American society. The first is an "ambition gap." Compared with the young, energetic Indians and Chinese, too many Americans have gotten too lazy. As David Rothkopf, a former official in the Clinton Commerce Department, puts it, "The real entitlement we need to get rid of is our sense of entitlement." Second, we have a serious numbers gap building. We are not producing enough engineers and scientists. We used to make up for that by importing them from India and China, but in a flat world, where people can now stay home and compete with us, and in a post-9/11 world, where we are insanely keeping out many of the first-round intellectual draft choices in the world for exaggerated security reasons, we can no longer cover the gap. That's a key reason companies are looking abroad. The numbers are not here. And finally we are developing an education gap. Here is the dirty little secret that no C.E.O. wants to tell you: they are not just outsourcing to save on salary. They are doing it because they can often get better-skilled and more productive people than their American workers.

These are some of the reasons that Bill Gates, the Microsoft chairman, warned the governors' conference in a Feb. 26 speech that American high-school education is "obsolete." As Gates put it: "When I compare our high schools to what I see when I'm traveling abroad, I am terrified for our work force of tomorrow. In math and science, our fourth graders are among the top students in the world. By eighth grade, they're in the middle of the pack. By 12th grade, U.S. students are scoring near the bottom of all industrialized nations. . . . The percentage of a population with a college degree is important, but so are sheer numbers. In 2001, India graduated almost a million more students from college than the United States did. China graduates twice as many students with bachelor's degrees as the U.S., and they have six times as many graduates majoring in engineering. In the international competition to have the biggest and best supply of knowledge workers, America is falling behind."

We need to get going immediately. It takes 15 years to train a good engineer, because, ladies and gentlemen, this really is rocket science. So parents, throw away the Game Boy, turn off the television and get your kids to work. There is no sugar-coating this: in a flat world, every individual is going to have to run a little faster if he or she wants to advance his or her standard of living. When I was growing up, my parents used to say to me, "Tom, finish your dinner—people in China are starving." But after sailing to the edges of the flat world for a year, I am now telling my own daughters, "Girls, finish your homework—people in China and India are starving for your jobs."

I repeat, this is not a test. This is the beginning of a crisis that won't remain quiet for long. And as the Stanford economist Paul Romer so rightly says, "A crisis is a terrible thing to waste."

Why the World Isn't Flat

PANKAJ GHEMAWAT

Republished with permission of *Foreign Policy*, from "Why the World Isn't Flat," Pankaj Ghemawat, No. 159 (Mar.–Apr., 2007), © 2007; permission conveyed through Copyright Clearance Center, Inc.

Globalization has bound people, countries, and markets closer than ever, rendering national borders relics of a bygone era—or so we're told. But a close look at the data reveals a world that's just a fraction as integrated as the one we thought we knew. In fact, more than 90 percent of all phone calls, Web traffic, and investment is local. What's more, even this small level of globalization could still slip away.

Ideas will spread faster, leaping borders. Poor countries will have immediate access to information that was once restricted to the industrial world and traveled only slowly, if at all, beyond it. Entire electorates will learn things that once only a few bureaucrats knew. Small companies will offer services that previously only giants could provide. In all these ways, the communications revolution is profoundly democratic and liberating, leveling the imbalance between large and small, rich and poor." The global vision that Frances Cairncross predicted in her *Death of Distance* appears to be upon us. We seem to live in a world that is no longer a collection of isolated, "local" nations, effectively separated by high tariff walls, poor communications networks, and mutual suspicion. It's a world that, if you believe the most prominent proponents of globalization, is increasingly wired, informed, and, well, "flat."

It's an attractive idea. And if publishing trends are any indication, globalization is more than just a powerful economic and political transformation; it's a booming cottage industry. According to the

U.S. Library of Congress's catalog, in the 1990s, about 500 books were published on globalization. Between 2000 and 2004, there were more than 4,000. In fact, between the mid-1990s and 2003, the rate of increase in globalization-related titles more than doubled every 18 months.

Amid all this clutter, several books on the subject have managed to attract significant attention. During a recent TV interview, the first question I was asked—quite earnestly—was why I still thought the world was round. The interviewer was referring of course to the thesis of *New York Times* columnist Thomas L. Friedman's bestselling book *The World Is Flat*. Friedman asserts that 10 forces—most of which enable connectivity and collaboration at a distance—are "flattening" the Earth and leveling a playing field of global competitiveness, the likes of which the world has never before seen.

It sounds compelling enough. But Friedman's assertions are simply the latest in a series of exaggerated visions that also include the "end of history" and the "convergence of tastes." Some writers in this vein view globalization as a good thing—an escape from the ancient tribal rifts that have divided humans, or an opportunity to sell the same thing to everyone on Earth. Others lament its cancerous spread, a process at the end of which everyone will be eating the same fast food. Their arguments are mostly characterized by emotional rather than cerebral appeals, a reliance on prophecy, semiotic arousal (that is, treating everything as a sign), a focus on technology as the driver of change, an emphasis on education that creates "new" people, and perhaps above all, a clamor for attention. But they all have one thing in common: They're wrong.

In truth, the world is not nearly as connected as these writers would have us believe. Despite talk of a new, wired world where information, ideas, money, and people can move around the planet faster than ever before, just a fraction of what we consider globalization actually exists. The portrait that emerges from a hard look at the way companies, people, and states interact is a world that's only beginning to realize the potential of true global integration. And what these trend's backers won't tell you is that globalization's future is more fragile than you know.

The 10 Percent Presumption

The few cities that dominate international financial activity—Frankfurt, Hong Kong, London, New York—are at the height of modern global integration; which is to say, they are all relatively well connected with one another. But when you examine the numbers, the picture is one of extreme connectivity at the local level, not a flat world. What do such statistics reveal? Most types of economic activity that could be conducted either within or across borders turn out to still be quite domestically concentrated.

One favorite mantra from globalization champions is how "investment knows no boundaries." But how much of all the capital being invested around the world is conducted by companies outside of their home countries? The fact is, the total amount of the world's capital formation that is generated from foreign direct investment (FDI) has been less than 10 percent for the last three years for which data are available (2003–05). In other words, more than 90 percent of the fixed investment around the world is still domestic. And though merger waves can push the ratio higher, it has never reached 20 percent. In a thoroughly globalized environment, one would expect this number to be much higher—about 90 percent, by my calculation. And FDI isn't an odd or unrepresentative example.

The levels of internationalization associated with cross-border migration, telephone calls, management research and education, private charitable giving, patenting, stock investment, and trade, as a fraction of gross domestic product (GDP), all stand much closer to 10 percent than 100 percent. The biggest exception in absolute terms—the trade-to-GDP ratio shown at the bottom of the chart—recedes most of the way back down toward 20 percent if you adjust for certain kinds of double-counting. So if someone asked me to guess the internationalization level of some activity about which I had no particular information, I would guess it to be much closer to 10 percent—the average for the nine categories of data in the chart—than to 100 percent. I call this the "10 Percent Presumption."

More broadly, these and other data on cross-border integration suggest a semiglobalized world, in which neither the bridges nor the barriers between countries can be ignored. From this perspective, the most astonishing aspect of various writings on globalization is the extent of exaggeration involved. In short, the levels of internationalization in the world today are roughly an order of magnitude lower than those implied by globalization proponents.

A Strong National Defense

If you buy into the more extreme views of the globalization triumphalists, you would expect to see a world where national borders are irrelevant, and where citizens increasingly view themselves as members of ever broader political entities. True, communications technologies have improved dramatically during the past 100 years. The cost of a three-minute telephone call from New York to London fell from $350 in 1930 to about 40 cents in 1999, and it is now approaching zero for voice-over-Internet telephony. And the Internet itself is just one of many newer forms of connectivity that have progressed several times faster than plain old telephone service. This pace of improvement has inspired excited proclamations about the pace of global integration. But it's a huge leap to go from predicting such changes to asserting that declining communication costs will obliterate the effects of distance. Although the barriers at borders have declined significantly, they haven't disappeared.

To see why, consider the Indian software industry—a favorite of Friedman and others. Friedman cites Nandan Nilekani, the CEO of the second-largest such firm, Infosys, as his muse for the notion of a flat world. But what Nilekani has pointed out privately is that while Indian software programmers can now serve the United States from India, access is assured, in part, by U.S. capital being invested—quite literally—in that outcome. In other words, the success of the Indian IT industry is not exempt from political and geographic constraints. The country of origin matters—even for capital, which is often considered stateless.

Or consider the largest Indian software firm, Tata Consultancy Services (TCS). Friedman has written at least two columns in the *New York Times* on TCS's Latin American operations: "[I]n today's world, having an Indian company led by a Hungarian-Uruguayan servicing American banks with Montevidean engineers managed by Indian technologists who have

learned to eat Uruguayan veggie is just the new normal," Friedman writes. Perhaps. But the real question is why the company established those operations in the first place. Having worked as a strategy advisor to TCS since 2000, I can testify that reasons related to the tyranny of time zones, languages, and the need for proximity to clients' local operations loomed large in that decision. This is a far cry from globalization proponents' oft-cited world in which geography, language, and distance don't matter.

Trade flows certainly bear that theory out. Consider Canadian-U.S. trade, the largest bilateral relationship of its kind in the world. In 1988, before the North American Free Trade Agreement (NAFTA) took effect, merchandise trade levels between Canadian provinces—that is, within the country—were estimated to be 20 times as large as their trade with similarly sized and similarly distant U.S. states. In other words, there was a built-in "home bias." Although NAFTA helped reduce this ratio of domestic to international trade—the home bias—to 10 to 1 by the mid-1990s, it still exceeds 5 to 1 today. And these ratios are just for merchandise; for services, the ratio is still several times larger. Clearly, the borders in our seemingly "borderless world" still matter to most people.

Geographical boundaries are so pervasive, they even extend to cyberspace. If there were one realm in which borders should be rendered meaningless and the globalization proponents should be correct in their overly optimistic models, it should be the Internet. Yet Web traffic within countries and regions has increased far faster than traffic between them. Just as in the real world, Internet links decay with distance. People across the world may be getting more connected, but they aren't connecting with each other. The average South Korean Web user may be spending several hours a day online—connected to the rest of the world in theory—but he is probably chatting with friends across town and e-mailing family across the country rather than meeting a fellow surfer in Los Angeles. We're more wired, but no more "global."

Just look at Google, which boasts of supporting more than 100 languages and, partly as a result, has recently been rated the most globalized Web site. But Google's operation in Russia (cofounder Sergey

Brin's native country) reaches only 28 percent of the market there, versus 64 percent for the Russian market leader in search services, Yandex, and 53 percent for Rambler. Indeed, these two local competitors account for 91 percent of the Russian market for online ads linked to Web searches. What has stymied Google's expansion into the Russian market? The biggest reason is the difficulty of designing a search engine to handle the linguistic complexities of the Russian language. In addition, these local competitors are more in tune with the Russian market, for example, developing payment methods through traditional banks to compensate for the dearth of credit cards. And, though Google has doubled its reach since 2003, it's had to set up a Moscow office in Russia and hire Russian software engineers, underlining the continued importance of physical location. Even now, borders between countries define—and constrain—our movements more than globalization breaks them down.

Turning Back the Clock

If globalization is an inadequate term for the current state of integration, there's an obvious rejoinder: Even if the world isn't quite flat today, it will be tomorrow. To respond, we have to look at trends, rather than levels of integration at one point in time. The results are telling. Along a few dimensions, integration reached its all-time high many years ago. For example, rough calculations suggest that the number of long-term international migrants amounted to 3 percent of the world's population in 1900—the high-water mark of an earlier era of migration—versus 2.9 percent in 2005.

Along other dimensions, it's true that new records are being set. But this growth has happened only relatively recently, and only after long periods of stagnation and reversal. For example, FDI stocks divided by GDP peaked before World War I and didn't return to that level until the 1990s. Several economists have argued that the most remarkable development over the long term was the declining level of internationalization between the two World Wars. And despite the records being set, the current level of trade intensity falls far short of completeness, as the Canadian-U.S. trade data suggest. In fact, when trade economists look at these figures,

they are amazed not at how much trade there is, but how little.

It's also useful to examine the considerable momentum that globalization proponents attribute to the constellation of policy changes that led many countries—particularly China, India, and the former Soviet Union—to engage more extensively with the international economy. One of the better-researched descriptions of these policy changes and their implications is provided by economists Jeffrey Sachs and Andrew Warner:

"The years between 1970 and 1995, and especially the last decade, have witnessed the most remarkable institutional harmonization and economic integration among nations in world history. While economic integration was increasing throughout the 1970s and 1980s, the extent of integration has come sharply into focus only since the collapse of communism in 1989. In 1995, one dominant global economic system is emerging."

Yes, such policy openings are important. But to paint them as a sea change is inaccurate at best. Remember the 10 Percent Presumption, and that integration is only beginning. The policies that we fickle humans enact are surprisingly reversible. Thus, Francis Fukuyama's *The End of History*, in which liberal democracy and technologically driven capitalism were supposed to have triumphed over other ideologies, seems quite quaint today. In the wake of Sept. 11, 2001, Samuel Huntington's *Clash of Civilizations* looks at least a bit more prescient. But even if you stay on the economic plane, as Sachs and Warner mostly do, you quickly see counterevidence to the supposed decisiveness of policy openings. The so-called Washington Consensus around market-friendly policies ran up against the 1997 Asian currency crisis and has since frayed substantially—for example, in the swing toward neopopulism across much of Latin America. In terms of economic outcomes, the number of countries—in Latin America, coastal Africa, and the former Soviet Union—that have dropped out of the "convergence club" (defined in terms of narrowing productivity and structural gaps vis-à-vis the advanced industrialized countries) is at least as impressive as the number of countries that have joined the club. At a multilateral level, the suspension of the Doha round of trade talks in the summer of 2006—prompting *The Economist* to run a cover titled "The Future of Globalization" and depicting a beached wreck—is no promising omen. In addition, the recent wave of cross-border mergers and acquisitions seems to be encountering more protectionism, in a broader range of countries, than did the previous wave in the late 1990s.

Of course, given that sentiments in these respects have shifted in the past 10 years or so, there is a fair chance that they may shift yet again in the next decade. The point is, it's not only possible to turn back the clock on globalization-friendly policies, it's relatively easy to imagine it happening. Specifically, we have to entertain the possibility that deep international economic integration may be inherently incompatible with national sovereignty—especially given the tendency of voters in many countries, including advanced ones, to support more protectionism, rather than less. As Jeff Immelt, CEO of GE, put it in late 2006, "If you put globalization to a popular vote in the U.S., it would lose." And even if cross-border integration continues on its upward path, the road from here to there is unlikely to be either smooth or straight. There will be shocks and cycles, in all likelihood, and maybe even another period of stagnation or reversal that will endure for decades. It wouldn't be unprecedented.

The champions of globalization are describing a world that doesn't exist. It's a fine strategy to sell books and even describe a potential environment that may someday exist. Because such episodes of mass delusion tend to be relatively short-lived even when they do achieve broad currency, one might simply be tempted to wait this one out as well. But the stakes are far too high for that. Governments that buy into the flat world are likely to pay too much attention to the "golden straitjacket" that Friedman emphasized in his earlier book, *The Lexus and the Olive Tree*, which is supposed to ensure that economics matters more and more and politics less and less. Buying into this version of an integrated world—or worse, using it as a basis for policymaking—is not only unproductive. It is dangerous.

Migration and Business: Weaving the World Together

Mass Migration in the Internet Age Is Changing the Way That People Do Business

THE ECONOMIST

In the flat world of maps, sharp lines show where one country ends and another begins. The real world is more fluid. Peoples do not have borders the way that parcels of land do. They seep from place to place; they wander; they migrate.

Consider the difference between China and the Chinese people. One is an enormous country in Asia. The other is a nation that spans the planet. More Chinese people live outside mainland China than French people live in France, with some to be found in almost every country. Then there are some 22m ethnic Indians scattered across every continent (the third Indian base in Antarctica will open next year). Hundreds of smaller diasporas knit together far-flung lands: the Lebanese in west Africa and Latin America, the Japanese in Brazil and Peru, the smiling Mormons who knock on your door wherever you live.

Diasporas have been a part of the world for millennia. Today two changes are making them matter much more. First, they are far bigger than they were. The world has some 215m first-generation migrants, 40% more than in 1990. If migrants were a nation, they would be the world's fifth-largest, a bit more numerous than Brazilians, a little less so than Indonesians.

Second, thanks to cheap flights and communications, people can now stay in touch with the places they came from. A century ago, a migrant might board a ship, sail to America and never see his friends or family again. Today, he texts his mother while still waiting to clear customs. He can wire her money in minutes. He can follow news from his hometown on his laptop. He can fly home regularly to visit relatives or invest his earnings in a new business.

Such migrants do not merely benefit from all the new channels for communication that technology provides; they allow this technology to come into its own, fulfilling its potential to link the world together in a way that it never could if everyone stayed put behind the lines on maps. No other social networks offer the same global reach—or commercial opportunity.

The Immigrant Song

This is because the diaspora networks have three lucrative virtues. First, they speed the flow of information across borders: a Chinese businessman in South Africa who sees a demand for plastic vuvuzelas will quickly inform his cousin who runs a factory in China.

Second, they foster trust. That Chinese factory-owner will believe what his cousin tells him, and act on it fast, perhaps sealing a deal worth millions with a single conversation on Skype.

Third, and most important, diasporas create connections that help people with good ideas collaborate with each other, both within and across ethnicities.

In countries where the rule of law is uncertain—which includes most emerging markets—it is hard to do business with strangers. When courts cannot be trusted to enforce contracts, people prefer to deal with those they have confidence in. Personal ties make this easier.

Chike Obidigbo, for example, runs a factory in Enugu, Nigeria, making soap and other household goods. He needs machines to churn palm oil and chemicals into soap, stamp it into bars and package it in plastic. He buys Chinese equipment, he says, because although it is not as good as European stuff, it is much cheaper. But it is difficult for a Nigerian firm to do business in China. Mr Obidigbo does not speak Chinese, and he cannot fly halfway around

the world every time he wants to buy a new soap machine. Worse, if something goes wrong neither the Chinese government nor the Nigerian one is likely to be much help.

Yet Mr Obidigbo's firm, Hardis and Dromedas, manages quite well with the help of middlemen in the African diaspora. When he wants to inspect a machine he has seen on the internet, he asks an agent from his tribe, the Igbo, who lives in China to go and look at it. He has met several such people at trade fairs. "When you hear people speaking Igbo outside Nigeria, you must go and greet them," he laughs.

He trusts them partly because they are his ethnic kin, but mostly because an Igbo middleman in Guangdong needs to maintain a good reputation. If a middleman cheats one Igbo, all the others who buy machinery in Guangdong will soon know about it. News travels fast on the diaspora grapevine.

Thanks in part to Mr Obidigbo's diaspora connections, Hardis and Dromedas is thriving. It employs 300 workers and sells about 300m naira-worth ($2m) of products each year. And it is just one of many African firms that use migrants as their eyes and ears in distant lands. The number of Africans living in China has exploded from hardly any two decades ago to tens of thousands today. One area of Guangzhou is now home to so many African traders that the locals call it Qiao-ke-li Cheng (Chocolate City).

The ability to use informal networks built on trust and a sense of belonging is not restricted to honest businesses such as soap making. Those with dirty hands can build criminal networks on a very similar basis. Many past diasporas have housed a "thing of our own", or Cosa Nostra, as the Sicilians put it, and some still do. But new technology may tip the scales in favour of those abiding by the law, at least a little. National police forces still do not co-operate seamlessly, but they are much easier to connect than once they were. And the ability of migrants to communicate with home directly leaves less room for sometimes criminal middlemen.

In Through the Out Door

The Chinese and Indian diasporas have long been commercially important. In previous generations, however, China and India themselves were closed economies, so overseas Chinese and Indian traders had to content themselves with linking foreign ports to each other (the Chinese in South-East Asia, for example, and the Indians in parts of Africa). That has completely changed. The overseas Chinese now connect the world to China and China to the world. The Indians do the same for India.

Consider the Riadys, an ethnic Chinese family who have lived in Indonesia for nearly a century. Mochtar Riady established the family fortune after the second world war, first as a bicycle trader, then by buying a bank, then by founding the Lippo Group, a conglomerate.

Throughout his career he relied on his relationships with other Chinese exiles. Rosabeth Moss Kanter, a professor at Harvard Business School (HBS) who has written a study of the Riady family, argues that for the Lippo Group, "networking is not just supportive of the business strategy; networking is the business strategy," and that ethnic ties serve as an "entrepreneurial springboard." Mr Riady would probably agree. "Without a network, we can do nothing," he once said.

The Riadys spread from Indonesia into Hong Kong and Singapore. In the 1980s they moved into America, hooking up with Chinese-American firms engaged in trans-Pacific trade. After Indonesia restored normal diplomatic ties with China in 1990, Mr Riady spent eight months touring the Middle Kingdom by car, sniffing out opportunities and forging new friendships. The Lippo Group—which has interests that range from property to supermarkets and newspapers—is investing in a variety of businesses in second-tier Chinese cities, where Western multinationals have been slow to penetrate. John Riady, Mochtar Riady's grandson, says Chinese contacts "really make us feel at home." The government in Beijing has set up a ministry to deal with the overseas Chinese.

Small wonder. Most of the foreign direct investment that flows into China is handled by the Chinese diaspora, loosely defined. Of the $105 billion of FDI in 2010, some two-thirds came from places where the population is more or less entirely ethnic Chinese (see chart). That includes Hong Kong and Taiwan, which are officially part of China. But these two places operate as if they are part of the diaspora. Citizens of

Taiwan are entirely outside Beijing's control. Hong Kongers are not, but they enjoy secure property rights and the rule of law in much the same way that Chinese Americans and Chinese Singaporeans do.

These data may be misleading. Mainland Chinese businesses sometimes launder money through Hong Kong to exploit Chinese government incentives for foreign investment. Nevertheless, it is clear that ethnic Chinese are far more confident about investing in China than anyone else. They understand the local business culture. They know whom to trust.

Which is why they also serve as a bridge for foreigners who wish to do business in China. A study by William Kerr and Fritz Foley of HBS showed that American firms that employ lots of Chinese Americans find it much easier to set up operations in China without the need for a joint venture with a local firm.

While some migrants settle down, others study or work abroad for a while and then return home, and others go first to one place, then another. "People don't have to choose between countries," says Kathleen Newland of the Migration Policy Institute in Washington, DC. "They can keep a foot in two or more." Their ceaseless circulation spreads ideas and expertise as the body's blood spreads oxygen and glucose.

Bringing It All Back Home

The benefits can be seen at places such as Fortis, a chain of 50 private hospitals in India. Malvinder and Shivinder Singh, the brothers who built the company up, both studied business in the United States. That imparted what Shivinder calls "a certain discipline". "If you live only in India, you naturally measure yourself against Indian standards," he says. "If you have lived abroad, you measure yourself against the best in the world."

During their father's terminal cancer the brothers had a sad opportunity to see the American healthcare system up close. Shivinder observed that the best American hospitals did not just have good doctors. They were also superbly organised. Doctors follow carefully documented procedures instead of relying solely on their instincts, as Indian doctors tended to. This might cramp the style of one or two medical geniuses, but it also raised ordinary physicians to a consistently high standard.

Fortis hospitals reimagined that American excellence to fit a frugal Indian setting. A leading surgeon in America might perform 250–350 operations a year. A surgeon at a Fortis hospital will perform 1,200. An army of helpers takes care of all the mundane tasks, leaving surgeons free to concentrate on the surgery. So even though the Singhs pay their doctors well, a kidney operation that might cost $100,000 in America costs less than $10,000.

To keep up with cutting-edge medicine, Fortis "very aggressively" recruits Indian doctors who have studied or worked abroad, says Shivinder. They bring back specialised skills, some of which were not previously available in India, such as transapical procedures for heart patients and ballooning techniques in spinal surgery. They also bring contacts: when a tough problem arises, they know whom to e-mail for advice.

Because migrants see the world through more than one cultural lens, they often spot opportunities invisible to their monocultural neighbours. For example, Cheung Yan, a Chinese woman living in America, noticed that Americans threw out mountains of waste paper and that ships carrying Chinese goods to America often steamed back half-empty. So she gathered up waste paper and shipped it to China for recycling into cardboard boxes, many of which were then returned to America with televisions inside. Her insight made Mrs Cheung a billionaire.

Going to California

The world is full of budding Cheung Yans. Immigrants are only an eighth of America's population, but a quarter of the engineering and technology firms started there between 1995 and 2005 had an immigrant founder, according to Vivek Wadhwa of Duke University.

The exceptional creativity of immigrants doubtless reflects the sort of people who up sticks and get visas. But work by William Maddux of INSEAD (a business school) and Adam Galinsky of Northwestern University suggests that exile itself makes people creative.

They compared MBA students who had lived abroad with otherwise similar students who had not, using an experiment in which each was given a candle, a box of matches and a box of drawing pins. The students' task was to attach the candle to a wall so that it burned properly and did not drip wax on the table or the floor. This Duncker candle problem, as it is known, is considered a good test of creativity because it requires you to imagine something being used for a purpose quite different from its usual one. Some 60% of the migrants saw the solution—pinning the drawing-pin box to the wall as a makeshift sconce—against 42% of non-migrants.

The creativity of migrants is enhanced by their ability to enroll collaborators both far-off and nearby. In Silicon Valley, more than half of Chinese and Indian scientists and engineers share tips about technology or business opportunities with people in their home countries, according to AnnaLee Saxenian of the University of California, Berkeley. A study by the Kauffman Foundation, a think-tank, found that 84% of returning Indian entrepreneurs maintain at least monthly contact with family and friends in America, and 66% are in contact at least that often with former colleagues. For entrepreneurs who return to China, the figures are 81% and 55%. The subjects they talk about most are customers (61% of Indians and 74% of Chinese mention this), markets (62% of Indians, 71% of Chinese), technical information (58% of Indians, 68% of Chinese) and business funding (31% of Indians, 54% of Chinese).

Mr Kerr has devised an ingenious study which uses patent information to measure how knowledge moves through diaspora networks. Looking at the names on American patent records, and guessing that an inventor called Zhang was probably ethnic Chinese, whereas someone called Rubio was probably Hispanic, he calculated that foreign researchers cite researchers of their own ethnicity based in America 30–50% more often than you would expect if ethnic ties made no difference.

It is not just that Brazilian scientists in São Paulo read papers written by Brazilian scientists in America. There's also gossip. Brazilian scientists in America will often alert their old classmates in São Paulo to intriguing research being done at the lab down the hall. And the information flows both ways.

A study in 2011 by the Royal Society found that cross-border scientific collaboration is growing more common, that it disproportionately involves scientists with diaspora ties and that it appears to lead to better science (using the frequency with which research is cited as a rough measure). A Chinese paper co-written with a scientist in America is cited three times as often as one produced solely in China.

Ramble On

Diaspora ties help businesses as well as scientists to collaborate. What may be the world's cheapest fridge was conceived from a marriage of ideas generated by Indians in India and Indians overseas. Uttam Ghoshal, Himanshu Pokharna and Ayan Guha, three Indian-American engineers, had an idea for a cooling engine, based on technology used to cool laptop computers, that they thought might work in a fridge. In India visiting relatives they decided to show their idea to Godrej & Boyce, an Indian manufacturing firm.

Mr Pokharna wheedled an introduction from a young member of the Godrej family, exploiting the fact that both had been at the University of Pennsylvania's Wharton business school. They discovered that Godrej was already working on a cheap fridge for rural Indians too poor to fork out the $200 normally required, let alone the subsequent electric bills.

Jamshyd Godrej, the firm's chairman, was determined to make a cheap battery-powered fridge. With the help of Mr Ghoshal's cooling chip, his team produced the Chotu Kool ("little cool"): light, portable, small and cheap. Mr Ghoshal's firm in Texas, Sheetak Inc, is working with Godrej to make it more efficient.

The "new type of hyperconnectivity" that enables such projects is fundamental to today's networked diasporas, according to Carlo Dade, of the Canadian Foundation for the Americas, a think-tank. "Migrants are now connected instantaneously, continuously, dynamically and intimately to their communities of origin... This is a fundamental and profound break from the past eras of migration." That break explains why diasporas, always marginalised in the flat-map world of national territories, find themselves in the thick of things as the world becomes networked.

Shrewd firms are taking notice. China's high-tech industry is dominated by returnees from abroad, such as Robin Li and Eric Xu, the founders of Baidu, China's leading search engine. Asked how many of his top people had worked or studied abroad, N. Chandrasekaran, the boss of Tata Consulting Services, a big Indian IT firm, replies: "All of them."

Peace in the Twenty-First Century?

BRUCE RUSSETT

"Peace in the Twenty-First Century?" by Bruce Russett. Reprinted with permission from *Current History* magazine. (Vol. 109, Issue 723, January 2010). © 2013 Current History, Inc.

One of the least-recognized global trends of the past 60 years is a decline in the number and especially the severity of violent conflicts between and within states. Daily news reports may seem to cast doubt on this trend's existence, but data collected by researchers on conflict, violence, and war clearly show that it is real.

Certainly, when it comes to conflict, no one should be nostalgic for the supposed good old days of the cold war. Thanks to some mixture of

intelligence and luck, no civilization-ending nuclear war occurred. Still, we are reminded in a recent book by Michael Dobbs—*One Minute to Midnight: Kennedy, Khrushchev, and Castro on the Brink of Nuclear War*—how close we came. At the height of the Cuban Missile Crisis, the United States reached the highest level of war readiness short of nuclear war itself.

During the cold war era, moreover, the Soviet Union and the United States, along with their allies and proxies, managed to kill millions of people—mostly in very poor countries. Yet even these conflicts inflicted considerably fewer fatalities than did earlier wars in the twentieth century. (Indeed, even the conflicts left over from World War II—chiefly the Greek and Chinese civil wars—left a record of casualties subsequently exceeded only by the Korean War.)

Figure 15.1 shows the huge decline in deaths overall, in both civil and international wars, since 1946. A longer-term perspective is even more striking, since it takes into account the two world wars, which set the past century's records for fatalities. Figure 15.2 shows that during World War II the average person's risk of dying in battle over the whole world was close to 0.3 percent—about 50 times higher than in any of the most recent 15 years. This longer view makes it clear that the decline in war-related deaths starting with the end of the cold war is not just a temporary spike downward.

What if we extend our view beyond battle deaths to consider one-sided, organized, deliberate killings of civilians? Even when we take into account

slaughters like the Cambodian and Rwandan genocides, the evidence tracks well with a bumpy but nonetheless steady and very sharp decline in fatalities since the horrors of World War II.

Or how about global terrorism? In fact, despite the publicity that terrorism attracts, it produces relatively low numbers of deaths. Many fatalities often counted among the recent victims of terrorism are already included under wars in Figure 15.1, in Afghanistan and especially Iraq. When these deaths are not double-counted, the worldwide total of fatalities from terrorism since 2000 has held steady at about 5,000 a year. This represents less than 10 percent of the Figure 15.1 totals since 2000. It is a blip not even discernible in Figure 15.2.

In short, something extraordinary has happened. We cannot know for certain, of course, that the decline in war deaths will continue. The trend might even be reversed, perhaps if a few really big terrorist attacks take place. Even so, it would take an enormous increase in carnage to match either World War II's death toll or what we barely escaped in the cold war.

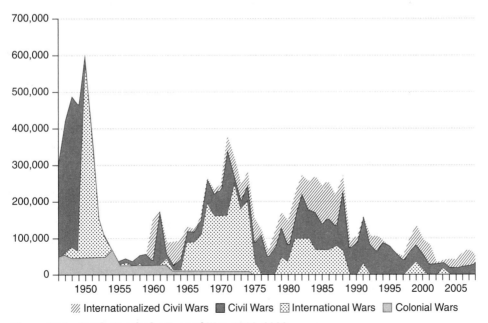

Figure 15.1   Battle Deaths by Type of War, 1946–2008
Source: Bethany Lacine and Nils Petter Gleditsch, "Monitoring Trends in Global Combat: A New Dataset of Battle Deaths," European Journal of Population *21 (2005):145–166*

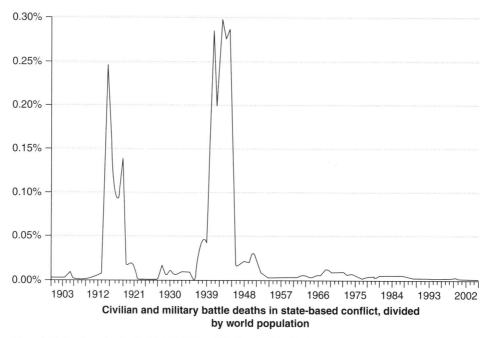

Figure 15.2   Average Individual's Risk of Dying in Battle, 1900–2005
Source: Bethany Lacina, Nils Petter Gleditsch, and Bruce Russett, "The Declining Risk of Death in Battle," International Studies Quarterly *50 (2006): 673–680*

And in the meantime, some other extraordinary things have occurred in recent decades—economic and political developments that, it is plausible to argue, have made a huge contribution to reducing organized violence, and may help hold it down in the future.

One of these developments is a rise in income levels and living standards around most of the world. Greater prosperity makes people less desperate and increases the costs of engaging in conflict. Where poverty is greatest (Africa), so is political violence. This fact alone does not prove a causal connection, but the theory and the evidence for such a connection are very strong.

Another possibility is that American hegemony has tamped down the ability and willingness of others to embark on large-scale violence. Maybe. We have certainly witnessed a short-term relationship between the end of the bipolar, cold war era and a decline in warfare. But the causal attribution between these two developments is questionable because the downward trend in war dates back to the end of World War II.

The Democracy Dividend

I am inclined to give stronger credit for the decline in warfare to factors identified by Immanuel Kant, the eighteenth century philosopher who was one of history's greatest international relations theorists. The title of his famous essay, *Perpetual Peace,* may sound squishy and naïve, but the work's substance is solid.

Kant was not just a theorist. He was a keen observer of governments, and of individual behavior. As a professor at the University of Königsberg, he taught anthropology and geography, among other subjects, and knew a lot about human behavior in many cultures. He lived in a trading city on the Baltic Sea that had once been a member of the Hanseatic League, an alliance of republics and other city-states.

Kant's ambition was to identify the circumstances under which peace might be secured—without establishing a world government, which he regarded as likely to become a "soulless tyranny." So he was not a Utopian thinker, but one who, in his own words, wanted to establish the conditions under which devils would act like angels because it was in their interest to do so. He did not expect to change devils' ways of thinking, just their incentives.

Kant identified three key characteristics that led countries to maintain peace, especially peace with similar countries: democracy (characterized by representative government, with separation of powers), commerce, and intergovernmental organizations (IGOS) and international law. Effectively these are the key elements of what we now call globalization. In recent decades they have been growing in the world—and have done so at the same time that the number and severity of armed conflicts have been declining. This is good news.

First, see Figure 15.3, on the spread of democracy and the relative decline of dictatorships (autocracies). In the 1940s, dictatorships outnumbered democracies in the world, but now more than half of all countries are democratic. The rest are either dictatorships or in a middle group called "anocracies," featuring mixed forms of government, often with weak central authorities. Why does this trend matter in terms of international security? Because democracies, though they are not necessarily peaceful in general, are peaceful toward each other.

Considerable evidence supports this assertion, and several plausible explanations for it are available. Different analysts favor different explanations, and as with most social phenomena, more than one influence probably operates. Perhaps the best explanation is that democratic leaders, or their parties, have to face reelection contests. If they fight long wars that are costly to a broad population—especially wars of choice rather than in self-defense against attackthey risk defeat at the polls. The leaders of any two democracies operate under the same electoral constraint, and they know this of each other.

In addition, democracies generally are good war fighters; they win most of their wars, including nearly 90 percent of those they initiate. They are often effective at mobilizing resources and motivating their populations. Opposing leaders know this about each other too. There are exceptions to all this, of coursepeace between democracies is not an iron law. But it is a strong generalization about what is likely to happen.

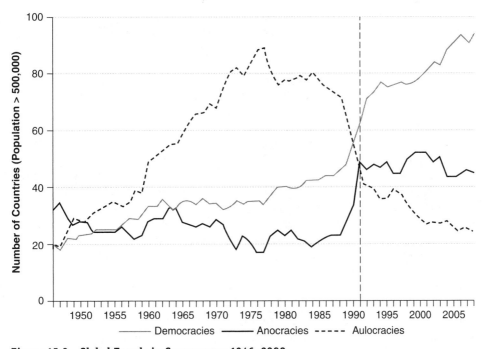

Figure 15.3 Global Trends in Governance, 1946–2008

Dictators, by contrast, can stay in power even if they lose wars, by repressing the populace and paying off cronies and security forces. They can even lose an unnecessary war and not be overthrown by their subjects. Iraq's Saddam Hussein managed this twice, once after losing the war he started with Iran and again after losing the first Gulf War, which followed his invasion of Kuwait.

The Interdependence Effect

Commerce, like democracy, also promotes peace. Trade and other commercial exchanges (such as investment) build economic interests in other countries. The greater the proportion of a country's gross domestic product that is accounted for by trade, the greater the interest of its population and leaders in maintaining orderly commerce.

And leaders and populations are especially concerned about maintaining peace with other trading countries. They do not want to destroy trading partners' export markets or their own imports, on which both partners depend. It is no coincidence that the number and severity of military conflicts declined sharply in recent decades as international trade grew in importance.

The same point can be made about the proliferation, during this same period, of intergovernmental organizations and international rules. IGOs do many things, among them settling diplomatic disputes before they get to the point of war or near-war. They also help establish and protect democratic governments by supervising and monitoring elections, setting up new media for free expression, and encouraging the development of independent police and legal systems.

The United Nations has become very important in these areas, but so have many regional, specialized IGOs, in which most of the member governments are democracies. These include the European Union, the Organization for Economic Cooperation and Development, the North Atlantic Treaty Organization, the Organization of American States, and Mercosur. (After the overthrow of dictators in several South American countries, new democratic leaders started Mercosur in 1991 as a free trade zone and mutual protection society.)

These regional organizations make membership in their groups conditional on being democratic, having free markets, and settling border disputes. Consequently, business groups and societal elites that stand to gain from admission of their states have greater leverage to make their governments adopt democratic norms and institutions, as has happened in Turkey.

Figure 15.4 shows the growth of the three "globalization" influences relative to their 1965 levels. The democracy trend is gleaned from Polity data, a set of coded information regarding characteristics of governments that is widely used in political science research. The Polity data rate countries on a 21-point scale from most dictatorial to most democratic. As more countries have achieved freedom and more dictatorships have fallen, the average democracy score has risen by 60 percent. Meanwhile, despite a dip during the cold war, the average country's trade-to-GDP ratio (the "economic openness" factor) is up by about 50 percent. And its number of IGO memberships is up by over 80 percent. So the world system has become more democratic, more commercially integrated, and more institutionalized.

Two more points should be made about IGOs. First, recent years have seen a marked rise in UN peacekeeping activity. The number of UN peacekeepers jumped from about 10,000 in 1991 to 90,000 in 2008. Most of these missions began during and especially after civil wars. They have aimed to stabilize peace settlements by demobilizing opposing armed forces, building economies and administrative and legal institutions, and promoting democratic elections. Not all these efforts have succeeded, but many have.

Second, membership in IGOs whose member states are democratic has risen over the years much more dramatically than it has for IGOs in general. These organizations help maintain democracy and stability among their members, and membership in them is about 15 times greater than it was in 1973. This is because new groups have been founded, old ones have expanded, and democratic rule has spread and consolidated in many countries. So this particular class of IGOs is especially important to the spread of peace.

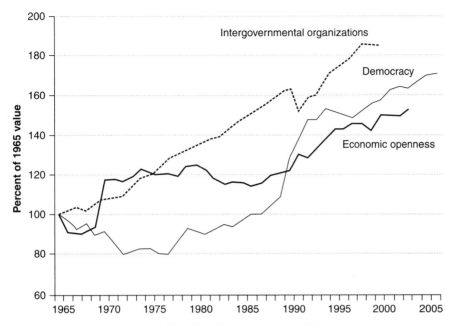

Figure 15.4   The Growth of "Liberal" Influences, 1965–2006
Source: Bruce Russett, David Kinsella, and Harvey Starr, World Politics: The Menu for Choice, 9th ed.,
Wadsworth, 2009

Something's Happening Here

The Kantian influences matter not just because Kant said so, of course, but because strong empirical evidence suggests that they do. Although scholars disagree about certain aspects of conflict and peace, it is clear that something big has been happening here. I will note here just one part of the evidence.

I have spent much of two decades, along with a lot of other people who have provided help and criticism (criticism is actually a form of help), looking at who fought whom in every year from 1885 to 2001. This is a very large set of information, entailing nearly half a million potential cases (pairs of countries). We have asked which pairs of countries fought each other, which pairs did not fight, and what their characteristics were.

The project is much like what epidemiologists do when they study large databases to identify risk factors for cancer or heart disease (smoking, bad diet, lack of exercise, environmental poisons, genetic endowment, and so on). They try to isolate the independent influence of each of these factors—that is, how the risk of disease is affected if one factor changes while the rest are held constant. An example would be to discern the effect of giving up smoking without improving diet or exercise. By doing this, medical researchers can give pretty good advice about how to lower our risk of disease. It is up to the patient to decide whether to take that advice.

Along with other scholars, I have followed much the same procedure in studying international conflicts. Figure 15.5 shows how we identify changes in the risk of what we call a "fatal militarized dispute" (that is, a military conflict in which at least one person is killed). The same sort of analysis has been performed for wars with more than 1,000 people killed, and the results are quite similar.

The table proceeds from a baseline risk of conflict between an average pair of countries. That risk is less than one-half of 1 percent per year. The table goes on to show how the risk changes if, for example, two countries are allied, or both countries

When both countries are allied	−9%
When their power disparity is 10 times greater than average	−61%
When both countries are over 90% on the democracy scale	−43%
When one country is over 90% and the other is below 10%	+197%
When both are over 90% in trade/GDP with each other	−56%
When both are in the top 10% of shared IGO memberships	−31%
When both are in the top 10% on all three influences	−83%

Figure 15.5 Percentage Change from the Average Risk That a Pair of Countries Will Begin a Fatal Militarized Dispute in Any One Year, 1886

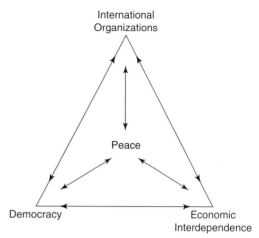

Figure 15.6 The Kantian Triangle

place in the top 10 percent of the Polity democracy scale, or have sizeable mutual trade, or are members of the same IGOs. Under such circumstances, how are the chances of fatal conflict affected?

Formal alliances do not help much, it turns out. Allies are almost as likely to fight each other as are countries not allied with each other. (Examples include Hungary and Czechoslovakia versus the Soviet Union during the cold war, and China versus the Soviet Union in the 1960s.)

Differences in relative power that are strong enough to create deterrence do matter. But for deterrence to make a significant difference, one state has to be much, much stronger than the other. This is not something that can be readily changed in a significant way. Thus, for example, even if China continues to post high rates of growth in economic strength and military capacity, decades will pass before US-Chinese relations will be affected in a major way.

But the data show that three other factors—the Kantian influences—make a big difference, especially when all three act together. Moreover, these three influences—democracy, trade, and IGO membership—are mutually reinforcing. They create a system of feedback loops that increasingly fosters peace.

The triangle in Figure 15.6 illustrates all the links—from the corners to the center, back to the corners, and around the sides. Everything is connected. Democracy, trade, and IGOs flourish best in

peacetime. They strengthen each other. And once the system gets going, it builds on itself. This is not to say that it cannot be reversed. But it builds powerful forces within and among countries not to slip back.

This process has worked in many parts of the world. The clearest case is the EU, but we see it among economically advanced countries generally, and for some poor countries as well. South America is an example, most notably among Argentina, Brazil, and Chile. Before the triad of democracy, commerce, and IGO membership took root in the region, these countries had been long-term rivals engaged in wars, near-wars, and arms races (including, in the case of Argentina and Brazil, a competition to develop nuclear arms capability).

Outside the Tent

Of course, some parts of the world are not part of this Kantian system. Some countries are at least potential threats to their neighbors, and to Americans. And yet, even these countries may be restrained by the norms and practices of the Kantian states. Our research has found that states embedded in the Kantian triangle have witnessed a great reduction in conflict—but even states outside the triangle are influenced by increases in the average level of Kantian ties for the system as a whole.

Peoples the world over want human rights and economic improvement. Traders and investors want peaceful, stable growth in their markets. As a result, autocratic governments may have to make concessions to stay in power.

Some countries must be deterred, and sometimes fought. Afghanistan under the Taliban displayed none of the Kantian characteristics: It was economically and politically isolated and certainly not democratic. It provided a haven for Al Qaeda to plan its attacks on the United States. Invading Afghanistan was the right decision, though prospects for stable democracy there are not bright.

But this is not an argument for invading other countries in general, nor for invading countries in order to establish democracy. Building democracy by imposing force from the outside is a long, costly, and high-risk job. Most such efforts fail. Germany and Japan after World War II are exceptions, but those countries were very different from Afghanistan or Iraq.

In fact, democratizing Iraq was only one minor motive for the invasion of that country, and the war was bungled. Nothing in our research suggests that this episode is a precedent worth repeating in the name of spreading democracy.

What our research *has* shown is this: Democratization, growing economic interdependence, and an increasingly dense network of IGOs each produces a great reduction in the risk of violent conflict between countries that share these characteristics. Together, the three links create a powerful self-reinforcing system for peaceful relations. Some improvement along even one of these dimensions is better than none.

The evidence suggests that democratic statesmen and international groups acting on these findings should focus on what is possible. They should rely on deterrence, peaceful change, and continuing economic integration to improve countries that do not already share the Kantian characteristics.

Democracy, trade, and international organizations and norms are not the only influences driving the decline in war. They have not brought an end to war, and probably will not. Yet they have been powerful factors in greatly reducing war across much of the world.

Human affairs do not progress in a nice linear advance, but rather by ups and downs. The Kantian peace project—gradually integrating more nations more firmly into the system—may be stalled for the moment, in part because of resistance in the Middle East. But it still shows a reasonable way forward for the long run.

DISCUSSION QUESTIONS

1) In what ways does Pankaj Ghemawat critique Thomas Friedman's argument about the world being "flat"? In what ways does Friedman suggest the world is flat, and to what extent (and why) does Ghemawat object?

2) Considering the article from *The Economist*, how should we understand the attachments migrants have to their home countries? Does this article suggest that people retain a strong sense of place and identity, even as they migrate and move around the world? Do you see migration as generally beneficial for the countries that attract or receive migrants? How about the countries from which people emigrate? Is it possible that both types of countries benefit, or that both lose out? How so?

3) Considering Bruce Russett's argument (and your own reaction to it), would you argue the causes of international war and peace are largely shaped by domestic political institutions within countries? Or would you argue that other factors account for when and where wars happen? If so, what might these causes be of major events in international relations? What does your perspective say for the question of whether understanding international relations between countries requires an understanding of comparative politics within countries?

Index

Page numbers followed by the italicized letter *f* indicate material found in Figures.